FIREBASE FOR ABSOLUTE BEGINNERS

From Zero Experience to Your First App

FIRST EDITION

Table of Contents

Table of Contents 1
Preface 12
Chapter 1: Introduction — Welcome to Firebase 13
   Overview of Firebase and Its Ecosystem 13
      Build 13
      Release & Monitor 14
      Engage 14
      The Firebase Ecosystem 15
      Firebase Use Cases 15
      Firebase's Limitations 15
      Why Use Firebase? 16
   Setting Up Your Development Environment 16
      Choosing the Right Tools for Firebase Development 16
      Setting Up a Firebase Project 17
      Setting Up an Emulator Environment 19
      Configuring Authentication 20
      Setting Up Database 21
      Setting Up Cloud Functions 22
      Conclusion 23
   What You Will Learn in This Book 23
      A Hands-On Approach to Learning Firebase 23
      Chapter-by-Chapter Breakdown 24
      Hands-On Projects and Practice Exercises 27
      Benefits of Firebase Development 27
Chapter 2: Getting Started with Firebase 29
   What is Firebase? 29
      The Firebase Ecosystem 29
      Firebase as a BaaS (Backend-as-a-Service) 29
      Key Features of Firebase 30
      How Firebase Helps in Application Development 33
      Limitations of Firebase 33
      When to Use Firebase? 33
      Summary 34

- Setting Up Firebase for Your Project 34
  - Creating a Firebase Project 34
  - Adding Firebase to Your Web App 35
  - Integrating Firebase Services 36
  - Firebase Project Settings and Configuration 39
  - Summary 39
- Connecting Firebase to Your App 40
  - Integrating Firebase with Web Apps 40
  - Using Firebase Authentication 42
  - Connecting Firebase to Android Apps 43
  - Integrating Firebase with iOS Apps 45
  - Summary 47
- Chapter 3: Firebase Authentication 48
  - Understanding Firebase Authentication 48
    - What is Firebase Authentication? 48
    - Why Use Firebase Authentication? 48
    - Authentication Flow in Firebase 49
    - Implementing Email and Password Authentication 49
    - Adding Error Handling and Security 52
    - Password Recovery 52
    - Email Verification 53
    - Security Best Practices for Firebase Authentication 54
  - Implementing Email and Password Authentication 54
    - Setting Up Email and Password Authentication in Firebase Console 55
    - Integrating Email and Password Authentication into Your App 55
    - Building the Registration Form 56
    - Building the Login Form 58
    - Handling User Authentication States 59
    - Password Reset 61
    - Securing Authentication with Firebase Security Rules 61
    - Error Handling and User Experience 62
    - Conclusion 63
  - Adding Social Logins 63
    - Benefits of Adding Social Logins 63
    - Configuring Social Login Providers in Firebase 64
    - Google Sign-In Implementation 64

Adding Facebook Login 67
Adding Twitter Login 69
Handling Sign-Out and Authentication State 70
Error Handling in Social Logins 72
Conclusion 73

Chapter 4: Real-time Database vs. Firestore 74
  Firebase Database Options 74
    Overview of Firebase Realtime Database 74
    Introduction to Cloud Firestore 75
    Choosing Between Realtime Database and Firestore 77
    Example Scenarios 77
    Performance Considerations 78
    Security Considerations 79
    Final Thoughts 80
  Getting Started with Realtime Database 80
    Setting Up Firebase Realtime Database 80
    Understanding the Data Structure 81
    Writing Data to the Realtime Database 82
    Reading Data from the Realtime Database 83
    Structuring Data for Efficient Reads 84
    Securing Your Data with Firebase Rules 85
    Offline Capabilities 86
    Handling Large Datasets 86
    Final Thoughts on Getting Started 86
  Exploring Firestore 87
    Firestore Structure and Data Model 87
    Setting Up Firestore 88
    Writing Data to Firestore 88
    Reading Data from Firestore 90
    Firestore Queries 92
    Firestore Security Rules 93
    Indexing in Firestore 94
    Offline Capabilities 94
    Final Thoughts on Firestore 94

Chapter 5: Firebase Storage 96
  Introduction to Firebase Storage 96

- Overview of Firebase Storage 96
- Firebase Storage Use Cases 96
- Setting Up Firebase Storage 96
- Uploading Files to Firebase Storage 98
- Downloading and Displaying Files 100
- Firebase Storage Security 101
- Best Practices for Using Firebase Storage 101
- Summary 102

Uploading and Managing Files 102
- Uploading Files: The Basics 102
- Managing File Uploads 104
- Organizing Files in Firebase Storage 106
- Deleting and Updating Files 106
- Working with File Metadata 108
- Handling Errors During Upload 109
- Summary 110

Downloading and Displaying Files 110
- Downloading Files from Firebase Storage 110
- Displaying Downloaded Files 113
- Handling Large File Downloads 115
- Error Handling in File Downloads 116
- Optimizing File Downloads 116
- Summary 117

Chapter 6: Cloud Functions for Beginners 118
What are Cloud Functions? 118
- 1. Why Use Cloud Functions? 118
- 2. Common Use Cases 118
- 3. Key Concepts of Cloud Functions 119
- 4. Writing Your First Cloud Function 120
- 5. Working with Background Functions 121
- 6. Testing and Debugging Cloud Functions 122
- 7. Best Practices for Cloud Functions 122
- Conclusion 123

Writing and Deploying Your First Function 123
- 1. Setting Up Your Local Development Environment 123
- 2. Initialize Firebase in Your Project 124

3. Writing Your First Cloud Function 125

4. Deploying Your Cloud Function 126

5. Testing Your Cloud Function Locally 126

6. Handling HTTP Methods 127

7. Working with Background Functions 127

8. Best Practices for Writing and Deploying Cloud Functions 128

Conclusion 129

Useful Cloud Function Examples 129

1. Sending Push Notifications on Database Changes 129

2. Automatically Adding User Metadata 131

3. Cleaning Up User Data on Account Deletion 132

4. Image Processing with Cloud Functions 133

5. Data Transformation with Firestore Triggers 134

6. Integrating with Third-Party APIs 135

Conclusion 136

Chapter 7: Firebase Hosting 137

Introduction to Firebase Hosting 137

1. Features of Firebase Hosting 137

2. Use Cases for Firebase Hosting 138

3. Getting Started with Firebase Hosting 138

4. Managing Hosting Releases 140

5. Firebase Hosting and Cloud Functions Integration 141

Conclusion 142

Deploying Your First Website 143

1. Setting Up Your Project for Deployment 143

2. Initializing Firebase Hosting 145

3. Preparing Your Website for Deployment 146

4. Deploying Your Website 148

5. Managing Your Hosting Configuration 148

6. Best Practices for Firebase Hosting 149

Conclusion 151

Custom Domains and Site Management 151

1. Setting Up Custom Domains in Firebase Hosting 152

2. SSL and Secure Connections 152

3. URL Rewrites and Redirects 153

4. Advanced Site Management 155

- 5. Caching Strategies and Custom Headers 156
- 6. Best Practices for Custom Domains and Site Management 159
- Conclusion 159

Chapter 8: Analytics with Firebase 161
- Why Use Firebase Analytics? 161
  - Key Features of Firebase Analytics 161
  - Setting Up Firebase Analytics 161
  - Understanding Firebase Analytics Dashboard 163
  - Tracking Custom Events 164
  - Understanding Audiences and Segmentation 165
  - Leveraging Firebase Analytics with Google Ads 165
  - Custom User Properties 166
  - Real-World Use Cases of Firebase Analytics 166
  - Conclusion 166
- Integrating Firebase Analytics 167
  - Setting Up Firebase Analytics 167
  - Tracking Events with Firebase Analytics 171
  - Using Firebase Analytics DebugView 172
  - Analyzing Data in Firebase Console 173
  - Leveraging Audience Segmentation 173
  - Best Practices for Integrating Firebase Analytics 173
  - Integrating Firebase Analytics with Other Firebase Products 174
  - Example: Using Firebase Analytics for E-commerce App Optimization 174
  - Conclusion 174
- Custom Events and User Insights 174
  - Understanding Custom Events 175
  - Defining Custom Events 175
  - Using Parameters with Custom Events 177
  - Best Practices for Custom Events 177
  - Creating and Analyzing User Insights 178
  - Custom Reporting with Google Analytics 179
  - Leveraging Firebase Predictions 179
  - A/B Testing with Firebase Analytics 180
  - Examples of Using User Insights for Marketing 180
  - Using User Properties 180
  - Conclusion 181

Chapter 9: Push Notifications with Firebase Cloud Messaging 182
Introduction to Firebase Cloud Messaging (FCM) 182
Why Use Firebase Cloud Messaging? 182
Setting Up Firebase Cloud Messaging 182
Requesting User Permission 184
Sending Your First Notification 185
Handling Incoming Notifications 187
Testing Your Setup 189
Best Practices for Using FCM 190
Conclusion 190
Setting Up FCM in Your App 190
Step 1: Adding Firebase to Your Project 190
Step 2: Adding Firebase SDK 191
Step 3: Configure Firebase Messaging in Your App 193
Step 4: Sending a Test Notification 196
Step 5: Handling Notifications in Your App 198
Step 6: Debugging and Troubleshooting 201
Conclusion 201
Advanced Notification Features 201
Customizing Notifications with Data Payloads 201
Topic Messaging for Segmentation 204
Condition-Based Messaging 206
Notification Customization with Platform-Specific Features 207
Interactive Notifications with Action Buttons 208
Silent Push Notifications 209
Using Analytics to Measure Notification Effectiveness 211
Conclusion 212
Chapter 10: Firebase Security and Best Practices 213
Securing Your Firebase Project 213
Understanding Firebase Security Rules 213
Key Strategies for Securing Your Firebase Project 214
Understanding Granular Security with Firebase Rules 215
Validating Data with Security Rules 216
Using Custom Claims for Role-Based Access Control 216
Protecting Firebase Storage 217
Best Practices for Firebase Security 217

Summary 219
Writing Effective Security Rules 219
    Overview of Firebase Security Rules 219
    Understanding the Firebase Security Rules Structure 220
    Defining Authentication-Based Rules 221
    Implementing Role-Based Access Control (RBAC) 221
    Validating Data with Firebase Security Rules 223
    Securing Nested Data Structures 224
    Using Firebase Storage Security Rules 225
    Combining Firebase Rules with Cloud Functions 225
    Testing and Debugging Security Rules 227
    Summary 227
Best Practices for Firebase Development 228
    Database Structuring and Management 228
    Managing Firebase Costs Effectively 229
    Cloud Functions Best Practices 230
    Security Best Practices 231
    Monitoring and Debugging 233
    Leveraging Analytics for Insights 234
    Optimizing for Performance 234
    Automating Deployment and Testing 235
    Summary 235

Chapter 11: Building and Launching Your First App 237
  Recap of Key Firebase Concepts 237
    Getting Started: App Overview 237
    Project Setup 237
    Firebase Authentication Integration 237
    Adding Notes: Firestore Database Integration 239
    Uploading Files: Firebase Storage 241
    Firebase Cloud Messaging: Notifications 242
    Putting It All Together 244
    Testing and Debugging 244
    Launching the App 244
  Developing a Simple App from Start to Finish 245
    Project Overview and Initial Setup 245
    Setting Up Firebase Configuration 246

- User Authentication ... 248
- Adding Tasks with Firestore ... 250
- Uploading Files with Firebase Storage ... 252
- Enabling Notifications with Firebase Cloud Messaging ... 254
- User Interface Enhancements ... 255
- Testing and Debugging Taskify ... 257
- Deploying Taskify ... 257
- Conclusion ... 258

Testing, Debugging, and Launching ... 258
- Importance of Testing and Debugging ... 258
- Types of Testing ... 258
- Writing Unit Tests ... 259
- Debugging Techniques ... 261
- Debugging Example: Fixing Sign-Up Errors ... 262
- Performance Testing ... 263
- Launching the Application ... 264
- Post-Launch Monitoring ... 265
- Continuous Improvement and Updates ... 265
- Conclusion ... 266

Chapter 12: Conclusion — Your Firebase Journey Begins ... 267

Reflecting on What You've Learned ... 267
- Firebase Authentication and User Management ... 267
- Real-time Database and Firestore ... 267
- Firebase Storage ... 268
- Cloud Functions for Scalability ... 268
- Hosting and Continuous Deployment ... 268
- Security and Best Practices ... 269
- Analytics, Messaging, and User Engagement ... 269
- The Power of the Firebase Ecosystem ... 270
- Moving Forward with Firebase ... 270
- Conclusion ... 270

Next Steps for Firebase Development ... 271
- Expand Your Knowledge with Advanced Firebase Features ... 271
- Build and Launch More Projects ... 272
- Leverage Firebase Extensions ... 273
- Contribute to Open Source Projects ... 273

- Explore Firebase Integration with Other Google Services 273
- Join the Firebase Community 274
- Firebase Certifications 274
- Conclusion 274
- Final Thoughts and Encouragement 275
  - Firebase as an Enabler of Creativity 275
  - Nurturing a Developer's Mindset 276
  - Developing for Scalability 277
  - Keep Innovating and Exploring 277
  - Turning Your Knowledge into Value 278
  - Final Words of Encouragement 278
- Chapter 13: Appendices 280
  - Glossary of Firebase Terms 280
    - Authentication 280
    - Firebase Realtime Database 280
    - Firestore (Cloud Firestore) 280
    - Firebase Storage 280
    - Cloud Functions 281
    - Firebase Hosting 281
    - Firebase Analytics 281
    - Firebase Cloud Messaging (FCM) 281
    - Firebase Security Rules 282
    - Firebase App Distribution 282
    - Firebase Crashlytics 282
    - Firebase Test Lab 282
    - Firebase Remote Config 283
    - Firebase Dynamic Links 283
    - Firebase Predictions 283
    - Firebase In-App Messaging 283
    - Firebase Extensions 284
    - Google Cloud Integration 284
    - Firebase Emulator Suite 284
    - Firebase SDK 284
    - Firebase Console 284
  - Resources for Further Learning 285
    - Official Documentation 285

- Firebase YouTube Channel 285
- Firebase Blog 286
- Firebase Community and Forums 286
- Online Learning Platforms 287
- GitHub Repositories and Open Source Projects 287
- Firebase Tools and Utilities 287
- Books and Reading Material 288
- Firebase Meetups and Conferences 289
- Firebase Podcasts and Newsletters 289
- Contributing to Firebase 289
- Conclusion 290

Sample Projects and Code Snippets 290
- Sample Project 1: Firebase Authentication and Firestore Integration 290
- Sample Project 2: Real-Time Chat Application 293
- Sample Project 3: Firebase Storage for User-Generated Content 295
- Sample Project 4: Cloud Functions for Automated Tasks 297
- Sample Project 5: Firebase Hosting with Static Site Deployment 299
- Conclusion 300

Firebase Reference Guide 300
- Firebase Authentication Reference 301
- Firebase Realtime Database Reference 303
- Firestore Reference 306
- Cloud Functions Reference 309
- Firebase Storage Reference 311
- Conclusion 313

Frequently Asked Questions 313
- General Firebase Questions 313
- Authentication FAQs 314
- Firestore and Realtime Database FAQs 316
- Cloud Functions FAQs 317
- Firebase Hosting FAQs 318
- Analytics and Notifications FAQs 319
- Conclusion 320

Preface

Firebase is an essential toolkit for modern app developers. From handling backend infrastructure to managing analytics, Firebase offers a comprehensive solution for building and scaling mobile and web applications. In this book, you'll embark on a journey through Firebase's rich ecosystem, exploring features like authentication, databases, storage, cloud functions, hosting, and more.

We've organized the book in a way that allows you to dive deep into each of Firebase's core functionalities while also offering practical, hands-on examples to get you started. Whether you're a beginner or an experienced developer seeking to enhance your skills, this book is designed to help you gain a robust understanding of Firebase and its ecosystem.

In Chapter 1, we provide an overview of Firebase and its ecosystem. We guide you through setting up your development environment and give you a taste of what you will be learning in the book. Chapter 2 introduces Firebase at a fundamental level, walking you through how to set up Firebase for your project and integrate it into your app.

The core functionalities of Firebase are broken down into subsequent chapters. Chapter 3 delves into Firebase Authentication, teaching you how to implement secure user logins, including email/password and social logins. Chapters 4 and 5 compare Firebase's real-time database options and explore Firebase Storage for managing your app's media.

Cloud Functions are covered in Chapter 6, giving you insight into serverless computing. Firebase Hosting, essential for deploying your web applications, is explained in Chapter 7. Analytics, a critical tool for understanding user behavior, is discussed in Chapter 8.

Chapter 9 covers Firebase Cloud Messaging (FCM) for push notifications, enabling you to keep your users engaged. We address Firebase security in Chapter 10, ensuring that your project is both secure and efficient. Chapter 11 brings all the knowledge together, guiding you through the process of building and launching a simple app.

The book wraps up with reflections and next steps in Chapter 12, followed by useful appendices in Chapter 13 that include resources for further learning, sample projects, and a glossary.

By the time you complete this book, you'll be comfortable using Firebase to develop, deploy, and manage your own applications. Whether you're a solo developer, part of a small team, or just curious about backend services, Firebase has something to offer you. This book will serve as both a comprehensive guide and a lasting reference for your Firebase journey.

We invite you to embark on this journey with us — let's get started!

Chapter 1: Introduction — Welcome to Firebase

Overview of Firebase and Its Ecosystem

Firebase is a comprehensive mobile and web application development platform provided by Google. Initially started as a Backend-as-a-Service (BaaS) to facilitate real-time data synchronization, it has since evolved into a full-fledged platform offering numerous tools that streamline every aspect of the development process. Firebase aims to eliminate much of the complexity that developers often face when dealing with backend infrastructure, thereby allowing them to focus on building feature-rich applications.

Firebase can be seen as a toolbox containing various essential services, each designed to solve different problems in app development. It includes options for managing real-time databases, user authentication, cloud storage, serverless computing, hosting, and analytics, all integrated under one platform. This integration greatly simplifies the backend and maintenance processes, offering developers a seamless way to manage data, scale servers, secure applications, and monitor user engagement.

Firebase is also particularly popular because it allows developers to leverage the same infrastructure that powers some of Google's most successful applications. As a managed platform, Firebase can scale effortlessly based on application requirements, meaning developers don't need to worry about managing servers, balancing loads, or handling infrastructure scaling.

Firebase is often described as having three main pillars: *Build*, *Release & Monitor*, and *Engage*. Let's dive into each of these pillars to better understand Firebase's capabilities:

Build

The first pillar is all about building your app. Firebase provides several features to help you create both the frontend and backend parts of your application with minimal effort:

1. **Authentication**: Firebase Authentication is an easy way to manage user sign-in using email, passwords, phone numbers, and popular identity providers like Google, Facebook, and Twitter. With this feature, you don't have to worry about setting up and securing user login flows yourself.
2. **Database Options**: Firebase offers two database types—*Realtime Database* and *Cloud Firestore*. While both databases are NoSQL and help store and synchronize data in real-time, they have their differences, and understanding them is key to choosing the right one for your app. The Realtime Database is Firebase's original database, suited for quick and straightforward syncing, whereas Firestore provides more structure and flexibility.
3. **Cloud Storage**: Firebase Cloud Storage helps you store and manage your app's media assets. With Firebase Storage, managing user-generated files, images, and

videos becomes easier, and it comes with built-in security provided by Google's infrastructure.
4. **Cloud Functions**: Cloud Functions for Firebase provides a way to run backend code without managing servers. These are functions triggered by events within Firebase services, allowing you to extend your app's backend functionalities in a serverless manner.
5. **Hosting**: Firebase Hosting helps you deploy web applications quickly and easily. It's useful for hosting static and dynamic content with simple deployment commands, allowing developers to focus more on writing code rather than configuring servers.

Release & Monitor

Firebase simplifies the process of releasing and monitoring applications, offering insight into how your app performs in real-world environments:

1. **Crashlytics**: Firebase Crashlytics is a lightweight, real-time crash reporting tool that helps developers prioritize and fix issues faster. It provides detailed crash reports along with insights that assist in addressing stability concerns to improve the user experience.
2. **Performance Monitoring**: Firebase Performance Monitoring provides insights into your app's performance characteristics. It helps developers understand how their app is performing on different devices, networks, and environments, making it easier to optimize slow or failing user experiences.
3. **Test Lab**: Firebase Test Lab is a cloud-based testing infrastructure that allows you to test your app across a wide variety of real devices and configurations. This helps developers ensure that their apps function correctly for all of their users before launching.

Engage

The third pillar of Firebase focuses on helping developers engage with their user base. Firebase provides tools to better understand users and keep them engaged with targeted campaigns:

1. **Analytics**: Firebase Analytics is a powerful, free-to-use analytics solution. It automatically captures certain key events and user properties, but it also allows developers to define custom events for more nuanced insights. This tool helps developers understand user behavior, identify trends, and make informed decisions to improve the app experience.
2. **Cloud Messaging**: Firebase Cloud Messaging (FCM) allows you to send notifications to users, either targeted to specific audiences or broadcast to all. It's one of the most effective tools for user engagement, allowing developers to craft personalized messages or send bulk notifications, which help in driving user retention.
3. **In-App Messaging**: Firebase In-App Messaging helps deliver targeted and contextual messages to users while they're actively using your application. This feature can prompt users to perform specific actions such as subscribing, watching a video, or completing a level in a game.

The Firebase Ecosystem

One of Firebase's biggest strengths is the ecosystem it offers. By seamlessly integrating various tools, Firebase ensures that developers can focus on building features rather than managing integrations. The seamless connection between Firebase services results in a cohesive development experience.

For example, using Firebase Authentication to sign in users can be directly linked to Firebase Database for storing and retrieving user data. Similarly, integrating Firebase Analytics allows you to understand user behavior in your app, which can then be used to trigger notifications using Firebase Cloud Messaging.

Moreover, Firebase's close integration with Google Cloud opens up possibilities for more complex application needs. If a particular feature or service is not directly available in Firebase, developers can often leverage Google Cloud services alongside Firebase, creating a more powerful and scalable infrastructure.

Firebase Use Cases

Firebase is often the go-to platform for applications that require rapid development cycles and real-time data synchronization, making it particularly popular among startups and solo developers. Here are a few typical use cases for Firebase:

1. **Mobile Applications**: Firebase's real-time database, user authentication, and analytics make it a popular choice for building both iOS and Android mobile applications. The platform's ability to handle data in real-time is particularly beneficial for chat and social networking apps.
2. **Single Page Applications (SPAs)**: Firebase Hosting, in conjunction with Cloud Firestore or Realtime Database, can be used to build SPAs that are secure, performant, and scalable. Firebase Authentication makes it easy to implement secure login for SPAs, while Firebase Analytics provides insights into user behavior.
3. **Games**: Firebase Realtime Database is an excellent choice for keeping multiple users in sync, making it suitable for multiplayer gaming. Using Firebase Cloud Messaging, developers can send game event notifications or offers, encouraging users to stay engaged.

Firebase's Limitations

While Firebase is an incredible platform that takes care of most backend tasks for you, it's also essential to understand some of its limitations:

1. **Vendor Lock-In**: Firebase is a proprietary Google platform. While it provides an easy development process, migrating away from Firebase can be challenging, as your entire backend system is tied to it.
2. **Pricing**: Firebase has a generous free tier, but pricing can escalate as your application grows. In particular, Firebase's pricing structure for databases like Realtime Database and Firestore is based on the number of reads and writes, which can become expensive if not optimized.

3. **Complex Queries**: Firebase databases have limitations when it comes to querying. Queries can be difficult if you require complex data operations, and Firestore, though more advanced than the Realtime Database, still doesn't offer SQL-like relational operations.

Why Use Firebase?

The reason Firebase has gained significant traction within the developer community is that it offers solutions that can accelerate development processes. You don't need to set up separate servers, worry about data security or scalability, or handle backend logic since Firebase manages most of these for you.

Firebase offers rapid prototyping capabilities, which allows developers to create proof-of-concepts with minimal time and effort. Its developer tools are well-documented, and integration with popular frontend frameworks is smooth.

Firebase's compatibility with Google Cloud Platform allows for limitless possibilities beyond its core offerings, which makes Firebase a powerful choice, especially when paired with more advanced Google services.

Firebase is essentially about convenience and speed — it's about focusing more on the front-facing aspects of your app while letting Google handle the backend complexities. Whether you are an indie developer looking for a managed backend solution or an enterprise looking for a reliable platform for user management and analytics, Firebase can help fulfill those needs efficiently.

In this book, we'll explore Firebase's different offerings and learn how to integrate them into a cohesive application. Firebase makes backend development accessible to all developers, empowering you to create robust applications without getting bogged down by complex server-side concerns. Let's continue on this journey to explore the depths of Firebase together.

Setting Up Your Development Environment

Before diving into Firebase's capabilities, it is crucial to set up a solid development environment to ensure smooth application development. Proper setup helps in avoiding unexpected issues down the line, ensures compatibility, and provides an optimized workspace. In this section, we will cover everything you need to set up your local environment, from selecting your tools to ensuring your Firebase configuration works correctly.

Choosing the Right Tools for Firebase Development

Firebase supports multiple platforms, including iOS, Android, and web. Each platform requires different tools for development, and this section will guide you through the most popular choices available.

- **Integrated Development Environment (IDE):** Your choice of IDE largely depends on the platform you're targeting. For Android, Android Studio is the most common IDE and provides deep integration with Firebase services. For iOS, Xcode is the preferred choice. For web development, VS Code is a popular choice due to its lightweight nature and extensive support for plugins. VS Code also works well for backend coding if you are using Firebase Cloud Functions.
- **Node.js and NPM:** Node.js is a JavaScript runtime that is essential for interacting with Firebase's backend services, such as Cloud Functions. NPM (Node Package Manager) is the default package manager for Node.js, which is used to install the Firebase tools.
  To install Node.js, follow these steps:
    - Visit the Node.js download page.
    - Download and install the latest LTS version. The LTS (Long-Term Support) version is recommended to ensure stability.

Once Node.js is installed, verify it by running the following command in your terminal:

```sh
node -v
npm -v
```

- These commands should return the versions of Node.js and NPM, respectively.

Firebase CLI: The Firebase Command-Line Interface (CLI) allows you to interact with Firebase directly from your terminal. You can use it to set up Firebase Hosting, Cloud Functions, and other Firebase services. To install Firebase CLI, run the following command:

```sh
npm install -g firebase-tools
```

After installing Firebase CLI, you can check if it was installed correctly by running:

```sh
firebase --version
```

-

Setting Up a Firebase Project

Firebase projects are at the core of Firebase development. All services, such as authentication, databases, and cloud storage, are tied to a specific Firebase project. Let's go step-by-step to set up your first Firebase project.

1. **Create a Firebase Project**: Go to the Firebase Console, and click on "Add Project". You will be asked to enter a project name, select an analytics account, and choose your project settings.

2. **Add an App to Your Project**: Once you've created your Firebase project, you need to add your app to it. Firebase supports Android, iOS, and web applications, so select the appropriate platform.
    - For Android, you will be required to provide the application package name.
    - For iOS, you need to provide the iOS bundle ID.
    - For web, you just need to give a nickname to the web app.
3. **Download and Integrate Configuration Files**: Depending on your chosen platform, Firebase provides different configuration files:
    - For Android, you will get a `google-services.json` file.
    - For iOS, you will get a `GoogleService-Info.plist` file.
    - For web, Firebase gives you JavaScript configuration keys to include in your project.
4. **Add the Firebase SDK to Your Project**: To access Firebase services from your app, you need to include the Firebase SDK.

Android: Add the Firebase SDK dependencies to your `build.gradle` file:
gradle
Copy code

```
// Top-level build.gradle file
buildscript {
    dependencies {
        classpath 'com.google.gms:google-services:4.3.10' // Google Services plugin
    }
}

// Module-level build.gradle file
dependencies {
    implementation platform('com.google.firebase:firebase-bom:31.0.2') // Firebase BOM (Bill of Materials)
    implementation 'com.google.firebase:firebase-analytics' // Example Firebase service
}
```

-

iOS: Add Firebase using CocoaPods by including Firebase dependencies in your `Podfile`:
ruby
Copy code

```
pod 'Firebase/Analytics'
pod 'Firebase/Auth'
```

- Run `pod install` in your project directory to install these dependencies.

Web: Add the Firebase JavaScript libraries to your project. You can add them via CDN links:

html

```
<script src="https://www.gstatic.com/firebasejs/10.0.0/firebase-app.js"></script>
<script src="https://www.gstatic.com/firebasejs/10.0.0/firebase-auth.js"></script>
<script src="https://www.gstatic.com/firebasejs/10.0.0/firebase-firestore.js"></script>
```

Then initialize Firebase in your JavaScript:

js

```
// Initialize Firebase
const firebaseConfig = {
  apiKey: "YOUR_API_KEY",
  authDomain: "YOUR_PROJECT_ID.firebaseapp.com",
  projectId: "YOUR_PROJECT_ID",
  storageBucket: "YOUR_PROJECT_ID.appspot.com",
  messagingSenderId: "YOUR_SENDER_ID",
  appId: "YOUR_APP_ID"
};

firebase.initializeApp(firebaseConfig);
```

o

Setting Up an Emulator Environment

Firebase provides local emulators that allow you to run and test your app locally without affecting your production data. This is especially useful when you're developing and testing new features. The Firebase Emulator Suite includes emulators for Authentication, Firestore, Realtime Database, Hosting, and Cloud Functions.

To set up the Emulator Suite, follow these steps:

1. **Install Firebase CLI Tools** (as discussed earlier).

Initialize Firebase in Your Project Directory: Run the following command from your terminal in your project's root directory:

sh

```
firebase init
```

2. You will be prompted to choose the features you want to use. Select "Emulators" along with other services you want to test locally.

20 | FIREBASE FOR ABSOLUTE BEGINNERS

Configure Emulator Settings: After initialization, you will get a `firebase.json` configuration file. It will contain the settings for which services to emulate, the ports they run on, and any other configurations. For example:

json
Copy code
```
{
  "emulators": {
    "firestore": {
      "port": 8080
    },
    "auth": {
      "port": 9099
    },
    "functions": {
      "port": 5001
    }
  }
}
```

3. **Start the Emulator Suite**: Use the following command to start all the emulators:

sh
Copy code
```
firebase emulators:start
```

4. Now, you can interact with Firebase services locally without the risk of modifying your production environment.

Configuring Authentication

Firebase Authentication allows you to manage user sign-ins easily. To set up Firebase Authentication, follow these steps:

1. **Navigate to Firebase Console**: From your Firebase project's dashboard, click on "Authentication" and then "Get Started".
2. **Enable Sign-In Methods**: Choose which methods you want to allow users to use for sign-in. Firebase offers several methods, such as:
   - **Email and Password**: You need to enable it from the console, and it allows users to create accounts using their email address.
   - **Social Logins (Google, Facebook, etc.)**: These options need extra configuration, like adding OAuth credentials for each service.

Here is an example of initializing Firebase Authentication in JavaScript:

js

Copy code

```js
// Firebase Auth Initialization
const auth = firebase.auth();

// Sign-up with email and password
function signUp(email, password) {
  auth.createUserWithEmailAndPassword(email, password)
    .then((userCredential) => {
      console.log("User created:", userCredential.user);
    })
    .catch((error) => {
      console.error("Error:", error.message);
    });
}
```

3.
4. **Testing Authentication with Emulator**: The Firebase Authentication emulator allows you to test authentication workflows in your local environment. You can use it to validate email-based sign-ups, sign-ins, and other flows without connecting to the real Firebase Authentication servers.

Setting Up Database

Firebase provides two main database options: **Realtime Database** and **Firestore**. Here's how to set up Firestore for your development:

1. **Create Firestore in Firebase Console**: Go to "Firestore Database" in the Firebase console and click on "Create Database". You will have options to set up Firestore either in *test mode* or *production mode*. Test mode is recommended while you're developing.

Integrate Firestore in Your App: js

Copy code

```
const db = firebase.firestore();

// Adding a document to the "users" collection
function addUser(userId, name, email) {
  db.collection("users").doc(userId).set({
    name: name,
    email: email
  })
  .then(() => {
    console.log("User added successfully!");
  })
```

```
  .catch((error) => {
    console.error("Error adding user:", error);
  });
}
```

2.

Setting Firestore Rules: Firestore rules determine who has read and write access to your data. In development mode, you might want more permissive rules, but in production, you need stricter control. Here's an example of a Firestore rule that allows only authenticated users to read and write data:

js
Copy code
```
service cloud.firestore {
  match /databases/{database}/documents {
    match /{document=**} {
      allow read, write: if request.auth != null;
    }
  }
}
```

3.

Setting Up Cloud Functions

Cloud Functions are Firebase's serverless solution, allowing you to extend Firebase with custom backend code. To set up Cloud Functions:

Initialize Functions: In your project directory, run:
sh
Copy code
```
firebase init functions
```

1. You will be asked if you want to use JavaScript or TypeScript. For this example, choose JavaScript.

Write Your First Function: Go to the `functions` folder created in your project. Open the `index.js` file and add the following function:
js
Copy code
```
const functions = require("firebase-functions");

// Hello World HTTP Function
exports.helloWorld = functions.https.onRequest((req, res) => {
  res.send("Hello from Firebase!");
```

```
});
```

2. **Deploy the Function**: Deploy the function using:

```sh
firebase deploy --only functions
```

3. After deployment, Firebase provides you with a URL where the function is accessible.

Conclusion

Setting up your development environment properly is the foundation for a successful Firebase project. By ensuring you have the right tools in place, creating a Firebase project, integrating it into your application, and setting up local emulators, you are well-prepared to make the most out of Firebase's powerful features. Firebase's integration with tools like Android Studio, Xcode, and VS Code, combined with its managed backend services, allows developers to focus more on their applications' core features, saving considerable time and effort in building and managing backend infrastructure.

With your development environment now set up, you're ready to dive into using Firebase to create dynamic and feature-rich applications. In the next chapter, we'll start exploring Firebase's core services and see how they help you build powerful apps efficiently.

What You Will Learn in This Book

This book is designed to help you navigate the wide-ranging features of Firebase, covering everything from basic project setup to implementing advanced features such as Cloud Functions and Firebase Analytics. The primary goal is to empower you with the skills needed to build, release, and maintain mobile and web applications using Firebase as your backend solution. We'll cover each Firebase component in depth, providing you with the knowledge and hands-on experience necessary to leverage these features for real-world application development.

A Hands-On Approach to Learning Firebase

In this book, we take a hands-on approach to understanding Firebase, meaning that theory is intertwined with practical exercises and real-world projects. Each chapter is dedicated to a core Firebase feature, allowing you to:

- **Understand the Concept**: We'll start by introducing you to the theoretical aspects of each Firebase feature. For example, when learning about Firebase Authentication, we'll discuss what makes it different from other authentication solutions, what benefits it offers, and how it integrates with other Firebase services.
- **Configure and Integrate**: Next, you'll learn how to configure each feature within the Firebase Console. For instance, we'll take you step-by-step through setting up a new

authentication provider, configuring database rules, and deploying web apps. This practical setup guide will ensure you get comfortable with Firebase Console navigation.
- **Code Along**: Each chapter includes code examples to demonstrate how to integrate Firebase services with your application. Whether you are building an Android app, an iOS app, or a web app, this book will provide the necessary code snippets. You'll learn how to make API calls, handle authentication states, and leverage Firebase SDKs to create powerful app features.

Let's look at what each part of the book covers and what you will learn from each of these components.

Chapter-by-Chapter Breakdown

This book is structured to help you master Firebase through logical progression—starting from the basics and gradually moving towards advanced topics. Here's a detailed look at what each chapter aims to teach:

Chapter 1: Introduction — Welcome to Firebase

The introductory chapter familiarizes you with Firebase and its ecosystem. We'll cover what Firebase offers, its main services, and how these services fit into the mobile and web application development process. You'll understand the role Firebase plays in app development, its target audience, and why it's a powerful tool for developers of all skill levels.

Chapter 2: Getting Started with Firebase

In this chapter, you will get acquainted with the fundamental setup processes. You'll learn how to create a Firebase project, add Firebase to your existing application, and understand how Firebase integrates into Android, iOS, and web projects. We'll guide you through adding Firebase SDKs to your projects and configuring your app to communicate with Firebase services. You will understand the prerequisites for each platform and how to efficiently start a project.

Chapter 3: Firebase Authentication

Firebase Authentication is at the core of many Firebase apps, providing a robust solution to manage user identities. We will cover user authentication with email/password, social logins (such as Google and Facebook), and phone authentication. By the end of this chapter, you will have implemented various types of sign-in methods and handled authentication states seamlessly within your application. You'll learn about best practices for authentication flows and securing user data.

```
// Example: Email and Password Authentication
const auth = firebase.auth();
```

```
function signUp(email, password) {
  auth.createUserWithEmailAndPassword(email, password)
    .then((userCredential) => {
      console.log("User signed up:", userCredential.user);
    })
    .catch((error) => {
      console.error("Error:", error.message);
    });
}
```

Chapter 4: Real-time Database vs. Firestore

Firebase offers two different database solutions, each tailored to specific use cases: Realtime Database and Firestore. In this chapter, you will learn the fundamental differences between these databases, including their respective strengths and weaknesses. You will gain practical knowledge on setting up and querying these databases, and you'll understand when to use one over the other for your projects. We will walk you through creating databases, adding data, and configuring data retrieval with real-time updates.

Chapter 5: Firebase Storage

Firebase Storage is essential for managing user-generated content like photos, videos, and documents. In this chapter, we will explore Firebase Storage, learning how to upload and manage files efficiently. You'll learn how to control access through security rules and how to integrate Firebase Storage into your app to allow users to upload and view content securely.

Chapter 6: Cloud Functions for Beginners

Firebase Cloud Functions allow you to execute backend code without managing servers. This chapter will provide you with an understanding of serverless computing and how Cloud Functions can extend the capabilities of your app. You will learn to write, deploy, and trigger functions based on Firebase events such as database updates or user creation. We'll also cover common use cases and examples of Cloud Functions that add essential functionalities to your application.

```
// Example: Simple Cloud Function
const functions = require("firebase-functions");

exports.sendWelcomeEmail = functions.auth.user().onCreate((user) =>
{
  console.log("Welcome email sent to:", user.email);
});
```

Chapter 7: Firebase Hosting

Firebase Hosting offers fast and secure hosting for web applications. In this chapter, you will learn how to deploy static and dynamic websites using Firebase Hosting. We will cover the Firebase CLI commands required to deploy and manage your website, and you'll learn how to set up custom domains, configure redirects, and manage website versioning. This chapter ensures that your web applications are easy to deploy, fast to access, and secure for end users.

Chapter 8: Analytics with Firebase

Analytics is key to understanding how your users interact with your app. Firebase Analytics is a powerful tool that provides insights into user behavior and app performance. In this chapter, you will learn how to integrate Firebase Analytics, track predefined and custom events, and use data to inform your development decisions. You'll understand user metrics, create audiences, and leverage data to create more personalized user experiences.

Chapter 9: Push Notifications with Firebase Cloud Messaging

Firebase Cloud Messaging (FCM) is used to send push notifications and keep users engaged with your application. This chapter will guide you through setting up FCM and sending notifications to targeted users or all users. You will learn how to create and schedule notifications, handle notifications in your mobile or web app, and add interactivity to your messages to improve user retention and engagement.

```javascript
// Example: Send Notification to All Users
const messaging = firebase.messaging();

function sendNotification(title, body) {
  messaging.send({
    notification: {
      title: title,
      body: body
    },
    topic: "allUsers"
  })
  .then((response) => {
    console.log("Notification sent successfully:", response);
  })
  .catch((error) => {
    console.error("Error sending notification:", error);
  });
}
```

Chapter 10: Firebase Security and Best Practices

Security is one of the most important aspects of app development. In this chapter, you will learn how to secure your Firebase project using security rules and authentication. We will cover writing security rules for Firestore and Realtime Database, ensuring only authorized users have the appropriate permissions. You'll learn best practices for securing data, managing user access, and protecting sensitive user information.

Chapter 11: Building and Launching Your First App

In this chapter, you will bring together everything you've learned and apply it to build a complete app. From setting up the Firebase backend to integrating services like Authentication, Database, Cloud Functions, and Analytics, this chapter is a culmination of your Firebase journey. You'll be guided through developing, testing, and launching your app. We will also cover debugging common issues, optimizing app performance, and handling deployment concerns.

Chapter 12: Conclusion — Your Firebase Journey Begins

This concluding chapter offers a reflection on what you've learned throughout the book. We will recap key Firebase concepts, and you'll be guided on the next steps you can take to further your Firebase development skills. You will learn about advanced Firebase topics and additional resources you can explore to keep growing as a developer.

Chapter 13: Appendices

The appendices include extra material like a glossary of Firebase terms, additional resources for further learning, sample projects, code snippets, and a Firebase reference guide. This chapter serves as an ongoing reference to help you refresh concepts and continue learning beyond the book.

Hands-On Projects and Practice Exercises

Theoretical knowledge is crucial, but hands-on experience is just as important when learning new technologies. This book contains numerous hands-on projects and exercises, allowing you to practice what you've learned and apply it in practical scenarios. Here are some of the projects you will complete:

1. **Authentication Project**: Create an authentication flow for an app with Firebase Authentication, including email/password and social logins.
2. **Chat Application**: Build a simple chat application using Firebase Realtime Database or Firestore to understand how to manage real-time data updates.
3. **File Upload Portal**: Implement a web interface to upload and download user-generated content using Firebase Storage. Learn how to handle file uploads securely and efficiently.
4. **Cloud Function Trigger**: Write a Cloud Function that performs backend operations when a user registers or updates their profile. Understand how to extend app features beyond frontend capabilities.
5. **Analytics and Engagement**: Integrate Firebase Analytics into an app and set up push notifications using FCM to engage with your users. Create and track custom events to measure the impact of notifications.

These projects are designed to give you real experience in integrating Firebase services and solving common app development challenges.

Benefits of Firebase Development

By the end of this book, you will understand how to leverage Firebase to develop complete applications without needing to manage your own backend infrastructure. You'll be comfortable using Firebase Authentication for user management, Firestore for data storage, Firebase Storage for media management, Cloud Functions for serverless backend logic, and Firebase Hosting for deploying web applications.

Firebase is an incredibly powerful tool, allowing you to bring applications to life quickly and efficiently. Whether you're an independent developer, a startup founder, or a part of a large development team, the skills you acquire from this book will be invaluable as you create engaging, scalable, and maintainable apps.

Firebase's philosophy is to reduce the barriers to mobile and web development, allowing you to focus on building features that matter most to your users. This book will enable you to make the most of Firebase's potential, ultimately improving your productivity as a developer and empowering you to create robust applications more easily than ever before.

We're excited for you to embark on this journey with Firebase. It's time to build, release, and monitor your applications like never before. Let's dive in!

Chapter 2: Getting Started with Firebase

What is Firebase?

Firebase is a comprehensive platform developed by Google, designed to help developers build and maintain mobile and web applications more easily. Firebase offers a wide array of tools and services that cover aspects like authentication, database management, file storage, and analytics—all seamlessly integrated to speed up development cycles and reduce the effort of managing backend infrastructure.

Firebase provides developers with tools to create applications without the need for setting up their own servers, databases, or custom backend services. This backend-as-a-service (BaaS) model is designed to help you focus more on building the front end of your application, enhancing user experiences, and reducing time to market. Firebase is particularly popular among mobile developers, and with Google's infrastructure behind it, it offers the scale and reliability that developers require.

The Firebase Ecosystem

At its core, Firebase consists of a suite of tools that together help create fully functional apps with less hassle:

- **Authentication**: Firebase Authentication provides easy integration for login services, supporting email-password combinations, social logins like Google and Facebook, and other third-party providers.
- **Realtime Database and Firestore**: Both Realtime Database and Firestore allow you to store and sync data in real time, with Firestore being more versatile for complex querying.
- **Firebase Storage**: Firebase Storage helps store and serve user-generated content such as images, videos, and other media files.
- **Cloud Functions**: Cloud Functions lets you run backend code without managing servers. It's perfect for executing server-side tasks in response to events from Firebase features.
- **Cloud Messaging**: Firebase Cloud Messaging (FCM) is used to send notifications to devices, keeping users engaged with the app.
- **Analytics**: Firebase Analytics provides insights into app usage, user behavior, and helps track performance metrics.

Firebase as a BaaS (Backend-as-a-Service)

Firebase is an excellent backend-as-a-service (BaaS) that saves developers the hassle of handling traditional backend setup and management. Imagine writing lines of code just to establish a REST API or manually configuring servers to support database connectivity. Firebase abstracts away all that complexity and provides a user-friendly SDK to do everything from authentication to file storage, allowing you to quickly set up services with just a few lines of code.

Firebase can be understood as a collection of services divided broadly into categories:

1. **Develop and Deploy**: Services like Authentication, Cloud Firestore, and Firebase Hosting fall into this category. They help developers build the foundational features of their app.
2. **Monitor and Engage**: Firebase Analytics and Cloud Messaging are tools that allow developers to understand how their application is used, identify any issues, and keep users engaged with the app.

Key Features of Firebase

1. Authentication

Firebase Authentication is one of the key components that help apps authenticate users effortlessly. It supports multiple methods, including:

- **Email and Password Authentication**: Allow users to register using their email and password.
- **Social Login**: Integrate with Google, Facebook, Twitter, etc.
- **Anonymous Authentication**: Let users use the app anonymously, providing a seamless user experience without requiring registration.

Here is an example of setting up Firebase authentication in a web application:

```
import { initializeApp } from 'firebase/app';
import { getAuth, createUserWithEmailAndPassword } from 'firebase/auth';

const firebaseConfig = {
  apiKey: "YOUR_API_KEY",
  authDomain: "YOUR_AUTH_DOMAIN",
  projectId: "YOUR_PROJECT_ID",
  storageBucket: "YOUR_STORAGE_BUCKET",
  messagingSenderId: "YOUR_MESSAGING_SENDER_ID",
  appId: "YOUR_APP_ID"
};

// Initialize Firebase
const app = initializeApp(firebaseConfig);
const auth = getAuth(app);

// Create a new user with email and password
```

```
createUserWithEmailAndPassword(auth,                 'user@example.com',
'password123')
  .then((userCredential) => {
    // Signed in
    const user = userCredential.user;
    console.log('User registered successfully:', user);
  })
  .catch((error) => {
    const errorCode = error.code;
    const errorMessage = error.message;
    console.error('Error during user registration:', errorCode,
errorMessage);
  });
```

This snippet demonstrates how easily Firebase allows us to create new users with email-password authentication using Firebase's Authentication service. The API handles all communication with the Firebase servers, ensuring security and ease of use.

2. Realtime Database and Firestore

Firebase offers two primary database solutions:

- **Realtime Database**: This is a NoSQL cloud database that stores data in JSON format and syncs it in real-time across all clients.
- **Firestore**: Cloud Firestore is a more advanced NoSQL document database that allows more complex data structures, indexing, and querying capabilities.

Firestore is generally preferred for modern applications because of its advanced features, including offline support, robust querying, and scalability.

Here is an example of adding a new document to Firestore:

```
import { getFirestore, doc, setDoc } from 'firebase/firestore';

// Initialize Firestore
const db = getFirestore(app);

// Add a new document to Firestore
async function addUser() {
  try {
    await setDoc(doc(db, "users", "user123"), {
      name: "John Doe",
      email: "john.doe@example.com",
```

```
      subscribed: true
    });
    console.log("Document successfully written!");
  } catch (error) {
    console.error("Error writing document: ", error);
  }
}

addUser();
```

In this example, a user document is added to the "users" collection in Firestore. The setDoc() method is used to create or overwrite the document data with the information specified.

3. Firebase Storage

Firebase Storage allows developers to store and serve user-generated content such as images, audio, and video. It is backed by Google Cloud Storage, ensuring scalability and reliability.

Here is an example of uploading a file to Firebase Storage:

```
import { getStorage, ref, uploadBytes } from 'firebase/storage';

// Initialize Firebase Storage
const storage = getStorage(app);

// Select a file input element
const fileInput = document.getElementById('file-input');

fileInput.addEventListener('change', async (event) => {
  const file = event.target.files[0];

  // Create a storage reference
  const storageRef = ref(storage, 'uploads/' + file.name);

  try {
    // Upload the file
    const snapshot = await uploadBytes(storageRef, file);
    console.log('Uploaded a blob or file!', snapshot);
  } catch (error) {
    console.error('Error uploading file:', error);
```

```
    }
});
```

Firebase Storage integrates seamlessly with Firebase Authentication, ensuring that only authenticated users have access to specific resources.

How Firebase Helps in Application Development

Firebase helps speed up application development in numerous ways:

1. **Eliminates Backend Development Needs**: Firebase takes care of backend infrastructure, such as servers, databases, and storage. Developers don't need to manage these, allowing them to focus on frontend development.
2. **Simplifies Authentication**: Adding authentication to an app is a significant challenge for many developers, especially when implementing OAuth or multi-factor authentication. Firebase provides easy-to-use authentication SDKs to integrate social logins.
3. **Real-time Synchronization**: The Realtime Database and Firestore allow applications to reflect data changes instantly across all users, ensuring a seamless experience for collaborative applications.
4. **Scalability and Reliability**: Firebase runs on Google Cloud, making it scalable and capable of handling millions of users without any additional configuration.
5. **Customizable Security Rules**: With Firebase's security rules, developers can protect their data while managing access for authenticated users.

Limitations of Firebase

Although Firebase is a powerful platform, there are certain limitations that developers should consider:

1. **Platform Lock-in**: Firebase uses proprietary tools and APIs. Switching to another platform in the future could be challenging if a project becomes highly reliant on Firebase-specific services.
2. **Pricing**: Firebase starts as a free service, but as the user base grows and application scales, costs may add up quickly, particularly if there are large storage or real-time database requirements.
3. **Database Structure Complexity**: Firestore and Realtime Database can be challenging to model correctly if you're coming from traditional relational databases like MySQL. Developers must be cautious about data structure to avoid costly read operations.
4. **Learning Curve**: Though Firebase services are intuitive, mastering all the available tools and understanding their use cases involves a learning curve, especially for those unfamiliar with NoSQL databases.

When to Use Firebase?

Firebase is best suited for projects that:

1. **Require Rapid Prototyping**: Firebase enables quick prototyping, allowing developers to focus on core features without managing infrastructure.
2. **Need Real-Time Data Synchronization**: Collaborative applications like chat apps, real-time games, or interactive dashboards are ideal use cases for Firebase's Realtime Database or Firestore.
3. **Don't Require Complex Queries**: If your application doesn't require complex relational database queries, Firebase's NoSQL databases can simplify development.
4. **Are Web and Mobile Centric**: Firebase is optimized for mobile and web apps, making it the perfect choice for startups and small-scale projects that need to go to market quickly.

Summary

Firebase offers a wide array of services that cover many aspects of mobile and web development. As a backend-as-a-service, Firebase allows developers to offload backend tasks like user authentication, real-time data syncing, file storage, and server-side code execution to the cloud, speeding up the development cycle.

While Firebase may not be ideal for every use case (e.g., projects requiring extensive relational data queries or those needing specific cloud infrastructure configurations), it is an excellent tool for developers looking to create powerful, scalable, and real-time applications efficiently. Its ability to handle backend services, coupled with Google Cloud's reliability, makes Firebase a popular choice for both beginners and experienced developers alike.

In the upcoming sections, we will dive deeper into Firebase features, exploring hands-on tutorials to implement them in real-world applications. Stay tuned as we proceed to connect Firebase to your application in the next section!

Setting Up Firebase for Your Project

Setting up Firebase for your project is one of the most crucial steps in utilizing Firebase's services and features effectively. In this section, we'll explore how to set up Firebase from scratch for a project, covering the process of creating a Firebase project, integrating it into your application, and configuring various services such as Authentication, Firestore, and Firebase Storage. By the end of this section, you will have a Firebase project ready to use, linked to your web or mobile app, and ready for further integration.

Creating a Firebase Project

The first step in setting up Firebase is to create a Firebase project using the Firebase Console. Firebase Console is a web-based interface that allows you to manage and monitor your Firebase resources.

1. **Go to Firebase Console**: Open your web browser and visit Firebase Console. You will need a Google account to use Firebase, so log in or create one if you haven't already.
2. **Create a New Project**:
    - Once logged in, click the "Add Project" button.

- Enter a name for your Firebase project. This name will help you identify the project in the console. It's usually a good idea to use a name similar to your application name.
- You may also be prompted to enable Google Analytics for your project. Enabling Analytics allows you to gather insights about your users, such as user engagement and app usage metrics.

3. **Select a Firebase Plan**:
   - Firebase offers a "Spark" plan, which is free, and a "Blaze" plan, which is pay-as-you-go. For development and small-scale projects, the Spark plan is usually sufficient, while larger projects may require the Blaze plan for scalability.

After following these steps, you will have successfully created a new Firebase project. You can now start configuring Firebase services and connect it to your app.

Adding Firebase to Your Web App

With your Firebase project set up, the next step is to integrate Firebase into your application. Firebase provides different SDKs for integrating its services into web and mobile apps. Here we'll focus on adding Firebase to a web application, but the process is similar for Android and iOS applications.

1. **Register Your Web App**:
   - From the Firebase Console, click on the "</>" icon (Web) to register a new web application with Firebase.
   - Enter a nickname for your web app, which helps identify it within the project.
   - You may also be prompted to set up Firebase Hosting, which we'll cover later.
2. **Firebase SDK Configuration**:
   - After registering your web app, you will receive a Firebase configuration object. This is JavaScript code that you need to include in your application to initialize Firebase.

The configuration code will look something like this:
javascript
Copy code
```
// Firebase configuration
const firebaseConfig = {
  apiKey: "YOUR_API_KEY",
  authDomain: "YOUR_AUTH_DOMAIN",
  projectId: "YOUR_PROJECT_ID",
  storageBucket: "YOUR_STORAGE_BUCKET",
  messagingSenderId: "YOUR_MESSAGING_SENDER_ID",
  appId: "YOUR_APP_ID"
};
```

3.

- Copy the configuration code and paste it into your JavaScript application. Typically, this would be in a `firebase.js` or similar file for easy reference.
4. **Install Firebase SDK**:
    - You can add Firebase to your project using either a CDN link or through a package manager such as npm or Yarn.

Option 1: Using CDN: Add the following script to your HTML file:

html
Copy code

```
<script src="https://www.gstatic.com/firebasejs/9.0.0/firebase-app.js"></script>
<script src="https://www.gstatic.com/firebasejs/9.0.0/firebase-auth.js"></script>
<script src="https://www.gstatic.com/firebasejs/9.0.0/firebase-firestore.js"></script>
<script src="https://www.gstatic.com/firebasejs/9.0.0/firebase-storage.js"></script>
```

Option 2: Using npm: Run the following command in your project directory:

bash
Copy code

```
npm install firebase
```

Import Firebase into Your Project:

javascript
Copy code

```
import { initializeApp } from 'firebase/app';
import { getAuth } from 'firebase/auth';
import { getFirestore } from 'firebase/firestore';
import { getStorage } from 'firebase/storage';

// Initialize Firebase
const app = initializeApp(firebaseConfig);
const auth = getAuth(app);
const db = getFirestore(app);
const storage = getStorage(app);
```

5. These steps will enable Firebase in your application and provide access to its Authentication, Firestore, and Storage services.

Integrating Firebase Services

Now that Firebase is connected to your application, let's dive deeper into setting up some of its most useful services—Firebase Authentication, Firestore, and Storage.

Setting Up Firebase Authentication

Firebase Authentication provides secure, simple, and effective methods to authenticate users in your application. To use Firebase Authentication:

1. **Enable Authentication Providers**:
   - Go to the Firebase Console.
   - Navigate to the "Authentication" tab on the left.
   - Click on "Sign-in method" and enable the desired sign-in providers. For example, you can enable **Email/Password**, **Google**, **Facebook**, and others.
2. **Code Implementation**:
   - Once the providers are enabled, you can start implementing them in your app. Here's an example of implementing email/password authentication:

```javascript
import { getAuth, createUserWithEmailAndPassword, signInWithEmailAndPassword } from 'firebase/auth';

// Register a new user
const registerUser = async (email, password) => {
  try {
    const userCredential = await createUserWithEmailAndPassword(auth, email, password);
    console.log('User registered successfully:', userCredential.user);
  } catch (error) {
    console.error('Error registering user:', error.message);
  }
};

// Sign in a user
const loginUser = async (email, password) => {
  try {
    const userCredential = await signInWithEmailAndPassword(auth, email, password);
    console.log('User logged in successfully:', userCredential.user);
  } catch (error) {
    console.error('Error logging in user:', error.message);
  }
};
```

3. This code snippet shows how to register and log in users using Firebase Authentication. With these methods, you can easily manage user sessions in your application.

Configuring Cloud Firestore

Cloud Firestore is a flexible, scalable database for storing and syncing data. Let's set up Firestore in your application.

1. **Enable Firestore**:
   - In the Firebase Console, navigate to the "Firestore Database" section.
   - Click on "Create Database."
   - Choose either production or test mode. For development, **test mode** can be used to avoid security restrictions initially. Remember to change to **production mode** before deployment to ensure data security.
2. **Create a Collection and Add Documents**:
   - Collections are containers for documents in Firestore.
   - For example, to create a `users` collection, navigate to Firestore in the console and click "Start Collection."
   - Add fields like `name`, `email`, `created_at`, etc.

Interacting with Firestore Programmatically: Here's how you can add a document to a Firestore collection:

javascript
Copy code

```javascript
import { collection, addDoc } from 'firebase/firestore';

const addUserToFirestore = async (user) => {
  try {
    const docRef = await addDoc(collection(db, 'users'), {
      name: user.name,
      email: user.email,
      created_at: new Date()
    });
    console.log('Document written with ID:', docRef.id);
  } catch (error) {
    console.error('Error adding document:', error);
  }
};
```

3. This code adds a new user document to the `users` collection in Firestore. You can also read, update, and delete documents as needed.

Setting Up Firebase Storage

Firebase Storage is used to store user-generated files such as images, audio, and video. Setting it up requires just a few steps:

1. **Enable Storage in Firebase Console**:
   - Go to the "Storage" section in the Firebase Console.

- Click "Get Started" and follow the setup prompts.

Upload Files to Storage: Here's an example of how to upload a file to Firebase Storage:
javascript
Copy code
```
import { ref, uploadBytes } from 'firebase/storage';

const uploadFile = async (file) => {
  const storageRef = ref(storage, 'uploads/' + file.name);
  try {
    const snapshot = await uploadBytes(storageRef, file);
    console.log('Uploaded a blob or file!', snapshot);
  } catch (error) {
    console.error('Error uploading file:', error);
  }
};
```

2. The above code takes a file and uploads it to the `uploads` directory in Firebase Storage.

Firebase Project Settings and Configuration

Firebase provides a wide range of settings that you can configure based on the needs of your project. Here are some common configurations you may need to adjust:

- **App Check**: Firebase App Check helps prevent unauthorized use of your resources by ensuring that only your app can access Firebase services. You can enable App Check in the Firebase Console under the App Check section.
- **Usage and Billing**: Firebase provides a dashboard where you can view your project's usage and billing information. This is especially useful when using the Blaze plan to monitor your spending and prevent unexpected costs.
- **Environment Settings**: When working with multiple environments (development, testing, production), Firebase allows you to create multiple Firebase projects and use different configurations. You can set up environment variables to manage configurations more effectively.

Summary

Setting up Firebase for your project is the first step in leveraging its powerful features for building real-time and engaging applications. By creating a Firebase project in the Firebase Console, integrating the Firebase SDK into your app, and configuring services like Authentication, Firestore, and Storage, you're establishing the foundation for a seamless, scalable application backend.

The next steps in your Firebase journey involve learning how to effectively use these services for your specific application requirements, understanding security rules to keep your data secure, and exploring advanced features like Firebase Hosting, Cloud Functions, and

Analytics. These powerful tools will help you build dynamic, real-time, and secure applications that delight users and simplify your development process.

Connecting Firebase to Your App

Connecting Firebase to your app is a pivotal step that allows you to leverage the full suite of Firebase services to enhance your application's functionality. Whether you are working on a mobile or web app, Firebase integration can streamline many of the backend complexities, such as user authentication, data management, file storage, and more. In this section, we will cover how to properly link Firebase to both web and mobile applications, including setting up configuration, initializing Firebase, and integrating core Firebase services.

Integrating Firebase with Web Apps

Connecting Firebase to a web application involves adding the Firebase SDK to your project, initializing the Firebase app, and integrating specific Firebase modules like Authentication, Firestore, or Storage.

Step 1: Add Firebase to Your Project

The first step is to add Firebase to your web project. Firebase provides multiple methods to do this—through a content delivery network (CDN) or by installing the Firebase SDK using npm.

1. **Using a CDN**:
    - Include the Firebase JavaScript libraries in your HTML by adding script tags.

html
Copy code
```
<script src="https://www.gstatic.com/firebasejs/9.0.0/firebase-app.js"></script>
<script src="https://www.gstatic.com/firebasejs/9.0.0/firebase-auth.js"></script>
<script src="https://www.gstatic.com/firebasejs/9.0.0/firebase-firestore.js"></script>
<script src="https://www.gstatic.com/firebasejs/9.0.0/firebase-storage.js"></script>
```

2.
3. **Using npm**:
    - If you prefer using a package manager, you can install Firebase using npm or Yarn.

bash
Copy code
```
npm install firebase
```

Chapter 2: Getting Started with Firebase

4.
   - Then, import the necessary modules into your project files:

```javascript
import { initializeApp } from 'firebase/app';
import { getAuth } from 'firebase/auth';
import { getFirestore } from 'firebase/firestore';
import { getStorage } from 'firebase/storage';
```

5.

Step 2: Firebase Project Configuration

Once Firebase is added to your project, the next step is to configure it with the project settings that you set up in the Firebase Console. This configuration object contains keys like `apiKey`, `authDomain`, `projectId`, and other identifiers unique to your Firebase project.

Here is an example configuration object:

```javascript
// Firebase configuration object
const firebaseConfig = {
  apiKey: "YOUR_API_KEY",
  authDomain: "YOUR_AUTH_DOMAIN",
  projectId: "YOUR_PROJECT_ID",
  storageBucket: "YOUR_STORAGE_BUCKET",
  messagingSenderId: "YOUR_MESSAGING_SENDER_ID",
  appId: "YOUR_APP_ID"
};

// Initialize Firebase
const app = initializeApp(firebaseConfig);
const auth = getAuth(app);
const db = getFirestore(app);
const storage = getStorage(app);
```

This configuration code is provided by Firebase Console when you add a new app to your Firebase project. Simply copy it and replace the placeholders (e.g., YOUR_API_KEY) with your actual values.

Step 3: Initialize Firebase

Firebase initialization is a crucial step that allows the SDK to start communicating with the Firebase backend services. Initializing Firebase typically occurs once, and all Firebase services are linked through this initialization.

The `initializeApp` method from `firebase/app` takes the configuration object and initializes it:

```javascript
// Initializing Firebase
const app = initializeApp(firebaseConfig);
```

This step needs to be done before accessing any Firebase services like Authentication or Firestore.

Using Firebase Authentication

Authentication is a critical part of most applications, and Firebase Authentication simplifies the process of managing users and their identities.

1. **Enabling Authentication Providers**:
    - Navigate to the Firebase Console and click on "Authentication."
    - Go to the "Sign-in method" tab and enable the sign-in providers you plan to use, such as **Email/Password**, **Google**, **Facebook**, etc.

Adding Authentication to Your App: With Firebase Authentication, you can allow users to register and log in easily. Here's how to create a registration and login feature using the **Email/Password** method.
javascript
Copy code

```javascript
import { createUserWithEmailAndPassword, signInWithEmailAndPassword } from 'firebase/auth';

// Register a new user
const registerUser = async (email, password) => {
  try {
    const userCredential = await createUserWithEmailAndPassword(auth, email, password);
    console.log('User registered:', userCredential.user);
  } catch (error) {
    console.error('Registration error:', error.message);
  }
};

// Sign in a user
const loginUser = async (email, password) => {
```

```
try {
    const userCredential = await signInWithEmailAndPassword(auth,
email, password);
    console.log('User signed in:', userCredential.user);
  } catch (error) {
    console.error('Login error:', error.message);
  }
};
```

2. This code creates simple functions to register and log in users using Firebase Authentication. By utilizing Firebase's authentication services, you can focus more on the user experience and less on the backend logic.

Connecting Firebase to Android Apps

Firebase offers a seamless integration process for Android apps, allowing developers to quickly add features like real-time databases, authentication, and cloud messaging.

Step 1: Set Up Firebase in Android Studio

1. **Add Firebase to Your Project**:
   - Open Android Studio and navigate to **Tools > Firebase**.
   - A Firebase Assistant pane will open on the right-hand side of the IDE.
   - Select the features you want to integrate (e.g., Authentication, Realtime Database) and follow the on-screen instructions.

Add Dependencies: Firebase Assistant will help add the required dependencies to your project's `build.gradle` file:
groovy
Copy code
```
dependencies {
    implementation platform('com.google.firebase:firebase-bom:31.0.2')
    implementation 'com.google.firebase:firebase-auth'
    implementation 'com.google.firebase:firebase-firestore'
}
```

2.
3. **Download the `google-services.json` File**:
   - Go to the Firebase Console.
   - Navigate to your project and add an Android app.
   - Download the `google-services.json` file provided by Firebase.
   - Place the file in your app's app/ directory in Android Studio.

Step 2: Initialize Firebase in Your Android App

To initialize Firebase in your Android app, modify your `MainActivity.java` or `MainActivity.kt`:

```java
import com.google.firebase.FirebaseApp;

public class MainActivity extends AppCompatActivity {
    @Override
    protected void onCreate(Bundle savedInstanceState) {
        super.onCreate(savedInstanceState);
        FirebaseApp.initializeApp(this);
        setContentView(R.layout.activity_main);
    }
}
```

This initialization step ensures that Firebase is ready for use when your app starts.

Step 3: Adding Firebase Authentication

With Firebase Authentication, you can add various sign-in options to your Android app.

Here's an example of adding email/password sign-in functionality in Android:

```java
FirebaseAuth auth = FirebaseAuth.getInstance();

public void registerUser(String email, String password) {
    auth.createUserWithEmailAndPassword(email, password)
        .addOnCompleteListener(this, task -> {
            if (task.isSuccessful()) {
                FirebaseUser user = auth.getCurrentUser();
                Log.d("FirebaseAuth", "Registration successful. User ID: " + user.getUid());
            } else {
                Log.e("FirebaseAuth", "Registration failed: " + task.getException().getMessage());
            }
        });
}

public void loginUser(String email, String password) {
    auth.signInWithEmailAndPassword(email, password)
        .addOnCompleteListener(this, task -> {
```

```java
            if (task.isSuccessful()) {
                FirebaseUser user = auth.getCurrentUser();
                Log.d("FirebaseAuth", "Login successful. User ID: " + user.getUid());
            } else {
                Log.e("FirebaseAuth", "Login failed: " + task.getException().getMessage());
            }
        });
}
```

In this example, the `registerUser` and `loginUser` methods allow users to create a new account and sign in, respectively, using their email and password.

Integrating Firebase with iOS Apps

Firebase also provides tools and SDKs for integrating with iOS apps, allowing iOS developers to take full advantage of Firebase's features.

Step 1: Set Up Firebase in Xcode

1. **Add Firebase to Your Xcode Project**:
   - Go to the Firebase Console and add a new iOS app.
   - Download the `GoogleService-Info.plist` file and add it to your Xcode project.
2. **Add Firebase SDK Dependencies**:
   - Firebase provides CocoaPods for managing dependencies. First, install CocoaPods if you haven't already:

bash
Copy code
```bash
sudo gem install cocoapods
```

   3.
   - Navigate to your project directory and create a `Podfile` by running:

bash
Copy code
```bash
pod init
```

   4.
   - Open the `Podfile` and add the Firebase dependencies you need:

ruby
Copy code
```ruby
pod 'Firebase/Auth'
```

```
pod 'Firebase/Firestore'
pod 'Firebase/Storage'
```

5.
   - Run pod install to install the dependencies.

Step 2: Initialize Firebase in Your iOS App

In your AppDelegate.swift file, add the following import and initialization:

```swift
import Firebase

@UIApplicationMain
class AppDelegate: UIResponder, UIApplicationDelegate {
    func application(_ application: UIApplication, didFinishLaunchingWithOptions launchOptions: [UIApplication.LaunchOptionsKey: Any]?) -> Bool {
        FirebaseApp.configure()
        return true
    }
}
```

This code initializes Firebase when your iOS application starts.

Step 3: Firebase Authentication for iOS

Firebase Authentication works similarly on iOS as it does on Android and web. Here's an example of adding email/password authentication:

```swift
import FirebaseAuth

func registerUser(email: String, password: String) {
    Auth.auth().createUser(withEmail: email, password: password) { authResult, error in
        if let error = error {
            print("Registration failed: \(error.localizedDescription)")
        } else {
            print("User registered successfully: \(authResult?.user.uid ?? "No User ID")")
        }
    }
}
```

```
}

func loginUser(email: String, password: String) {
    Auth.auth().signIn(withEmail: email, password: password) { authResult, error in
        if let error = error {
            print("Login failed: \(error.localizedDescription)")
        } else {
            print("User logged in successfully: \(authResult?.user.uid ?? "No User ID")")
        }
    }
}
```

These methods help register and log in users, similar to the process on Android and web platforms.

Summary

Connecting Firebase to your application—whether it's a web, Android, or iOS app—is a straightforward but essential step in utilizing the full range of Firebase services. By following the steps outlined above, you can link Firebase to your app, set up Authentication, configure Firestore and Storage, and ensure that the app is ready to provide a rich, dynamic experience to users.

Firebase's unified SDK and streamlined integration process make it an excellent choice for developers looking to incorporate powerful backend services with minimal setup. Once connected, Firebase allows you to focus on building great features and enhancing the user experience without the burden of managing infrastructure, servers, and data synchronization complexities.

Chapter 3: Firebase Authentication

Understanding Firebase Authentication

Firebase Authentication is a powerful and easy-to-use authentication system that allows developers to add various sign-in methods to their applications. It offers several ways for users to authenticate, including email/password, phone numbers, and social providers like Google, Facebook, and Twitter. This flexibility makes Firebase Authentication suitable for a wide variety of applications, ranging from small personal projects to large-scale commercial apps.

The importance of authentication in modern applications cannot be overstated. It forms the backbone of securing user data, ensuring that only authorized users can access specific features and content. Firebase simplifies the process of integrating robust authentication features, allowing you to focus more on building your application's core functionalities rather than managing and securing user credentials.

What is Firebase Authentication?

Firebase Authentication is a service that provides backend services, easy-to-use SDKs, and ready-made UI libraries to authenticate users to your app. By utilizing Firebase Authentication, you can handle the entire user sign-in process, complete with email verification, password resets, and multi-factor authentication without writing your own server code. Firebase takes care of complex tasks like encryption, token generation, and validation, so you don't have to reinvent the wheel.

Some of the key features of Firebase Authentication are:

- **Multiple Authentication Providers**: Support for email/password, social logins (Google, Facebook, Twitter), and anonymous authentication.
- **Integration with Firebase Products**: Firebase Authentication integrates seamlessly with other Firebase products like Firestore and Realtime Database.
- **Custom Authentication System**: The flexibility to use custom authentication systems and identity providers.

Why Use Firebase Authentication?

Firebase Authentication brings a lot of convenience and security to your application. Let's explore some of the reasons why it stands out:

- **Ease of Use**: Firebase offers straightforward APIs and libraries that help you implement authentication with minimal effort. The provided SDKs are well-documented and allow integration with different types of applications, including mobile (iOS, Android) and web applications.

- **Pre-built UI and Security**: Firebase provides pre-built UI libraries that you can use to create beautiful, customizable sign-in forms, helping you save time on building forms from scratch. Additionally, Firebase manages security for you, providing industry-standard encryption and authentication flows.
- **Scalability**: Firebase Authentication is built on Google infrastructure, ensuring high scalability to accommodate growing user bases without changing your authentication logic.
- **Support for Multiple Sign-in Providers**: It includes support for all major identity providers, such as Google, Facebook, GitHub, and Twitter. You can even create a custom provider if needed.

Authentication Flow in Firebase

The authentication process generally follows these steps:

1. **User Initiates Sign-in**: The user initiates the authentication by selecting their preferred authentication method (e.g., email/password, Google).
2. **Firebase Authentication Request**: The application sends the user credentials (or provider token) to Firebase Authentication via SDK.
3. **Token Verification and Response**: Firebase verifies the user credentials and generates an authentication token for a valid user.
4. **Access Granted**: Once authenticated, the application uses the generated token to grant access to restricted areas or resources.

Implementing Email and Password Authentication

Firebase offers multiple authentication options, but one of the simplest and most widely used is **email and password authentication**. Below, we'll walk through the process of implementing this in your application using Firebase.

Step 1: Enable Email and Password Authentication in Firebase Console

1. Go to the **Firebase Console**.
2. Select your project, then click on **Authentication** from the left-hand menu.
3. Navigate to the **Sign-in Method** tab and enable **Email/Password**.

Step 2: Setting Up Authentication in Your Application

You'll need to add Firebase to your application to use its authentication features. Ensure you have Firebase SDK installed and properly configured.

For **Web Applications**:

Add the Firebase JavaScript SDK to your project by including the script in your HTML:

```
<script     src="https://www.gstatic.com/firebasejs/9.x.x/firebase-app.js"></script>
```

```
<script        src="https://www.gstatic.com/firebasejs/9.x.x/firebase-
auth.js"></script>
<script>
  // Your web app's Firebase configuration
  const firebaseConfig = {
    apiKey: "YOUR_API_KEY",
    authDomain: "YOUR_AUTH_DOMAIN",
    projectId: "YOUR_PROJECT_ID",
    storageBucket: "YOUR_STORAGE_BUCKET",
    messagingSenderId: "YOUR_MESSAGING_SENDER_ID",
    appId: "YOUR_APP_ID"
  };

  // Initialize Firebase
  firebase.initializeApp(firebaseConfig);
</script>
```

For **Android Applications**:

Add Firebase Authentication to your project by including the required dependency in your build.gradle file:

```
implementation 'com.google.firebase:firebase-auth:21.0.1'
```

Then, ensure Firebase is initialized properly in your app by including:

```
FirebaseApp.initializeApp(this);
```

Step 3: Sign Up New Users with Email and Password

Once Firebase Authentication is enabled, you can allow users to sign up with their email and password. Here's an example for a **Web Application**:

```
import { getAuth, createUserWithEmailAndPassword } from
"https://www.gstatic.com/firebasejs/9.x.x/firebase-auth.js";

const auth = getAuth();
function signUpUser(email, password) {
    createUserWithEmailAndPassword(auth, email, password)
```

Chapter 3: Firebase Authentication

```
    .then((userCredential) => {
        // Signed up successfully
        const user = userCredential.user;
        console.log("User created:", user);
    })
    .catch((error) => {
        const errorCode = error.code;
        const errorMessage = error.message;
        console.error("Error creating user:", errorCode,
errorMessage);
    });
}
```

For Android, you could implement a similar flow:

```
FirebaseAuth mAuth = FirebaseAuth.getInstance();

mAuth.createUserWithEmailAndPassword(email, password)
    .addOnCompleteListener(this, task -> {
        if (task.isSuccessful()) {
            // Sign up success, update UI with the user's
information
            FirebaseUser user = mAuth.getCurrentUser();
            Log.d("Auth", "User registered successfully");
        } else {
            // If sign in fails, display a message to the user.
            Log.w("Auth", "User registration failed",
task.getException());
        }
    });
```

Step 4: Sign In Users

After registering users, they can sign in with their email and password. Here's how:

For Web:

```
import { getAuth, signInWithEmailAndPassword } from
"https://www.gstatic.com/firebasejs/9.x.x/firebase-auth.js";
```

```javascript
function signInUser(email, password) {
    signInWithEmailAndPassword(auth, email, password)
    .then((userCredential) => {
        // Signed in successfully
        const user = userCredential.user;
        console.log("User signed in:", user);
    })
    .catch((error) => {
        const errorCode = error.code;
        const errorMessage = error.message;
        console.error("Error signing in:", errorCode, errorMessage);
    });
}
```

For Android:

```java
mAuth.signInWithEmailAndPassword(email, password)
    .addOnCompleteListener(this, task -> {
        if (task.isSuccessful()) {
            FirebaseUser user = mAuth.getCurrentUser();
            Log.d("Auth", "User signed in successfully");
        } else {
            Log.w("Auth", "Sign-in failed", task.getException());
        }
    });
```

Adding Error Handling and Security

Error handling is critical to providing a good user experience, especially during authentication. Here are some common errors you need to handle:

- **Invalid Email Format**: Ensure users are entering a properly formatted email address.
- **Weak Password**: Firebase may reject weak passwords. Ensure you prompt users to create strong passwords.
- **User Not Found**: Handle cases where users try to sign in but the account doesn't exist.
- **Network Errors**: Handle network connectivity issues gracefully to avoid a poor user experience.

Adding **recaptcha verification** to your email/password flow can further enhance the security of your authentication process.

Password Recovery

Firebase Authentication makes it easy to implement password recovery if users forget their password. You can use the **sendPasswordResetEmail** method:

For Web:

```
import { getAuth, sendPasswordResetEmail } from "https://www.gstatic.com/firebasejs/9.x.x/firebase-auth.js";

function resetPassword(email) {
    sendPasswordResetEmail(auth, email)
    .then(() => {
        // Password reset email sent
        console.log("Password reset email sent");
    })
    .catch((error) => {
        console.error("Error sending password reset email:", error);
    });
}
```

For Android:

```
mAuth.sendPasswordResetEmail(email)
    .addOnCompleteListener(task -> {
        if (task.isSuccessful()) {
            Log.d("Auth", "Password reset email sent");
        } else {
            Log.w("Auth", "Failed to send password reset email", task.getException());
        }
    });
```

Email Verification

Sending an email verification link after a user has signed up adds another layer of security. Firebase provides a convenient method for this:

For Web:

```
import { getAuth, sendEmailVerification } from
"https://www.gstatic.com/firebasejs/9.x.x/firebase-auth.js";

function verifyEmail() {
    sendEmailVerification(auth.currentUser)
    .then(() => {
        // Email verification sent
        console.log("Verification email sent");
    });
}
```

For Android:

```
FirebaseUser user = mAuth.getCurrentUser();
if (user != null) {
    user.sendEmailVerification()
        .addOnCompleteListener(task -> {
            if (task.isSuccessful()) {
                Log.d("Auth", "Verification email sent");
            }
        });
}
```

Security Best Practices for Firebase Authentication

- **Enforce Strong Passwords**: Enforce policies requiring users to use strong passwords.
- **Monitor Login Attempts**: Use Firebase's **Analytics** to monitor suspicious login activity.
- **Multi-Factor Authentication (MFA)**: For higher security, consider implementing **MFA** to provide a second layer of authentication.
- **Rules and Database Security**: Integrate **Firebase Security Rules** to prevent unauthorized access to your database even after successful authentication.

Firebase Authentication provides a feature-rich, secure, and easy-to-use solution to manage user sign-in and sign-up. Its built-in features, including support for multiple identity providers, security measures, and easy integration with other Firebase products, make it a preferred choice for many developers.

By understanding how to implement, manage, and secure authentication using Firebase, you'll be well on your way to developing applications that are not only functional but also safe and user-friendly. Firebase Authentication is the cornerstone for creating a seamless user experience that maintains high security standards, a crucial element for any successful app.

Implementing Email and Password Authentication

Email and Password Authentication is one of the most common authentication methods for web and mobile applications. Firebase makes it extremely simple to add this type of authentication to your project. This section will guide you through the process of setting up email and password authentication, implementing the necessary forms, and managing the authentication flow, covering both client-side and backend considerations.

Setting Up Email and Password Authentication in Firebase Console

Before diving into the code, it's essential to configure Firebase to allow users to sign in using their email and password. To do this:

1. Navigate to the **Firebase Console**.
2. Select your project, and then click on **Authentication** in the left-hand menu.
3. Under the **Sign-in method** tab, locate the **Email/Password** option and click to enable it.
4. Save your settings.

This enables your Firebase backend to accept and authenticate users who register using an email and password.

Integrating Email and Password Authentication into Your App

Step 1: Install and Configure Firebase SDK

To start integrating Firebase Authentication into your app, you need to install the Firebase SDK. The installation and configuration process varies based on your platform:

For Web Applications:

First, add Firebase to your project by including the JavaScript SDK in your HTML:

```
<script       src="https://www.gstatic.com/firebasejs/9.x.x/firebase-app.js"></script>
<script       src="https://www.gstatic.com/firebasejs/9.x.x/firebase-auth.js"></script>
<script>
  // Your web app's Firebase configuration
  const firebaseConfig = {
    apiKey: "YOUR_API_KEY",
    authDomain: "YOUR_AUTH_DOMAIN",
    projectId: "YOUR_PROJECT_ID",
```

```
    storageBucket: "YOUR_STORAGE_BUCKET",
    messagingSenderId: "YOUR_MESSAGING_SENDER_ID",
    appId: "YOUR_APP_ID"
  };

  // Initialize Firebase
  firebase.initializeApp(firebaseConfig);
</script>
```

For Android Applications:

In Android, add the Firebase Authentication dependency to your `build.gradle` file:

```
implementation 'com.google.firebase:firebase-auth:21.0.1'
```

Initialize Firebase in your app by adding the following to your `onCreate()` method in your main activity:

```
FirebaseApp.initializeApp(this);
```

Building the Registration Form

Now that Firebase is set up, the next step is to build a registration form. This form will allow users to enter their email and password to sign up.

For Web Applications:

Here's a simple example of a registration form in HTML:

```
<form id="registrationForm">
  <input type="email" id="email" placeholder="Enter your email" required />
  <input type="password" id="password" placeholder="Enter your password" required />
  <button type="submit">Register</button>
</form>

<script>
```

```
document.getElementById('registrationForm').addEventListener('submit
', (e) => {
    e.preventDefault();
    const email = document.getElementById('email').value;
    const password = document.getElementById('password').value;
    signUpUser(email, password);
  });
</script>
```

JavaScript Code for Registration:

To register a new user using Firebase Authentication, use the following JavaScript function:

```
import { getAuth, createUserWithEmailAndPassword } from
"https://www.gstatic.com/firebasejs/9.x.x/firebase-auth.js";

const auth = getAuth();

function signUpUser(email, password) {
  createUserWithEmailAndPassword(auth, email, password)
    .then((userCredential) => {
      // User registered successfully
      const user = userCredential.user;
      console.log("User signed up:", user);
    })
    .catch((error) => {
      const errorCode = error.code;
      const errorMessage = error.message;
      console.error("Error during sign-up:", errorCode, errorMessage);
    });
}
```

This function handles user registration by taking the email and password inputs, using the createUserWithEmailAndPassword function to communicate with Firebase, and then handling the response.

For Android Applications:

To implement user registration on Android, use the following Java code:

```java
FirebaseAuth mAuth = FirebaseAuth.getInstance();

public void signUpUser(String email, String password) {
    mAuth.createUserWithEmailAndPassword(email, password)
        .addOnCompleteListener(this, task -> {
            if (task.isSuccessful()) {
                // Registration successful
                FirebaseUser user = mAuth.getCurrentUser();
                Log.d("Auth", "User registered successfully: " + user.getEmail());
            } else {
                // Registration failed
                Log.w("Auth", "User registration failed", task.getException());
            }
        });
}
```

Building the Login Form

After registration, users need to log in to access their accounts. Let's implement a login form to authenticate users.

For Web Applications:

Here's a simple login form in HTML:

```html
<form id="loginForm">
  <input type="email" id="loginEmail" placeholder="Enter your email" required />
  <input type="password" id="loginPassword" placeholder="Enter your password" required />
  <button type="submit">Log In</button>
</form>

<script>
  document.getElementById('loginForm').addEventListener('submit', (e) => {
    e.preventDefault();
    const email = document.getElementById('loginEmail').value;
    const password = document.getElementById('loginPassword').value;
```

```
    loginUser(email, password);
  });
</script>
```

JavaScript Code for Login:

To log in a user using Firebase Authentication, use the following JavaScript function:

```
import { getAuth, signInWithEmailAndPassword } from
"https://www.gstatic.com/firebasejs/9.x.x/firebase-auth.js";

function loginUser(email, password) {
  signInWithEmailAndPassword(auth, email, password)
    .then((userCredential) => {
      // User signed in successfully
      const user = userCredential.user;
      console.log("User logged in:", user);
    })
    .catch((error) => {
      const errorCode = error.code;
      const errorMessage = error.message;
      console.error("Error during login:", errorCode, errorMessage);
    });
}
```

For Android Applications:

To implement user login on Android, use the following Java code:

```
mAuth.signInWithEmailAndPassword(email, password)
    .addOnCompleteListener(this, task -> {
        if (task.isSuccessful()) {
            // Sign in success
            FirebaseUser user = mAuth.getCurrentUser();
            Log.d("Auth", "User signed in successfully: " + user.getEmail());
        } else {
            // Sign in failed
            Log.w("Auth", "User sign-in failed", task.getException());
```

        }
    });

Handling User Authentication States

Handling user authentication states is crucial for managing user sessions. Firebase makes it easy to monitor the authentication state of users and act accordingly.

For Web Applications:

```
import { getAuth, onAuthStateChanged } from "https://www.gstatic.com/firebasejs/9.x.x/firebase-auth.js";

onAuthStateChanged(auth, (user) => {
  if (user) {
    // User is signed in
    console.log("User is signed in:", user);
  } else {
    // User is signed out
    console.log("No user is signed in");
  }
});
```

For Android Applications:

In Android, you can use an `AuthStateListener` to monitor user authentication:

```
FirebaseAuth.AuthStateListener authListener = firebaseAuth -> {
    FirebaseUser user = firebaseAuth.getCurrentUser();
    if (user != null) {
        // User is signed in
        Log.d("Auth", "User is signed in: " + user.getEmail());
    } else {
        // User is signed out
        Log.d("Auth", "No user is signed in");
    }
};

@Override
protected void onStart() {
```

```
    super.onStart();
    mAuth.addAuthStateListener(authListener);
}

@Override
protected void onStop() {
    super.onStop();
    if (authListener != null) {
        mAuth.removeAuthStateListener(authListener);
    }
}
```

Password Reset

It's common for users to forget their passwords. Firebase makes it simple to add a password reset feature.

For Web Applications:

To allow users to reset their password, use the `sendPasswordResetEmail` function:

```
import { getAuth, sendPasswordResetEmail } from
"https://www.gstatic.com/firebasejs/9.x.x/firebase-auth.js";

function resetPassword(email) {
  sendPasswordResetEmail(auth, email)
    .then(() => {
      // Password reset email sent
      console.log("Password reset email sent");
    })
    .catch((error) => {
      console.error("Error sending password reset email:", error);
    });
}
```

For Android Applications:

```
mAuth.sendPasswordResetEmail(email)
    .addOnCompleteListener(task -> {
        if (task.isSuccessful()) {
```

```
            Log.d("Auth", "Password reset email sent");
        } else {
            Log.w("Auth", "Failed to send password reset email",
task.getException());
        }
    });
```

Securing Authentication with Firebase Security Rules

Firebase allows you to define security rules to protect your authentication system and ensure that data access is restricted only to authenticated users. When setting up Firebase Authentication, you should ensure the proper security rules are in place to prevent unauthorized access.

For example, you might want to write rules in Firebase Firestore that only allow authenticated users to access data:

```
service cloud.firestore {
  match /databases/{database}/documents {
    match /{document=**} {
      allow read, write: if request.auth != null;
    }
  }
}
```

These rules ensure that only authenticated users can read or write data to your Firestore database, enhancing the overall security of your application.

Error Handling and User Experience

Handling errors appropriately is crucial to maintaining a good user experience. Firebase Authentication provides several error codes that you need to handle:

- **Invalid Email**: Ensure users provide a valid email address.
- **User Not Found**: Display appropriate messages if a user tries to sign in with an unregistered email.
- **Wrong Password**: Inform users when they provide an incorrect password.
- **Weak Password**: During sign-up, enforce the use of strong passwords.

For instance, here's a way to handle these errors in JavaScript:

```
function handleAuthError(error) {
  const errorCode = error.code;
```

```javascript
  switch (errorCode) {
    case 'auth/invalid-email':
      console.error("Invalid email address.");
      break;
    case 'auth/user-not-found':
      console.error("No user found with this email.");
      break;
    case 'auth/wrong-password':
      console.error("Incorrect password.");
      break;
    case 'auth/weak-password':
      console.error("Password is too weak. Please use a stronger password.");
      break;
    default:
      console.error("An unknown error occurred:", error.message);
  }
}
```

Using these error-handling techniques ensures that users receive informative feedback, which can help them resolve issues and improve their experience.

Conclusion

Email and password authentication is a fundamental part of most applications today, and Firebase makes implementing this feature straightforward. By following the steps outlined in this section, you can set up a robust authentication system, allowing users to securely register, log in, and manage their accounts.

Firebase provides all the tools you need for a reliable authentication system—ranging from managing user sessions, handling forgotten passwords, and integrating secure authentication flows to monitoring authentication states. The combination of simplicity, flexibility, and security makes Firebase Authentication an ideal choice for most projects.

Whether you're building a small personal app or a large-scale platform, using Firebase Authentication helps you focus on your core application logic while ensuring users can authenticate safely and efficiently.

Adding Social Logins

Adding social logins to your application can significantly enhance user experience by allowing users to sign in with their existing accounts on platforms like Google, Facebook, Twitter, or GitHub. This reduces friction, as users do not need to create new credentials and remember additional passwords. Firebase Authentication makes it easy to integrate these providers, offering pre-built solutions and simplified APIs for most major identity providers.

In this section, we will explore how to add social login features to your Firebase Authentication flow, including the setup steps and code examples for different platforms.

Benefits of Adding Social Logins

Before diving into implementation, let's look at why adding social logins can benefit your application:

1. **Better User Experience**: Users can quickly sign up or log in with a single click, avoiding the need to fill out lengthy registration forms.
2. **Higher Conversion Rates**: Simplified registration processes lead to more users completing the sign-up process.
3. **Reduced Password Fatigue**: Social logins reduce the burden of remembering yet another password, which can enhance user satisfaction.
4. **Verification and Data**: Social logins can provide verified information like email addresses, making it easier to trust user inputs and streamline app onboarding.

Configuring Social Login Providers in Firebase

To add social logins, you need to enable the desired providers in the Firebase Console:

1. **Go to the Firebase Console** and select your project.
2. Click on **Authentication** from the left-hand menu.
3. Navigate to the **Sign-in Method** tab.
4. You will see options for **Google, Facebook, Twitter, GitHub**, and other providers.
5. Click on the provider you want to enable and follow the instructions to configure it. Each provider requires some credentials:
   - For **Google**: No additional setup is required; just enable it.
   - For **Facebook**: You will need the **App ID** and **App Secret** from the Facebook Developers portal.
   - For **Twitter** and **GitHub**: You will need similar keys and secrets from their developer platforms.

Google Sign-In Implementation

Let's begin with **Google Sign-In**, one of the most popular social login options. Firebase provides an easy-to-use API for adding Google as an authentication provider.

Step 1: Enable Google Sign-In in Firebase Console

To enable Google Sign-In:

- Go to the **Sign-in Method** tab in the Firebase Console.
- Select **Google** from the list of providers.
- Click **Enable** and save your changes.

Step 2: Setting Up Google Sign-In in Your App

For Web Applications:

Add the necessary scripts to your HTML file to include Firebase and Google provider functionality:

```html
<script src="https://www.gstatic.com/firebasejs/9.x.x/firebase-app.js"></script>
<script src="https://www.gstatic.com/firebasejs/9.x.x/firebase-auth.js"></script>
<script>
  // Your web app's Firebase configuration
  const firebaseConfig = {
    apiKey: "YOUR_API_KEY",
    authDomain: "YOUR_AUTH_DOMAIN",
    projectId: "YOUR_PROJECT_ID",
    storageBucket: "YOUR_STORAGE_BUCKET",
    messagingSenderId: "YOUR_MESSAGING_SENDER_ID",
    appId: "YOUR_APP_ID"
  };

  // Initialize Firebase
  firebase.initializeApp(firebaseConfig);
</script>
```

Now, add a Google Sign-In button and implement the sign-in function:

```html
<button id="googleSignInButton">Sign in with Google</button>

<script>
  import { getAuth, GoogleAuthProvider, signInWithPopup } from "https://www.gstatic.com/firebasejs/9.x.x/firebase-auth.js";

  const auth = getAuth();
  const provider = new GoogleAuthProvider();


document.getElementById('googleSignInButton').addEventListener('click', () => {
    signInWithPopup(auth, provider)
```

```javascript
      .then((result) => {
        // User signed in successfully
        const user = result.user;
        console.log("User signed in with Google:", user);
      })
      .catch((error) => {
        console.error("Error signing in with Google:", error);
      });
  });
</script>
```

For Android Applications:

Add the Google Sign-In dependency to your `build.gradle` file:

```
implementation 'com.google.android.gms:play-services-auth:20.0.0'
```

Configure Google Sign-In options:

```java
GoogleSignInOptions gso = new GoogleSignInOptions.Builder(GoogleSignInOptions.DEFAULT_SIGN_IN)
    .requestIdToken(getString(R.string.default_web_client_id))
    .requestEmail()
    .build();
GoogleSignInClient mGoogleSignInClient = GoogleSignIn.getClient(this, gso);
```

Handle sign-in intent:

```java
@Override
public void onClick(View v) {
    switch (v.getId()) {
        case R.id.google_sign_in_button:
            signIn();
            break;
    }
}

private void signIn() {
```

```java
        Intent signInIntent = mGoogleSignInClient.getSignInIntent();
        startActivityForResult(signInIntent, RC_SIGN_IN);
    }

    @Override
    public void onActivityResult(int requestCode, int resultCode, Intent data) {
        super.onActivityResult(requestCode, resultCode, data);

        if (requestCode == RC_SIGN_IN) {
            Task<GoogleSignInAccount> task = GoogleSignIn.getSignedInAccountFromIntent(data);
            try {
                GoogleSignInAccount account = task.getResult(ApiException.class);
                firebaseAuthWithGoogle(account);
            } catch (ApiException e) {
                Log.w(TAG, "Google sign in failed", e);
            }
        }
    }

    private void firebaseAuthWithGoogle(GoogleSignInAccount acct) {
        AuthCredential credential = GoogleAuthProvider.getCredential(acct.getIdToken(), null);
        mAuth.signInWithCredential(credential)
            .addOnCompleteListener(this, task -> {
                if (task.isSuccessful()) {
                    FirebaseUser user = mAuth.getCurrentUser();
                    Log.d("Auth", "signInWithCredential:success");
                } else {
                    Log.w("Auth", "signInWithCredential:failure", task.getException());
                }
            });
    }
```

Adding Facebook Login

Facebook is another widely used social login option. Setting it up involves getting credentials from the Facebook Developer Console.

Step 1: Get App Credentials from Facebook Developer Console

- Create a new app in the **Facebook Developer Console**.
- Under **Settings > Basic**, you will find the **App ID** and **App Secret**.
- Copy these credentials and use them in the Firebase Console to enable Facebook login.

Step 2: Enable Facebook Login in Firebase Console

- Go to the Firebase Console.
- Under **Authentication > Sign-in Method**, select **Facebook**.
- Enter the **App ID** and **App Secret**, and save your changes.

Step 3: Implement Facebook Login in Your App

For Web Applications:

Add the Facebook login button and handle the login process:

```html
<button id="facebookSignInButton">Sign in with Facebook</button>

<script>
  import { getAuth, FacebookAuthProvider, signInWithPopup } from "https://www.gstatic.com/firebasejs/9.x.x/firebase-auth.js";

  const auth = getAuth();
  const provider = new FacebookAuthProvider();


document.getElementById('facebookSignInButton').addEventListener('click', () => {
    signInWithPopup(auth, provider)
      .then((result) => {
        // User signed in successfully
        const user = result.user;
        console.log("User signed in with Facebook:", user);
      })
      .catch((error) => {
        console.error("Error signing in with Facebook:", error);
      });
  });
</script>
```

For Android Applications:

Add the Facebook SDK to your project:

```
implementation 'com.facebook.android:facebook-android-sdk:[5,6)'
```

Configure Facebook login:

```java
CallbackManager mCallbackManager = CallbackManager.Factory.create();
LoginButton loginButton = findViewById(R.id.login_button);
loginButton.setReadPermissions("email", "public_profile");
loginButton.registerCallback(mCallbackManager,                          new
FacebookCallback<LoginResult>() {
    @Override
    public void onSuccess(LoginResult loginResult) {
        Log.d(TAG, "facebook:onSuccess:" + loginResult);
        handleFacebookAccessToken(loginResult.getAccessToken());
    }

    @Override
    public void onCancel() {
        Log.d(TAG, "facebook:onCancel");
    }

    @Override
    public void onError(FacebookException error) {
        Log.d(TAG, "facebook:onError", error);
    }
});

private void handleFacebookAccessToken(AccessToken token) {
    AuthCredential                       credential                      =
FacebookAuthProvider.getCredential(token.getToken());
    mAuth.signInWithCredential(credential)
        .addOnCompleteListener(this, task -> {
            if (task.isSuccessful()) {
                Log.d(TAG, "signInWithCredential:success");
                FirebaseUser user = mAuth.getCurrentUser();
            } else {
                Log.w(TAG,                   "signInWithCredential:failure",
task.getException());
            }
```

        });
}

Adding Twitter Login

Twitter login is also popular, particularly for applications that have a user base active on that platform.

Step 1: Obtain Twitter App Credentials

- Go to the **Twitter Developer Console**.
- Create an application and generate the **API Key** and **API Secret Key**.
- Enable **3-legged OAuth**.

Step 2: Enable Twitter Login in Firebase Console

- Go to the Firebase Console.
- Under **Authentication** > **Sign-in Method**, select **Twitter**.
- Enter the **API Key** and **API Secret Key** from Twitter.

Step 3: Implement Twitter Login in Your App

For Web Applications:

Add the necessary code to implement Twitter login using Firebase:

```
import { getAuth, TwitterAuthProvider, signInWithPopup } from "https://www.gstatic.com/firebasejs/9.x.x/firebase-auth.js";

const auth = getAuth();
const provider = new TwitterAuthProvider();

function twitterLogin() {
  signInWithPopup(auth, provider)
    .then((result) => {
      // Twitter login successful
      const user = result.user;
      console.log("User signed in with Twitter:", user);
    })
    .catch((error) => {
      console.error("Error signing in with Twitter:", error);
    });
}
```

```
document.getElementById('twitterSignInButton').addEventListener('cli
ck', twitterLogin);
```

Handling Sign-Out and Authentication State

After implementing various social login providers, you need to handle **sign-out** and monitor **authentication states** effectively.

Sign-Out Functionality:

To sign out a user:

For Web Applications:

```
import { getAuth, signOut } from
"https://www.gstatic.com/firebasejs/9.x.x/firebase-auth.js";

function logOut() {
  signOut(auth).then(() => {
    console.log("User signed out successfully.");
  }).catch((error) => {
    console.error("Error signing out:", error);
  });
}
```

For Android Applications:

```
FirebaseAuth.getInstance().signOut();
```

Handling Authentication State:

Monitoring the authentication state allows you to detect whether a user is signed in or not, making it easy to tailor your app's user interface accordingly.

For Web Applications:

```
import { getAuth, onAuthStateChanged } from
"https://www.gstatic.com/firebasejs/9.x.x/firebase-auth.js";

onAuthStateChanged(auth, (user) => {
  if (user) {
```

```
    // User is signed in
    console.log("User signed in:", user.displayName);
  } else {
    // User is signed out
    console.log("No user is signed in.");
  }
});
```

For Android Applications:

```
FirebaseAuth.AuthStateListener authListener = firebaseAuth -> {
    FirebaseUser user = firebaseAuth.getCurrentUser();
    if (user != null) {
        Log.d(TAG, "User is signed in: " + user.getEmail());
    } else {
        Log.d(TAG, "No user is signed in.");
    }
};
```

Error Handling in Social Logins

Error handling is crucial when integrating social logins, as users can face a variety of issues, such as denied permissions or network errors.

Common Errors:

- **Popup Blocked**: Browsers might block popups, especially for the first-time sign-in attempt.
- **Network Errors**: Ensure your application is prepared to handle scenarios where network availability is poor.
- **Denied Permissions**: Users may deny permissions requested by the app, leading to incomplete authentication.

An example of handling common errors in a web app:

```
function handleAuthError(error) {
  switch (error.code) {
    case 'auth/popup-blocked':
      console.error("Popup was blocked by the browser.");
      break;
    case 'auth/network-request-failed':
```

```
      console.error("Network   error   occurred.   Please   check   your
connection.");
      break;
    case 'auth/cancelled-popup-request':
      console.error("User   closed   the   popup   before   completing   the
sign-in process.");
      break;
    default:
      console.error("An unknown error occurred:", error.message);
  }
}
```

Conclusion

Adding social logins to your application can dramatically improve the user experience by offering fast, convenient ways to sign up and sign in. Firebase Authentication provides a simple, unified approach to integrating multiple identity providers, including Google, Facebook, Twitter, and more.

Throughout this section, we have covered how to enable and implement social login providers in Firebase, with examples for both web and Android applications. By implementing social logins, you are helping users avoid the hassle of managing new accounts and passwords, making your app more attractive and accessible.

From setting up provider credentials to handling user authentication states, Firebase makes it easier to manage a secure and flexible login system that meets your application's needs while enhancing user satisfaction.

Chapter 4: Real-time Database vs. Firestore

Firebase Database Options

Firebase provides two main database services for app development: the **Realtime Database** and **Cloud Firestore**. While both offer powerful cloud-hosted NoSQL database solutions, they cater to slightly different use cases and have distinct architectures, which makes understanding their differences crucial for choosing the right option for your project.

Overview of Firebase Realtime Database

The Firebase **Realtime Database** is a NoSQL cloud database that stores data as a JSON tree. Its key characteristic is the capability to synchronize data in real-time across all clients connected to it. This means that whenever data changes, every client with a listener receives the updated data instantly. Realtime Database is particularly well-suited for applications that require live, synchronized data, such as chat apps, collaborative tools, and games.

Key Features of Realtime Database
Real-time Synchronization: The primary feature of the Realtime Database is that it synchronizes data across connected clients instantly. For example, in a chat application, new messages are instantly available to all users without needing a manual refresh.
javascript
Copy　　　　　　　　　　　　　　　　　　　　　　　　　　　　　　　　　　code
```javascript
const db = firebase.database();
db.ref('/messages').on('value', (snapshot) => {
    const messages = snapshot.val();
    updateUI(messages);
});
```

1. In this snippet, the on('value', ...) listener ensures that whenever the /messages path changes, the UI is automatically updated.

Offline Support: Realtime Database also provides offline support. When users lose connectivity, data remains accessible locally and syncs when they regain a connection. This feature is handy for mobile apps where network issues are common.
javascript
Copy　　　　　　　　　　　　　　　　　　　　　　　　　　　　　　　　　　code
```javascript
firebase.database().ref('/todos').once('value')
  .then((snapshot) => {
    // Data is available locally, even if offline
```

```javascript
    const todos = snapshot.val();
    displayTodos(todos);
});
```

2.
3. **Simple Data Model**: Data is represented in JSON format. While this makes the Realtime Database easy to use, it also presents challenges with complex data structures. All data is nested, meaning you may need to be careful to avoid deeply nested JSON that can become cumbersome to maintain.

Pros and Cons of Realtime Database

Pros:

- **Real-time Updates**: Immediate synchronization between clients.
- **Offline Capabilities**: Support for offline mode, enabling data persistence on clients.
- **Ease of Use**: A simple JSON-based data model makes getting started easy.

Cons:

- **Scalability Challenges**: As data size grows, performance might degrade. Realtime Database is ideal for small to medium-sized applications but may require workarounds for scaling with massive data.
- **Data Nesting**: The JSON structure can become difficult to manage if the data grows complex, leading to increased maintenance efforts.

Introduction to Cloud Firestore

Cloud **Firestore** is Firebase's newer database service, which addresses many of the limitations of the Realtime Database. Firestore is a NoSQL document-based database, where data is organized into collections and documents. It was built with scalability and complex queries in mind, making it a more suitable option for modern applications that need advanced data management.

Key Features of Firestore

Document-Based Structure: Firestore uses a document and collection hierarchy. Data is stored in documents, and documents are organized into collections. Unlike the Realtime Database's JSON tree, this structure allows for a more flexible and organized data schema.
javascript
Copy   code
```
const db = firebase.firestore();
const userRef = db.collection('users').doc('user123');
userRef.set({
    name: 'Alice',
    age: 30,
    email: 'alice@example.com'
});
```

1. In this snippet, the `users` collection contains documents, each with fields like name, age, and email. The structure is more modular compared to Realtime Database's nested JSON.

Advanced Query Capabilities: Firestore provides advanced querying options, such as compound queries, ordering, and range queries. This allows for a more robust interaction with your data.

```javascript
db.collection('users')
  .where('age', '>', 18)
  .orderBy('age')
  .get()
  .then((querySnapshot) => {
    querySnapshot.forEach((doc) => {
        console.log(doc.id, " => ", doc.data());
    });
  });
```

2. This example demonstrates the use of both a range filter (age > 18) and ordering (`orderBy('age')`) to retrieve users older than 18.
3. **Automatic Scaling**: Firestore is built with scalability in mind, automatically scaling as your app grows. It can handle large datasets and high request rates without manual intervention.

Real-time and Offline Support: Similar to Realtime Database, Firestore supports real-time listeners and offline persistence. The real-time aspect of Firestore enables developers to set up listeners that react to changes as they happen.

```javascript
db.collection('messages')
  .onSnapshot((snapshot) => {
    snapshot.docChanges().forEach((change) => {
        if (change.type === 'added') {
            console.log('New message: ', change.doc.data());
        }
    });
  });
```

4. The `onSnapshot()` listener allows for real-time updates when documents are added, removed, or modified.

Pros and Cons of Firestore

Pros:

- **Structured Data**: Documents and collections make data modeling more intuitive.
- **Advanced Queries**: More robust querying capabilities allow for complex data retrieval.
- **Scalable Architecture**: Designed to scale automatically with the growth of your application.

Cons:

- **Pricing**: Firestore's pricing model can be more complex and potentially more expensive than Realtime Database, especially with high read and write rates.
- **Learning Curve**: For developers accustomed to simpler data models like JSON, getting used to documents and collections may take some time.

Choosing Between Realtime Database and Firestore

Choosing between the Realtime Database and Firestore largely depends on your application's requirements and growth plans. Let's break down the scenarios where each is most suitable.

Use Cases for Realtime Database

- **Real-time Sync**: If your application relies heavily on real-time updates, such as chat applications, collaborative tools, or multiplayer games, the Realtime Database's synchronized nature makes it an excellent choice.
- **Simple Data Structures**: For smaller applications with relatively straightforward data, the JSON tree structure of Realtime Database is easy to implement and maintain.
- **Lower Budget Projects**: Realtime Database can sometimes be more cost-effective, depending on the data structure and access pattern.

Use Cases for Firestore

- **Complex Data Relationships**: If your data is complex, involving multiple interlinked entities, Firestore's document-based structure is more suitable.
- **Scalable Applications**: Firestore scales automatically and is better at handling a large number of concurrent users and extensive datasets.
- **Advanced Query Requirements**: If you need complex querying capabilities, such as compound filtering, range queries, or ordering, Firestore is more adept than Realtime Database.

Example Scenarios

To understand better, consider the following scenarios:

1. **Chat Application**: For a chat application, the Realtime Database might be the best fit due to its real-time synchronization. Messages need to be pushed to clients immediately as they are sent, and the Realtime Database is optimized for this type of behavior.

E-commerce Platform: An e-commerce platform involves handling products, orders, and customer data with multiple interconnected relationships. Firestore is a better fit here, as its document-based structure allows for easy separation of products, users, and orders while maintaining links between them.

javascript
Copy code

```javascript
// Firestore data structure example for an e-commerce platform
db.collection('products').doc('prod123').set({
    name: 'Gaming Laptop',
    price: 1500,
    category: 'Electronics'
});

db.collection('orders').doc('order456').set({
    userId: 'user123',
    productId: 'prod123',
    quantity: 2,
    total: 3000
});
```

2.

Performance Considerations

Performance is another factor that can influence your decision. The Realtime Database uses a single, giant JSON tree, which can lead to performance issues if data grows without proper structure. Firestore, on the other hand, benefits from its hierarchical structure, where data is logically separated into documents and collections, reducing the risk of performance bottlenecks.

For example, consider a social media app where each user has numerous posts. In the Realtime Database, you might end up with a deeply nested JSON structure:

```
{
  "users": {
    "user123": {
      "name": "John Doe",
      "posts": {
        "post1": {
          "title": "My first post",
          "content": "Hello, world!"
        }
      }
    }
```

        }
    }

In Firestore, you would instead separate users and posts into their own collections:

```
db.collection('users').doc('user123').set({
    name: 'John Doe'
});

db.collection('posts').add({
    userId: 'user123',
    title: 'My first post',
    content: 'Hello, world!'
});
```

This approach not only keeps the data model clean but also improves performance and query efficiency.

Security Considerations

Firebase provides **security rules** for both databases, but the way you implement them differs.

- **Realtime Database Rules**: These rules are written in a JSON-like syntax and apply at various node levels.
- **Firestore Security Rules**: Firestore rules are more flexible, allowing for condition-based security at both collection and document levels.

For example, in Firestore, you can write granular security rules that restrict access based on a user's role:

```
service cloud.firestore {
  match /databases/{database}/documents {
    match /orders/{order} {
      allow read: if request.auth != null && request.auth.token.role == 'admin';
      allow write: if request.auth != null;
    }
  }
}
```

In this example, only authenticated users with an admin role can read from the orders collection, while any authenticated user can write to it.

Final Thoughts

In summary, both the Firebase **Realtime Database** and **Firestore** offer robust cloud-hosted NoSQL solutions for application development, each catering to specific use cases. If you need real-time synchronization with simple data models, the Realtime Database may be your choice. If you require scalability, structured data management, and complex querying, then Firestore is likely the better fit.

While it's possible to use both databases together in a single application, it's typically better to choose the one that aligns most closely with your current and future application needs. When selecting between them, consider aspects like data complexity, need for real-time syncing, scalability, and security requirements to make an informed decision.

Getting Started with Realtime Database

The Firebase Realtime Database is a powerful tool for building data-driven applications with real-time, collaborative features. In this section, we will dive deep into how to get started with Firebase Realtime Database. This involves setting up the database, learning the core concepts of data modeling, understanding how to read and write data, and integrating it into an app effectively. By the end of this section, you'll be able to confidently use Firebase Realtime Database for your projects.

Setting Up Firebase Realtime Database

The first step to using the Firebase Realtime Database is to set up your Firebase project. You will need to add the Firebase SDK to your app and configure it to connect to the Realtime Database.

Step-by-Step Setup

1. **Create a Firebase Project**: To begin, navigate to the Firebase Console (https://console.firebase.google.com/). If you don't already have a project, create one by clicking on **Add Project**. Provide a project name and configure any necessary settings like Google Analytics.
2. **Add Firebase to Your Application**: Depending on the platform you're developing for (e.g., Android, iOS, or Web), you need to add Firebase to your application:
    - For **Android**, you will be required to add the google-services.json file to your project, update build.gradle, and add the Firebase Realtime Database dependency.
    - For **iOS**, you'll need to add the Firebase SDK using CocoaPods and configure Info.plist.
    - For **Web**, you will need to integrate Firebase using a script tag and initialize the Firebase app with your configuration details.

```javascript
// Firebase configuration object for Web projects
const firebaseConfig = {
  apiKey: "YOUR_API_KEY",
  authDomain: "YOUR_PROJECT_ID.firebaseapp.com",
  databaseURL: "https://YOUR_PROJECT_ID.firebaseio.com",
  projectId: "YOUR_PROJECT_ID",
  storageBucket: "YOUR_PROJECT_ID.appspot.com",
  messagingSenderId: "YOUR_MESSAGING_SENDER_ID",
  appId: "YOUR_APP_ID"
};

// Initialize Firebase
firebase.initializeApp(firebaseConfig);
```

3.
4. **Enable Realtime Database**: Go to the **Database** section in the Firebase Console and click on **Create Database** under Realtime Database. Choose a suitable location for your data (depending on your target audience), and decide whether to start in locked or test mode. For initial development, test mode is convenient, but be mindful of changing the security rules later to protect your data.

Understanding the Data Structure

Firebase Realtime Database is structured as a JSON tree, which means data is stored in a hierarchical format. This allows you to easily nest data under nodes, but it also requires careful planning to avoid data duplication and unwieldy structures.

For example, a basic JSON data structure in Firebase could look like this:

```
{
  "users": {
    "user123": {
      "name": "John Doe",
      "email": "john@example.com",
      "age": 25
    },
    "user456": {
      "name": "Jane Smith",
      "email": "jane@example.com",
      "age": 30
    }
```

```
    },
    "posts": {
      "post1": {
        "title": "My First Post",
        "content": "This is my first post!",
        "author": "user123"
      },
      "post2": {
        "title": "Hello World",
        "content": "Excited to join this community.",
        "author": "user456"
      }
    }
  }
}
```

Writing Data to the Realtime Database

Writing data to Firebase Realtime Database involves referencing the correct location in the JSON tree and setting the data you want to store. Firebase provides different methods for interacting with the database, such as .set(), .update(), and .push(). Let's go over each one in detail.

Using .set() to Write Data

The .set() method writes data to a specific reference. If the reference already has data, it is completely overwritten.

```
// Reference the Firebase Realtime Database
const dbRef = firebase.database().ref();

// Write a new user to the "users" node
dbRef.child("users/user123").set({
    name: "John Doe",
    email: "john@example.com",
    age: 25
});
```

In the above example, the .set() method is used to write data for a user. If the path /users/user123 already exists, the new data will replace the existing value.

Using .update() for Partial Updates

The `.update()` method is useful for updating specific fields without affecting the entire object. This is especially useful when you need to make minor changes to data.

```
// Update the age of user123
dbRef.child("users/user123").update({
    age: 26
});
```

Here, the `.update()` method modifies only the age field without affecting the other fields like `name` and `email`.

Using `.push()` to Add New Items

The `.push()` method generates a unique key under the specified reference, which is helpful when adding new items like messages or posts.

```
// Adding a new post
const postsRef = dbRef.child("posts");
postsRef.push({
    title: "New Blog Post",
    content: "This is a new blog post.",
    author: "user123"
});
```

The `.push()` method automatically creates a new, unique key for each entry. This is particularly useful for dynamic data where you don't need to define the key yourself.

Reading Data from the Realtime Database

Firebase offers several ways to read data from the Realtime Database, including `.once()` and `.on()`. Let's go through each method and explore their use cases.

Using `.once()` for One-Time Reads

The `.once()` method reads data a single time. This is ideal for data that doesn't require constant updating, such as loading a user profile page.

```
// Get user123 data once
dbRef.child("users/user123").once('value').then((snapshot) => {
    const userData = snapshot.val();
    console.log(userData);
```

```
});
```

In this example, the data for user123 is read once, and the snapshot contains all fields of that user.

Using .on() for Real-Time Listeners

The .on() method listens for changes at the specified reference. Whenever the data changes, the listener is triggered, providing real-time synchronization across devices.

```
// Listen for changes in user123's data
dbRef.child("users/user123").on('value', (snapshot) => {
    const userData = snapshot.val();
    console.log("Updated User Data: ", userData);
});
```

The .on('value', callback) method keeps listening for changes in the database reference, making it suitable for real-time applications like chat or collaborative tools.

Structuring Data for Efficient Reads

When designing a Firebase Realtime Database, consider how you will access the data. For example, storing posts directly under a user's node might seem intuitive, but it makes querying posts by different criteria challenging. Instead, separate entities like users and posts into different nodes, as in the earlier example.

Denormalization for Faster Access

Firebase Realtime Database lacks a traditional querying system, so data needs to be structured for efficient access. This often means denormalizing data — storing copies of the same data at multiple locations to optimize reads.

For instance, if you have a social media app and you want to display a user's posts alongside their profile, you could store some post data under both the users node and the posts node:

```
{
  "users": {
    "user123": {
      "name": "John Doe",
      "email": "john@example.com",
      "posts": {
```

```
        "post1": true,
        "post2": true
      }
    }
  },
  "posts": {
    "post1": {
      "title": "My First Post",
      "content": "This is my first post!",
      "author": "user123"
    },
    "post2": {
      "title": "Hello World",
      "content": "Excited to join this community.",
      "author": "user456"
    }
  }
}
```

In the above structure, under each user's data, we have a reference to their posts using a Boolean (true), which makes it easy to fetch a user's posts without deeply traversing the database.

Securing Your Data with Firebase Rules

Security is crucial when working with a cloud-hosted database. Firebase Realtime Database uses **security rules** to control read and write access at various paths in the database.

Setting Security Rules

You can configure rules to allow or restrict access based on authentication status. For instance, you might want to allow users to write to their own profile but restrict write access to other users' data.

```
{
  "rules": {
    "users": {
      "$userId": {
        ".read": "$userId === auth.uid",
        ".write": "$userId === auth.uid"
      }
    }
```

```
    }
}
```

In this example, the rules restrict read and write permissions to authenticated users, ensuring that users can only access their own data.

Offline Capabilities

The Firebase Realtime Database has built-in support for offline data access. When the device goes offline, data remains available locally, and all changes are synchronized once the device is back online. This feature is particularly useful for mobile apps where network connectivity might be unreliable.

To enable offline persistence for the web:

```
firebase.database().setPersistenceEnabled(true);
```

Handling Large Datasets

When dealing with large datasets, it's essential to use queries to avoid downloading unnecessary data. Firebase allows you to use `.orderByChild()`, `.limitToFirst()`, `.limitToLast()`, and other methods to manage large datasets effectively.

```
// Querying posts ordered by title
postsRef.orderByChild('title').limitToFirst(10).once('value').then((snapshot) => {
    snapshot.forEach((childSnapshot) => {
        console.log(childSnapshot.key, childSnapshot.val());
    });
});
```

In this example, `.orderByChild('title')` orders the posts alphabetically by title, and `.limitToFirst(10)` limits the number of results to the first ten.

Final Thoughts on Getting Started

Getting started with Firebase Realtime Database involves not only understanding how to read and write data but also making deliberate design choices to ensure scalability, efficient reads, and security. A well-structured database can save you time and effort in the long run and improve the performance of your application.

As you grow more comfortable with Firebase, consider exploring advanced features like data denormalization, query optimization, and real-time syncing to make the most of the Realtime Database. Each of these elements plays a crucial role in building responsive and robust applications that deliver a seamless user experience.

Exploring Firestore

Firestore is Firebase's advanced, scalable, cloud-hosted NoSQL database solution designed to help developers build serverless, interactive, and scalable applications. In this section, we will explore Firestore in depth, including its document-based structure, key features, how to read and write data, indexing, querying capabilities, and security rules. By the end, you'll have a comprehensive understanding of Firestore's capabilities and how to utilize them effectively in your applications.

Firestore Structure and Data Model

Firestore follows a document and collection-based data model, unlike the Realtime Database's JSON tree. Data in Firestore is stored in documents, which are organized into collections. This structure is more hierarchical, which offers better separation of data and helps in creating scalable and maintainable applications.

Collections and Documents

A **collection** is a container that holds multiple **documents**. A document, in turn, holds various fields, which can be of several data types, including strings, numbers, arrays, nested objects, or even references to other documents.

- **Collections** are containers of documents. Collections cannot directly contain other collections, but they can contain documents that contain **sub-collections**.
- **Documents** are individual records within a collection. Each document is identified by a unique ID and contains a set of key-value pairs.

Let's see an example structure:

- `users` (collection)
    - `user123` (document)
        - `name`: "John Doe"
        - `age`: 25
        - `email`: "john@example.com"
        - `posts` (sub-collection)
            - `post1` (document)
                - `title`: "My First Post"
                - `content`: "Hello World!"
            - `post2` (document)
                - `title`: "Another Day"
                - `content`: "Having a great time!"

In the above example, users is a collection that contains multiple documents (user123, user456, etc.). Each user document can have different fields, and also include **sub-collections**, such as posts.

Setting Up Firestore

To use Firestore, you need to set it up in your Firebase project. Here's how to do it:

1. **Create a Firebase Project**: First, log in to the Firebase Console (https://console.firebase.google.com/), and either create a new project or select an existing one.
2. **Add Firestore to Your App**:
   - For **Web**: Add Firebase SDK to your project and initialize Firestore.
   - For **Android/iOS**: Add the Firebase SDK and dependencies to your project using Gradle (Android) or CocoaPods (iOS).

Initialize Firestore:

javascript
Copy code

```javascript
// Initialize Firestore for Web
import { initializeApp } from "firebase/app";
import { getFirestore } from "firebase/firestore";

const firebaseConfig = {
  apiKey: "YOUR_API_KEY",
  authDomain: "YOUR_PROJECT_ID.firebaseapp.com",
  projectId: "YOUR_PROJECT_ID",
  storageBucket: "YOUR_PROJECT_ID.appspot.com",
  messagingSenderId: "YOUR_MESSAGING_SENDER_ID",
  appId: "YOUR_APP_ID"
};

const app = initializeApp(firebaseConfig);
const db = getFirestore(app);
```

3. This code snippet shows how to initialize Firestore within a web application. Firestore can now be used to read from and write to your database.

Writing Data to Firestore

Firestore provides multiple methods to write data, such as .set(), .add(), and .update(). Each of these methods is suited for different scenarios.

Using .set() to Write Data

The .set() method writes data to a specified document. If the document does not exist, it will be created; if it already exists, the data will be overwritten.

```
import { doc, setDoc } from "firebase/firestore";

// Reference to the document
const userRef = doc(db, "users", "user123");

// Write data to the document
await setDoc(userRef, {
  name: "John Doe",
  age: 25,
  email: "john@example.com"
});
```

In this example, we reference a document (user123) under the users collection and use .set() to write data to that document. If user123 already exists, its data is overwritten.

Using .add() to Create a Document with a Generated ID

If you don't want to specify a document ID manually, you can use the .add() method. This automatically generates a unique ID for each document.

```
import { collection, addDoc } from "firebase/firestore";

// Reference to the collection
const usersCollectionRef = collection(db, "users");

// Add a new document to the collection
const newUserRef = await addDoc(usersCollectionRef, {
  name: "Jane Smith",
  age: 30,
  email: "jane@example.com"
});

console.log("Document written with ID: ", newUserRef.id);
```

Here, Firestore creates a new document under the users collection with a unique identifier, and we write the provided data into that document.

Using `.update()` to Update Specific Fields

The `.update()` method allows you to modify specific fields in an existing document without affecting other fields.

```
import { doc, updateDoc } from "firebase/firestore";

// Reference to the document
const userRef = doc(db, "users", "user123");

// Update the age field
await updateDoc(userRef, {
  age: 26
});
```

The `.update()` method only updates the specified field (age in this case) without altering other fields in the document.

Reading Data from Firestore

Firestore provides several ways to read data, including `.getDoc()`, `.getDocs()`, and real-time listeners (`.onSnapshot()`). Let's take a look at each approach.

Getting a Single Document

To read a specific document, you can use the `.getDoc()` function. This function is useful when you need to retrieve data from a single known document.

```
import { doc, getDoc } from "firebase/firestore";

// Reference to the document
const userRef = doc(db, "users", "user123");

// Get the document data
const userSnap = await getDoc(userRef);

if (userSnap.exists()) {
  console.log("Document data:", userSnap.data());
} else {
  console.log("No such document!");
}
```

The `.getDoc()` function retrieves data from the `user123` document. If the document exists, it prints the data; otherwise, it indicates that the document does not exist.

Getting Multiple Documents

To retrieve multiple documents from a collection, you can use the `.getDocs()` function. This is helpful when you need to fetch data for an entire collection or a subset of it.

```
import { collection, getDocs } from "firebase/firestore";

// Reference to the collection
const usersCollectionRef = collection(db, "users");

// Get all documents in the collection
const usersSnapshot = await getDocs(usersCollectionRef);

usersSnapshot.forEach((doc) => {
  console.log(doc.id, " => ", doc.data());
});
```

The `.getDocs()` function fetches all the documents from the `users` collection. The callback function (`.forEach()`) iterates through each document in the collection and logs its data.

Using Real-Time Listeners

If you need real-time synchronization between Firestore and your app, use `.onSnapshot()` to listen for changes. Real-time listeners are great for applications where data updates frequently, such as chat applications.

```
import { collection, onSnapshot } from "firebase/firestore";

// Reference to the collection
const usersCollectionRef = collection(db, "users");

// Set up a real-time listener
onSnapshot(usersCollectionRef, (snapshot) => {
  snapshot.docChanges().forEach((change) => {
    if (change.type === "added") {
      console.log("New user: ", change.doc.data());
    }
    if (change.type === "modified") {
```

```
        console.log("Modified user: ", change.doc.data());
      }
      if (change.type === "removed") {
        console.log("Removed user: ", change.doc.data());
      }
    });
  });
```

The .onSnapshot() function listens to changes in the collection and logs newly added, modified, or removed documents.

Firestore Queries

Firestore offers powerful querying capabilities that allow you to retrieve a specific subset of data based on certain criteria. Let's explore some of these features.

Simple Queries

You can use queries to retrieve documents that meet specific conditions. For instance, you can query for users over a certain age.

```
import { collection, query, where, getDocs } from "firebase/firestore";

// Reference to the collection
const usersCollectionRef = collection(db, "users");

// Create a query to filter users over the age of 25
const q = query(usersCollectionRef, where("age", ">", 25));

// Execute the query
const querySnapshot = await getDocs(q);
querySnapshot.forEach((doc) => {
  console.log(doc.id, " => ", doc.data());
});
```

In this example, we create a query (q) that filters users whose age is greater than 25, and then use .getDocs() to retrieve the matching documents.

Compound Queries

Firestore supports **compound queries**, which allow you to combine multiple conditions. However, Firestore requires you to create **indexes** for compound queries to optimize their performance.

```
import { collection, query, where, getDocs } from "firebase/firestore";

// Reference to the collection
const usersCollectionRef = collection(db, "users");

// Create a compound query
const q = query(usersCollectionRef, where("age", ">", 25), where("email", "==", "john@example.com"));

// Execute the query
const querySnapshot = await getDocs(q);
querySnapshot.forEach((doc) => {
  console.log(doc.id, " => ", doc.data());
});
```

The above example retrieves users who are older than 25 **and** have an email address of "john@example.com".

Firestore Security Rules

Security is crucial when dealing with databases, and Firestore provides a rich security rules engine to protect your data. Firestore security rules determine who can access what data, and under what conditions.

Writing Firestore Security Rules

Here's an example of Firestore security rules that enforce read and write permissions based on user authentication:

```
service cloud.firestore {
  match /databases/{database}/documents {
    match /users/{userId} {
      allow read, write: if request.auth != null && request.auth.uid == userId;
    }
    match /posts/{postId} {
      allow read: if request.auth != null;
```

```
        allow    write:    if    request.auth    !=    null    &&
request.auth.token.role == 'admin';
    }
  }
}
```

In this example:

- Users can read and write their own data if they are authenticated and their user ID matches the document ID.
- Posts can be read by any authenticated user, but only users with an admin role can write to the `posts` collection.

Indexing in Firestore

Firestore automatically indexes fields within documents, but for advanced queries or compound queries, it may require explicit indexing. When a query that requires an index is run, Firestore will provide a link in the error message to create the required index.

Indexes help to improve query performance and ensure that data retrieval is efficient, especially when working with large datasets.

Offline Capabilities

Firestore supports offline data persistence, which means that your application can still read and write data when there is no network connection. Once the connection is restored, Firestore syncs local changes with the server.

To enable offline persistence in a web app:

```
import { enableIndexedDbPersistence } from "firebase/firestore";

enableIndexedDbPersistence(db)
  .catch((err) => {
    if (err.code == 'failed-precondition') {
      console.log('Persistence can only be enabled in one tab at a time.');
    } else if (err.code == 'unimplemented') {
      console.log('The current browser does not support offline persistence.');
    }
  });
```

This feature is beneficial for mobile and web applications where the network connection may be unreliable, providing a seamless user experience.

Final Thoughts on Firestore

Firestore's flexible data model, powerful query capabilities, real-time synchronization, and robust security features make it an ideal choice for a wide range of applications. Whether you're building a small personal project or a large-scale application, Firestore can handle the complexity and provide the performance you need.

To make the most out of Firestore, always plan your data structure carefully, leverage indexing for optimal query performance, use real-time listeners for dynamic updates, and write secure access rules to protect your data.

By understanding the foundational aspects of Firestore and applying best practices, you can build secure, efficient, and highly responsive applications that provide a great user experience.

Chapter 5: Firebase Storage

Introduction to Firebase Storage

Firebase Storage is a powerful and easy-to-use solution provided by Firebase for handling and storing user-generated content, such as images, videos, and other files. With Firebase Storage, you can save and retrieve any type of binary data directly from your app, leveraging Google's robust and scalable infrastructure. This makes Firebase Storage a great option for both small projects and large applications that require extensive file management capabilities.

In this section, we will explore the fundamentals of Firebase Storage and walk through how to integrate it into your mobile or web applications. We will cover the key features, advantages, and best practices of Firebase Storage, followed by practical examples and code snippets that will help you store, retrieve, and manage your files effectively.

Overview of Firebase Storage

Firebase Storage is built on top of Google Cloud Storage, which means it benefits from the same level of security, performance, and scalability that Google offers to its Cloud customers. The main objective of Firebase Storage is to make it easy for developers to handle and manage user-uploaded files in a way that integrates seamlessly with other Firebase services.

Some of the key features of Firebase Storage include:

1. **Simple SDK Integration**: Firebase provides SDKs for iOS, Android, and web platforms, allowing you to easily add file storage and retrieval functionality to your apps.
2. **Secure File Access**: Firebase Security Rules let you control access to stored files by defining conditions based on the authenticated state of users or other criteria.
3. **Scalability**: Firebase Storage is highly scalable, making it suitable for storing large volumes of files, no matter the size of your user base.
4. **Reliability and Performance**: Files are stored in Google Cloud Storage, ensuring high availability, reliability, and quick response times.

Firebase Storage Use Cases

Firebase Storage can be used for various purposes across different types of applications. Some common use cases include:

- **Social Media Apps**: Users can upload profile pictures, share images, videos, and other media content.
- **E-commerce Apps**: Storing product images and promotional material.

- **Content Sharing Apps**: Users can upload files for others to view or download, such as documents, presentations, or PDFs.

Let's dive deeper into Firebase Storage and learn how to integrate it into your app.

Setting Up Firebase Storage

To use Firebase Storage in your project, you need to set up a Firebase project and add the necessary SDKs to your app. Below, we'll cover the general setup steps for both Android and web applications.

Step 1: Create a Firebase Project

First, you need to create a Firebase project if you haven't done so already. Follow these steps:

1. Go to the Firebase Console.
2. Click on **Add Project** and enter the name for your project.
3. Follow the prompts to configure Google Analytics (optional).
4. Once the project is created, you will be redirected to the Firebase dashboard.

Step 2: Add Firebase to Your App

Firebase Storage is a part of the broader Firebase ecosystem, and you'll need to add Firebase to your app to start using Storage.

For Android:

1. In the Firebase Console, click on the **Android** icon to add an Android app to your project.
2. Enter your app's package name and click **Register App**.
3. Download the `google-services.json` file and add it to your Android app module's app/ directory.

In your app-level `build.gradle` file, add the following dependencies:
groovy
Copy code
```
implementation platform('com.google.firebase:firebase-bom:32.0.0')
implementation 'com.google.firebase:firebase-storage'
```

4.
5. Sync your project with Gradle to apply the changes.

For Web:

1. In the Firebase Console, click on the **Web** icon to add a web app to your project.
2. Register your app by providing a name.

98 | FIREBASE FOR ABSOLUTE BEGINNERS

Add the Firebase SDK to your project by including the following script tags in your HTML:
html
Copy code

```
<script src="https://www.gstatic.com/firebasejs/10.3.0/firebase-app.js"></script>
<script src="https://www.gstatic.com/firebasejs/10.3.0/firebase-storage.js"></script>
```

   3.

Initialize Firebase in your JavaScript code:
javascript
Copy code

```
const firebaseConfig = {
  apiKey: "YOUR_API_KEY",
  authDomain: "YOUR_AUTH_DOMAIN",
  projectId: "YOUR_PROJECT_ID",
  storageBucket: "YOUR_STORAGE_BUCKET",
  messagingSenderId: "YOUR_MESSAGING_SENDER_ID",
  appId: "YOUR_APP_ID"
};

// Initialize Firebase
firebase.initializeApp(firebaseConfig);
```

   4.

Uploading Files to Firebase Storage

Uploading files to Firebase Storage is simple and straightforward. Let's go over the process for both Android and web apps.

Uploading Files from Android

To upload files to Firebase Storage from an Android application, you will need to interact with the Firebase Storage API. Below is an example of how to upload an image from a local file URI.

```
// Get an instance of FirebaseStorage
FirebaseStorage storage = FirebaseStorage.getInstance();
StorageReference storageRef = storage.getReference();

// Create a reference to the folder where the file will be stored
StorageReference imagesRef = storageRef.child("images/myImage.jpg");
```

```
// Get the file URI (this could be a local file path)
Uri fileUri = Uri.fromFile(new File("/path/to/images/myImage.jpg"));

// Upload the file
imagesRef.putFile(fileUri)
    .addOnSuccessListener(taskSnapshot -> {
        // File uploaded successfully
        Log.d("FirebaseStorage", "File uploaded successfully");
    })
    .addOnFailureListener(e -> {
        // Handle any errors
        Log.e("FirebaseStorage", "Failed to upload file", e);
    });
```

In the above example, we create a reference to a storage location (images/myImage.jpg) and then call putFile(fileUri) to upload the file.

Uploading Files from Web

On the web, Firebase Storage allows you to easily upload files, such as from an <input type="file"> element. Below is an example of how to upload an image from a file input:

```
<input type="file" id="fileInput" />

<script>
  // Get a reference to the storage service
  const storage = firebase.storage();
  const storageRef = storage.ref();

  // Listen for file input changes
  document.getElementById("fileInput").addEventListener("change", (event) => {
    const file = event.target.files[0];

    // Create a storage reference for the file
    const imagesRef = storageRef.child("images/" + file.name);

    // Upload the file
    imagesRef.put(file).then((snapshot) => {
      console.log("File uploaded successfully");
```

```
    }).catch((error) => {
      console.error("Failed to upload file", error);
    });
  });
</script>
```

In this example, the user selects a file using an `<input>` element, and the file is then uploaded to the `images` folder in Firebase Storage.

Downloading and Displaying Files

Firebase Storage makes it easy to download files, either to use them locally in your app or to display them directly to users.

Downloading Files in Android

To download a file from Firebase Storage in an Android app, you can use the `getFile()` method to download the file to the local storage, or you can use `getDownloadUrl()` to get a URL that can be used to access the file.

```
// Get an instance of FirebaseStorage
FirebaseStorage storage = FirebaseStorage.getInstance();
StorageReference storageRef = storage.getReference();

// Create a reference to the file you want to download
StorageReference fileRef = storageRef.child("images/myImage.jpg");

// Download to a local file
File localFile = new File(getFilesDir(), "myImage.jpg");
fileRef.getFile(localFile)
    .addOnSuccessListener(taskSnapshot -> {
        // File downloaded successfully
        Log.d("FirebaseStorage", "File downloaded successfully");
    })
    .addOnFailureListener(e -> {
        // Handle any errors
        Log.e("FirebaseStorage", "Failed to download file", e);
    });
```

In this example, we create a reference to the file `images/myImage.jpg` and use `getFile(localFile)` to download it locally.

Displaying Files on Web

In web applications, you can use the `getDownloadURL()` method to obtain a URL for displaying files, such as images, directly in the browser.

```
<img id="image" />

<script>
  // Get a reference to the storage service
  const storage = firebase.storage();
  const storageRef = storage.ref();

  // Reference to the file
  const fileRef = storageRef.child("images/myImage.jpg");

  // Get the download URL
  fileRef.getDownloadURL().then((url) => {
    // Set the image source to the download URL
    document.getElementById("image").src = url;
  }).catch((error) => {
    console.error("Failed to get download URL", error);
  });
</script>
```

In this code, we obtain the download URL of the `myImage.jpg` file and set it as the `src` of an `<img>` element to display the image on the web page.

Firebase Storage Security

Firebase Storage allows you to secure access to your files using **Firebase Security Rules**. These rules allow you to specify who can read or write files based on various conditions, such as user authentication.

For example, if you want to allow only authenticated users to upload files, you can write rules like the following:

```
{
  "rules": {
    ".read": "auth != null",
    ".write": "auth != null"
  }
}
```

This rule ensures that both read and write operations are allowed only for authenticated users. You can also define more fine-grained rules based on specific file paths or user data.

Best Practices for Using Firebase Storage

When using Firebase Storage, keep in mind the following best practices:

1. **Use Security Rules**: Always define comprehensive security rules to protect user data and prevent unauthorized access.
2. **Organize Files Logically**: Use meaningful folder structures and file names to keep your storage organized. This makes it easier to manage files, especially as your app grows.
3. **Handle Errors Gracefully**: Always handle errors that may occur during file uploads or downloads, such as network issues or permission errors.
4. **Optimize Image Size**: When uploading images, consider resizing them to reduce the file size and improve the user experience, especially for users on slower networks.

Summary

Firebase Storage is a robust solution for managing user-generated content within your apps. With simple SDK integration, secure access, and scalability, it provides everything needed for effective file storage and retrieval. Whether you're building a social media app, an e-commerce platform, or any application that requires handling user-uploaded files, Firebase Storage has the tools and features to make the process seamless.

In the next sections, we will dive deeper into managing uploaded files, exploring advanced functionalities like metadata management, and implementing best practices for an optimized storage experience.

Uploading and Managing Files

Firebase Storage is a highly versatile tool that allows developers to upload, store, and manage various types of files efficiently. This section will focus on understanding how to work with Firebase Storage to upload files, manage uploaded content, and make use of the built-in features to enhance the overall user experience of your application.

Uploading files is a core feature of Firebase Storage, and it allows developers to easily handle user-generated content, such as profile images, documents, and other media. We will start with the basics of file uploads, move into organizing and managing those files effectively, and finally, discuss some advanced techniques that make Firebase Storage even more powerful.

Uploading Files: The Basics

The process of uploading files to Firebase Storage is straightforward, thanks to the SDKs provided by Firebase. Firebase Storage lets you create references, which can be thought of as unique file paths within the storage bucket. These references allow you to easily store and retrieve files in a structured manner.

The following examples illustrate how to upload files from Android and web applications.

Uploading Files from Android

In Android, Firebase Storage allows you to upload files either from a local device path or a file URI. Here is a basic example that demonstrates how to upload an image from a local file URI.

```
// Step 1: Get an instance of FirebaseStorage
FirebaseStorage storage = FirebaseStorage.getInstance();

// Step 2: Create a reference to the storage location
StorageReference storageRef = storage.getReference().child("images/myUploadedFile.jpg");

// Step 3: Get the file URI (e.g., a local file path or from the gallery)
Uri fileUri = Uri.fromFile(new File("/storage/emulated/0/Download/myImage.jpg"));

// Step 4: Upload the file
storageRef.putFile(fileUri)
    .addOnSuccessListener(taskSnapshot -> {
        // File uploaded successfully
        Log.d("FirebaseStorage", "Upload successful: " + taskSnapshot.getMetadata().getPath());
    })
    .addOnFailureListener(e -> {
        // Handle any errors
        Log.e("FirebaseStorage", "Upload failed", e);
    });
```

In this example, we create a reference to the location where the file will be stored (images/myUploadedFile.jpg) and call putFile(fileUri) to upload the file. The use of addOnSuccessListener and addOnFailureListener helps in handling the result of the upload operation, allowing you to confirm a successful upload or manage errors as needed.

Uploading Files from Web

The Firebase web SDK makes it equally simple to upload files in web applications. Below is a sample implementation that allows users to select a file from their local system and upload it to Firebase Storage.

```
<input type="file" id="fileInput" />

<script>
  // Step 1: Get a reference to the storage service
  const storage = firebase.storage();
  const storageRef = storage.ref();

  // Step 2: Add a listener for file input changes
  document.getElementById("fileInput").addEventListener("change",
(event) => {
    const file = event.target.files[0];

    // Step 3: Create a storage reference for the file
    const fileRef = storageRef.child("images/" + file.name);

    // Step 4: Upload the file
    fileRef.put(file).then((snapshot) => {
      console.log("File uploaded successfully");
    }).catch((error) => {
      console.error("Failed to upload file", error);
    });
  });
</script>
```

In this example, a file is selected using an HTML file input element. When the user selects a file, it is uploaded to the Firebase Storage location specified by `fileRef`.

Managing File Uploads

Uploading files is only one part of using Firebase Storage effectively. To ensure the best user experience, you need to manage uploaded files, monitor their progress, and provide users with relevant feedback during the upload process. Below, we will explore different strategies to achieve this.

Tracking Upload Progress

Tracking the progress of an upload operation is an important feature, especially for applications that deal with large files or operate on unreliable networks. Firebase provides

Chapter 5: Firebase Storage

the ability to monitor upload progress through the `UploadTask` object, which allows you to create progress indicators.

Android Example:

```
// Create a reference to the storage location
StorageReference storageRef = FirebaseStorage.getInstance().getReference().child("videos/myVideo.mp4");

// Upload the file and track progress
UploadTask uploadTask = storageRef.putFile(fileUri);
uploadTask.addOnProgressListener(taskSnapshot -> {
    double progress = (100.0 * taskSnapshot.getBytesTransferred()) / taskSnapshot.getTotalByteCount();
    Log.d("FirebaseStorage", "Upload is " + progress + "% done");
}).addOnSuccessListener(taskSnapshot -> {
    Log.d("FirebaseStorage", "Upload complete");
}).addOnFailureListener(e -> {
    Log.e("FirebaseStorage", "Upload failed", e);
});
```

The `addOnProgressListener` method allows you to keep track of how many bytes have been transferred, providing a way to inform users of the progress. This is especially useful in scenarios where you want to show an upload progress bar.

Web Example:

```
<input type="file" id="fileInput" />
<progress value="0" max="100" id="uploadProgress"></progress>

<script>
  const storage = firebase.storage();
  const storageRef = storage.ref();

  document.getElementById("fileInput").addEventListener("change", (event) => {
    const file = event.target.files[0];
    const fileRef = storageRef.child("images/" + file.name);

    const uploadTask = fileRef.put(file);
```

```
  // Track upload progress
  uploadTask.on('state_changed', (snapshot) => {
    const       progress      =     (snapshot.bytesTransferred    /
snapshot.totalBytes) * 100;
    document.getElementById("uploadProgress").value = progress;
    console.log('Upload is ' + progress + '% done');
  }, (error) => {
    console.error('Upload failed', error);
  }, () => {
    console.log('Upload complete');
  });
});
</script>
```

In this example, the state_changed event is used to track the upload progress. The <progress> HTML element is updated accordingly to reflect the percentage of bytes transferred.

Organizing Files in Firebase Storage

Organizing files in Firebase Storage is crucial for ensuring that your app's data remains manageable and easy to locate. Firebase Storage uses a folder-like structure, and it's up to you as the developer to decide how to organize your files.

Folder Structure and File Naming

Using descriptive folder structures and meaningful file names is a best practice when storing files. For example:

- **User Content**: Store files in folders named by user IDs. This way, each user has their own set of files, which makes it easy to locate user-specific content.
    - /users/user123/profile.jpg
    - /users/user123/posts/postImage.jpg
- **Category-Based Organization**: For applications dealing with different content categories, create folders based on the content type.
    - /products/electronics/itemImage.jpg
    - /products/clothing/shirt.jpg

It is important to consider how files will be accessed and modified, as this affects not only the performance of the app but also the readability and security of your storage structure.

Deleting and Updating Files

Managing Firebase Storage also involves updating and deleting files. Let's go over how to accomplish these tasks effectively.

Deleting Files

You can easily delete a file from Firebase Storage by calling the delete() method on a storage reference.

Android Example:

```
// Reference to the file to delete
StorageReference fileRef = FirebaseStorage.getInstance().getReference().child("images/myOldImage.jpg");

// Delete the file
fileRef.delete().addOnSuccessListener(aVoid -> {
    Log.d("FirebaseStorage", "File deleted successfully");
}).addOnFailureListener(e -> {
    Log.e("FirebaseStorage", "Failed to delete file", e);
});
```

Web Example:

```
// Reference to the file
const storage = firebase.storage();
const fileRef = storage.ref().child("images/myOldImage.jpg");

// Delete the file
fileRef.delete().then(() => {
  console.log("File deleted successfully");
}).catch((error) => {
  console.error("Failed to delete file", error);
});
```

Deleting unused or outdated files helps in maintaining the storage bucket, ensuring that you're not paying for unused data.

Updating Files

To update a file in Firebase Storage, you simply upload a new version of the file with the same name. Firebase will replace the old file with the new one.

Example:

```
// Reference to the existing file
StorageReference fileRef = FirebaseStorage.getInstance().getReference().child("images/myImage.jpg");

// Upload a new version of the file
fileRef.putFile(newFileUri).addOnSuccessListener(taskSnapshot -> {
    Log.d("FirebaseStorage", "File updated successfully");
}).addOnFailureListener(e -> {
    Log.e("FirebaseStorage", "Failed to update file", e);
});
```

Firebase Storage does not provide a separate "update" method since uploading a file with the same reference will overwrite the existing one.

Working with File Metadata

Firebase Storage allows you to store metadata alongside your files. This metadata can include information such as file type, size, creation date, and custom data.

Adding Metadata

You can include metadata when uploading a file to Firebase Storage. Metadata can help you categorize files, add descriptions, or store any custom information that your app might need.

Example:

```
// Define metadata for the file
StorageMetadata metadata = new StorageMetadata.Builder()
    .setContentType("image/jpeg")
    .setCustomMetadata("description", "Profile picture")
    .build();

// Upload the file with metadata
StorageReference storageRef = FirebaseStorage.getInstance().getReference().child("images/profile.jpg");
storageRef.putFile(fileUri, metadata)
    .addOnSuccessListener(taskSnapshot -> {
        Log.d("FirebaseStorage", "File uploaded with metadata");
```

```
})
.addOnFailureListener(e -> {
    Log.e("FirebaseStorage", "Failed to upload file", e);
});
```

Retrieving Metadata

To retrieve metadata of a file, you can use the `getMetadata()` method on a storage reference.

Example:

```
// Reference to the file
StorageReference fileRef = FirebaseStorage.getInstance().getReference().child("images/profile.jpg");

// Retrieve metadata
fileRef.getMetadata().addOnSuccessListener(metadata -> {
    String contentType = metadata.getContentType();
    String description = metadata.getCustomMetadata("description");
    Log.d("FirebaseStorage", "Content Type: " + contentType);
    Log.d("FirebaseStorage", "Description: " + description);
}).addOnFailureListener(e -> {
    Log.e("FirebaseStorage", "Failed to retrieve metadata", e);
});
```

Handling Errors During Upload

Handling errors is an important aspect of working with Firebase Storage, as file uploads can fail for various reasons, such as network issues or permission errors. Firebase provides comprehensive error handling through its API.

Typical errors you might encounter include:

- **Network Error**: When a user's internet connection is lost during an upload.
- **Storage Quota Exceeded**: If the storage limit is reached for your Firebase project.
- **Permission Denied**: When the user does not have permission to perform a particular action.

You can handle these errors in your code by adding error listeners to your upload tasks:

Android Example:

```
storageRef.putFile(fileUri)
    .addOnFailureListener(e -> {
        if (e instanceof StorageException) {
            StorageException se = (StorageException) e;
            switch (se.getErrorCode()) {
                case StorageException.ERROR_QUOTA_EXCEEDED:
                    Log.e("FirebaseStorage", "Storage quota exceeded");
                    break;
                case StorageException.ERROR_NOT_AUTHORIZED:
                    Log.e("FirebaseStorage", "User not authorized");
                    break;
                default:
                    Log.e("FirebaseStorage", "Unknown error", e);
            }
        }
    });
```

Summary

In this section, we explored how to upload files to Firebase Storage and manage those files effectively. We covered the basics of uploading files from Android and web applications, monitoring upload progress, organizing files using folder structures, and handling file deletion and updates. We also looked at working with file metadata and managing errors that might occur during uploads.

Firebase Storage provides powerful features that make file management a seamless experience for developers. By following best practices and using the provided SDK features effectively, you can build robust applications that provide users with a smooth and reliable experience when interacting with user-generated content.

Downloading and Displaying Files

Firebase Storage not only provides the capability to upload and store files, but also offers a seamless way to download and display them in your applications. Whether it's user-generated content like profile pictures, product images for an e-commerce platform, or media files for a social app, Firebase Storage makes it straightforward to retrieve these files and present them to your users.

In this section, we will cover how to download files from Firebase Storage and display them in your application. We will look at implementations for both Android and web applications, explore various methods for retrieving files, and discuss best practices to optimize the download experience for users.

Downloading Files from Firebase Storage

Downloading files from Firebase Storage involves creating a reference to the file and then retrieving it. Firebase provides several methods for downloading files, depending on your specific use case. You can either:

1. **Download the file to a local storage location**, which is useful when you need offline access.
2. **Get a download URL**, which allows you to use the URL to display the file directly in your application.

Let's begin by exploring these methods for different platforms.

Downloading Files in Android

In Android, you can download files from Firebase Storage either by saving them to the device's local storage or by retrieving a download URL to access them. Both approaches are useful depending on your app's requirements.

Method 1: Downloading to Local Storage

To download a file from Firebase Storage to a local path, use the getFile() method. This method is useful when you need to store the file locally for offline use or when you need to manipulate it further.

Here is an example of how to download a file and save it to the local storage of an Android device:

```
// Get an instance of FirebaseStorage
FirebaseStorage storage = FirebaseStorage.getInstance();

// Create a reference to the file to be downloaded
StorageReference storageRef = storage.getReference().child("images/sampleImage.jpg");

// Define the local file path where the file will be saved
File localFile = new File(getFilesDir(), "downloadedImage.jpg");

// Start the download
storageRef.getFile(localFile)
    .addOnSuccessListener(taskSnapshot -> {
        // File downloaded successfully
        Log.d("FirebaseStorage", "File downloaded successfully to: " + localFile.getAbsolutePath());
    })
```

```
    .addOnFailureListener(e -> {
        // Handle any errors
        Log.e("FirebaseStorage", "Failed to download file", e);
    });
```

In this example:

- We create a reference to the file stored in Firebase Storage (images/sampleImage.jpg).
- We then specify a local file path (downloadedImage.jpg) to which the downloaded file should be saved.
- The getFile() method is used to download the file, and appropriate listeners are attached to handle success or failure cases.

Method 2: Getting a Download URL

Alternatively, you can get a URL that can be used to access the file directly. This is particularly useful if you want to load the file into an ImageView or use it in an external component.

```
// Create a reference to the file in Firebase Storage
StorageReference fileRef = storage.getReference().child("images/sampleImage.jpg");

// Get the download URL
fileRef.getDownloadUrl().addOnSuccessListener(uri -> {
    String downloadUrl = uri.toString();
    Log.d("FirebaseStorage", "Download URL: " + downloadUrl);

    // You can use the URL to load the image using an image loading library
    // For example, using Glide to load the image into an ImageView
    ImageView imageView = findViewById(R.id.myImageView);
    Glide.with(this).load(downloadUrl).into(imageView);
}).addOnFailureListener(e -> {
    // Handle any errors
    Log.e("FirebaseStorage", "Failed to get download URL", e);
});
```

In this example:

- We use getDownloadUrl() to get a URL that points to the file stored in Firebase Storage.
- The URL can be used directly in your application, for instance, by passing it to an image loading library like **Glide** or **Picasso** to load an image into an ImageView.

Downloading Files in Web Applications

For web applications, Firebase Storage allows you to easily download and display files using JavaScript. You can use the getDownloadURL() method to retrieve a URL for the file, and then use it to display or download the content.

Getting a Download URL

The getDownloadURL() method is used to obtain a URL that can be used to access the file from Firebase Storage. Here is an example that illustrates this approach:

```html
<img id="imageDisplay" />

<script>
  // Get a reference to the storage service
  const storage = firebase.storage();
  const storageRef = storage.ref();

  // Reference to the file you want to download
  const fileRef = storageRef.child("images/sampleImage.jpg");

  // Get the download URL
  fileRef.getDownloadURL().then((url) => {
    // Use the download URL to set the image source
    document.getElementById("imageDisplay").src = url;
    console.log("Image URL: " + url);
  }).catch((error) => {
    console.error("Failed to get download URL", error);
  });
</script>
```

In this example:

- We use the getDownloadURL() method to retrieve the URL for a file.
- The URL is then set as the src attribute of an <img> element, which will display the image in the browser.

Displaying Downloaded Files

114 | FIREBASE FOR ABSOLUTE BEGINNERS

Displaying files is a common use case, especially for applications that deal with images, documents, or other types of media. Firebase Storage provides an easy way to fetch and display these files directly within your app's UI.

Displaying Images in Android

To display an image that is stored in Firebase Storage, you can use the download URL along with popular image loading libraries like **Glide** or **Picasso**. Below is an example of how you can achieve this:

```java
// Create a reference to the file in Firebase Storage
StorageReference storageRef = FirebaseStorage.getInstance().getReference().child("images/profilePicture.jpg");

// Get the download URL
storageRef.getDownloadUrl().addOnSuccessListener(uri -> {
    String imageUrl = uri.toString();

    // Load the image using Glide
    ImageView imageView = findViewById(R.id.profileImageView);
    Glide.with(this).load(imageUrl).into(imageView);
}).addOnFailureListener(e -> {
    Log.e("FirebaseStorage", "Failed to load image", e);
});
```

In this example, **Glide** is used to load the image from the download URL into an ImageView. This approach provides efficient memory management and caching, which improves the overall performance of the app.

Displaying Images in Web

For web applications, displaying an image or any file type is straightforward with the getDownloadURL() method. You can use this URL to set the source attribute of HTML elements like <img>, <video>, or even to download documents.

Example: Displaying an Image:

```html
<img id="profileImage" alt="User Profile Image" />

<script>
  // Reference to Firebase Storage
  const storage = firebase.storage();
```

```
  const storageRef = storage.ref();

  // Reference to the image file
  const                         profileImageRef                     =
storageRef.child('images/userProfile.jpg');

  // Get the download URL
  profileImageRef.getDownloadURL().then((url) => {
    // Set the image element source to the URL
    document.getElementById('profileImage').src = url;
  }).catch((error) => {
    console.error('Failed to retrieve download URL', error);
  });
</script>
```

This example retrieves the download URL and uses it to set the `src` attribute of an HTML `<img>` tag, which will cause the image to be rendered on the webpage.

Handling Large File Downloads

When dealing with large files, such as videos or high-resolution images, it is essential to optimize the download process to ensure that the user experience is smooth. There are several techniques you can use to handle large file downloads more effectively.

Streaming Video Content

If your application involves streaming video content, you can use Firebase Storage to host and serve video files. By getting the download URL, you can load the video into an HTML `<video>` element and enable users to stream content directly from Firebase Storage.

```
<video id="videoPlayer" controls>
  <source id="videoSource" type="video/mp4" />
</video>

<script>
  // Reference to Firebase Storage
  const storage = firebase.storage();
  const videoRef = storage.ref().child('videos/sampleVideo.mp4');

  // Get the download URL for the video
  videoRef.getDownloadURL().then((url) => {
    // Set the video source URL
```

```
    document.getElementById('videoSource').src = url;
    document.getElementById('videoPlayer').load();
  }).catch((error) => {
    console.error('Error fetching video URL:', error);
  });
</script>
```

By using this approach, you can take advantage of the browser's native video streaming capabilities, which will allow the video to buffer and play as it is being downloaded.

Error Handling in File Downloads

Errors can occur during the file download process due to several reasons, such as network issues, insufficient permissions, or incorrect file paths. Handling these errors gracefully is important for a seamless user experience.

Android Example: Handling Errors

```
StorageReference                         fileRef                         =
FirebaseStorage.getInstance().getReference().child("images/sampleIma
ge.jpg");

fileRef.getDownloadUrl().addOnSuccessListener(uri -> {
    String downloadUrl = uri.toString();
    // Use the URL for further processing
}).addOnFailureListener(e -> {
    if (e instanceof StorageException) {
        StorageException se = (StorageException) e;
        switch (se.getErrorCode()) {
            case StorageException.ERROR_OBJECT_NOT_FOUND:
                Log.e("FirebaseStorage", "File not found");
                break;
            case StorageException.ERROR_NOT_AUTHORIZED:
                Log.e("FirebaseStorage", "User not authorized to access this file");
                break;
            case StorageException.ERROR_RETRY_LIMIT_EXCEEDED:
                Log.e("FirebaseStorage", "Retry limit exceeded");
                break;
            default:
                Log.e("FirebaseStorage", "Unknown error", e);
        }
    }
```

```
        }
});
```

In this example, the errors are handled based on their specific type, allowing you to display appropriate error messages to the user.

Optimizing File Downloads

Optimizing file downloads from Firebase Storage is essential for ensuring that your application remains performant and responsive, especially when dealing with large files or slow network conditions. Below are some best practices for optimizing file downloads:

1. Use Caching

Caching helps to reduce redundant network requests and speeds up the loading of frequently accessed files. Firebase Storage can work with popular image loading libraries like **Glide** or **Picasso**, which have built-in caching mechanisms to store files locally and reuse them when needed.

2. Compress Large Files

Before uploading large files to Firebase Storage, consider compressing them to reduce their size. This not only saves on storage costs but also speeds up download times, improving the user experience. For instance, image files can be compressed using lossy or lossless algorithms, depending on your requirements.

3. Download Files on Demand

Instead of downloading all files at once, download them on demand when the user requests them. This is particularly useful for applications with user-generated content, where not all content may be relevant to every user. By downloading files only when needed, you save bandwidth and reduce the amount of data the user's device has to process.

4. Monitor Network Conditions

Firebase provides tools like **Firebase Performance Monitoring** to track network requests and identify bottlenecks. Using this information, you can determine whether your application is struggling due to network issues and make adjustments accordingly.

Summary

Downloading and displaying files from Firebase Storage is an essential feature for applications that need to provide users with access to images, videos, documents, or other types of content. In this section, we covered how to use Firebase Storage to download files in both Android and web applications. We explored different methods for downloading files—either directly to local storage or by obtaining a download URL—and demonstrated how to display the files in your application's user interface.

We also discussed error handling and shared best practices for optimizing file downloads to ensure a smooth user experience. Whether you are dealing with small images or large video files, Firebase Storage provides the tools necessary to manage and retrieve your data effectively, making it a powerful choice for content-driven applications.

Chapter 6: Cloud Functions for Beginners

What are Cloud Functions?

Firebase Cloud Functions are a powerful feature of the Firebase platform that allows you to execute backend code in response to various events triggered by Firebase services and HTTPS requests. In simple terms, they are serverless, event-driven pieces of code that run in the cloud. This enables you to build highly scalable backend logic without the need for managing servers or dealing with the complexities of traditional backend infrastructure.

Firebase Cloud Functions are particularly useful for creating custom business logic that responds to user interactions, database changes, file uploads, or other events occurring within your Firebase project. These functions are written in JavaScript or TypeScript and are deployed using Firebase's infrastructure, which means they are automatically scaled, and the associated compute resources are managed for you. This makes Cloud Functions ideal for creating robust, scalable backend services for your mobile or web applications.

In this section, we'll dive deeper into understanding what Firebase Cloud Functions are, their common use cases, and how they can be used to enrich the functionality of your applications.

1. Why Use Cloud Functions?

Firebase Cloud Functions provide several benefits for developers:

1. **Scalability**: Cloud Functions automatically scale based on demand. You don't need to worry about managing servers or ensuring the system can handle spikes in usage. Google's infrastructure takes care of the scaling for you.
2. **Serverless Approach**: With Firebase Cloud Functions, you can build and deploy backend logic without having to maintain or manage physical servers. This reduces the overhead and costs associated with server maintenance.
3. **Event-Driven Architecture**: Cloud Functions can be triggered by a variety of Firebase events, such as changes in the Realtime Database or Firestore, new file uploads to Firebase Storage, or user authentication events.
4. **Custom Business Logic**: Cloud Functions are great for adding server-side custom logic to your app. This can include validating database entries, transforming data, sending notifications, and more.
5. **Integration with Other Firebase Products**: Since Cloud Functions are tightly integrated with the Firebase ecosystem, you can easily respond to Firebase Authentication, Database, Firestore, and Storage events.

These benefits make Firebase Cloud Functions an excellent choice for many types of applications. They allow you to focus more on building features, rather than worrying about backend infrastructure and scaling.

2. Common Use Cases

Here are some common use cases where Firebase Cloud Functions can be highly effective:

- **Data Validation**: Automatically validate and sanitize data before it's written to the database to ensure the integrity of your data.
- **Push Notifications**: Send push notifications to users when certain events occur, such as when they receive a new message or a friend request.
- **Image Processing**: Automatically resize images uploaded to Firebase Storage, generate thumbnails, or apply image filters.
- **Automated Email Sending**: Trigger email notifications when a specific event happens, like user registration or password reset.
- **Analytics Transformation**: Process analytics data, like custom user events, and store the transformed data for further insights.

3. Key Concepts of Cloud Functions

Firebase Cloud Functions can be categorized into two primary types:

- **HTTP Functions**: These functions are triggered by HTTPS requests. You can use them to create APIs or other web services that can be called from your app or even from outside the Firebase ecosystem.
- **Background Functions**: These are functions triggered by Firebase events such as changes in the Realtime Database, Firestore, Authentication, or Storage. They are useful for adding business logic that runs automatically in response to specific actions in Firebase.

For example:

HTTP Trigger: To create an HTTP endpoint, you can write an HTTP function and then deploy it. This endpoint can be used to handle requests and respond to them.
javascript
Copy code
```
const functions = require('firebase-functions');

// Create a simple HTTP function
exports.helloWorld = functions.https.onRequest((request, response) => {
  response.send("Hello from Firebase!");
});
```

- In the above code, `exports.helloWorld` creates an HTTP endpoint. Whenever the endpoint is hit, it sends back a response with the text "Hello from Firebase!".

Background Trigger: A background function that listens to changes in Firestore might look like this:

javascript
Copy code
```javascript
const functions = require('firebase-functions');
const admin = require('firebase-admin');
admin.initializeApp();

// Triggered when a new document is created in Firestore
exports.newUserCreated = functions.firestore
  .document('users/{userId}')
  .onCreate((snapshot, context) => {
    const newValue = snapshot.data();
    console.log('A new user has signed up:', newValue.name);
    // Perform additional operations, such as sending a welcome email
  });
```

- In this example, `exports.newUserCreated` listens for new documents added to the users collection in Firestore. Whenever a new user is created, it logs their name and performs additional operations.

4. Writing Your First Cloud Function

To write and deploy your first Cloud Function, you need to follow these steps:

Step 1: Set Up Firebase Tools

Before you start, you need to install the Firebase CLI. The Firebase CLI allows you to initialize and deploy your Cloud Functions.

```
npm install -g firebase-tools
```

After installing, log in to Firebase using your Google account:

```
firebase login
```

Navigate to the root directory of your project and initialize Firebase Functions:

```
firebase init functions
```

The initialization process will create a `functions` directory and add a `package.json` file to it.

Step 2: Write the Function

After initializing, open the `functions/index.js` file. This is where you will write your Cloud Functions. For this example, let's create a simple HTTP function:

```
const functions = require('firebase-functions');

exports.greetUser = functions.https.onRequest((request, response) => {
  const name = request.query.name || "Guest";
  response.send(`Hello, ${name}! Welcome to our service.`);
});
```

This function will respond with a personalized greeting when called. For example, calling `https://<your-cloud-function-url>?name=John` will return Hello, John! Welcome to our service..

Step 3: Deploy the Function

Once you've written your function, deploy it using:

```
firebase deploy --only functions
```

Firebase will then build and deploy your function to Google Cloud, and provide you with a URL where your HTTP function can be accessed.

5. Working with Background Functions

Cloud Functions for Firebase can also respond to changes in your database, file storage, or user management services. Let's create a function that sends a welcome email to new users when they register.

First, we need to initialize Firebase Admin SDK in our Cloud Function:

```
const admin = require('firebase-admin');
admin.initializeApp();
```

Now, let's create the function that will be triggered when a new user account is created:

```javascript
const functions = require('firebase-functions');

exports.sendWelcomeEmail = functions.auth.user().onCreate((user) => {
  const email = user.email;
  const displayName = user.displayName;

  console.log(`Sending welcome email to ${displayName} at ${email}`);

  // Here you would integrate with an email service like SendGrid to send the email.
  return null; // For simplicity, we won't implement the actual email sending here.
});
```

This function listens for new user sign-ups using Firebase Authentication and logs a welcome message.

6. Testing and Debugging Cloud Functions

Testing and debugging Cloud Functions can sometimes be challenging because they are run in a cloud environment. Here are some tools and strategies you can use:

1. **Firebase Logs**: Firebase provides logging capabilities for Cloud Functions. You can use `console.log()` statements in your code to output messages to the Firebase console.
2. **Firebase Emulator Suite**: The Firebase Emulator Suite allows you to run and test your Cloud Functions locally before deploying them to production. This helps in debugging functions without incurring cloud costs.

To start the emulator, use:

```
firebase emulators:start
```

7. Best Practices for Cloud Functions

Here are some best practices to keep in mind while working with Firebase Cloud Functions:

1. **Minimize Cold Starts**: Cold starts occur when a Cloud Function hasn't been used for a while, resulting in longer execution times. To mitigate this, keep your function's

code lightweight, and consider using a dedicated plan that keeps instances warm if low latency is crucial.

Use Environment Variables: For sensitive information like API keys, use Firebase environment configuration rather than hardcoding them.

bash
Copy code
```
firebase functions:config:set api.key="YOUR_API_KEY"
```

2.
3. **Avoid Infinite Loops**: Be careful when writing functions that update databases, as they might trigger themselves, creating an infinite loop. Always use conditional logic to ensure that such loops are avoided.
4. **Proper Error Handling**: Always include error handling in your Cloud Functions to make debugging easier and to improve resilience.

Conclusion

Firebase Cloud Functions provide a powerful way to run backend code without managing servers, making them ideal for quickly adding server-side logic to your Firebase projects. Whether you're building RESTful APIs, processing database changes, or automating file operations, Cloud Functions are versatile enough to handle a wide variety of use cases.

In the next sections, we will explore how you can leverage Firebase Hosting to deploy your web applications and make them accessible to users around the globe.

Writing and Deploying Your First Function

Firebase Cloud Functions offer a seamless way to extend the functionality of your application by allowing you to write server-side logic without managing your own servers. In this section, we will take a hands-on approach to writing and deploying your first Cloud Function. We'll go through the entire process, starting from setting up your local environment to writing, testing, and deploying a simple Cloud Function.

1. Setting Up Your Local Development Environment

Before we can start writing Cloud Functions, we need to set up our local environment. The following steps will guide you through the installation and configuration of the Firebase CLI, which is required for initializing and deploying Cloud Functions.

Step 1: Install Node.js and NPM

Firebase Cloud Functions are written in JavaScript or TypeScript and require Node.js to run. Therefore, the first step is to install Node.js and npm (Node Package Manager) if they are not already installed.

To check if you already have Node.js and npm installed, open your terminal and run:

```
node -v
npm -v
```

If you see version numbers for both, you are good to go. If not, you can download and install Node.js from nodejs.org. This installation will also include npm.

Step 2: Install Firebase CLI

The Firebase CLI (Command Line Interface) is used to manage your Firebase projects and deploy your Cloud Functions. To install it globally on your system, use the following command:

```
npm install -g firebase-tools
```

After the installation, verify that the Firebase CLI has been installed correctly by running:

```
firebase --version
```

Step 3: Authenticate with Firebase

Next, you need to authenticate with your Firebase account to allow the CLI to interact with your projects. Run the following command:

```
firebase login
```

This will open a browser window asking you to log in with your Google account.

2. Initialize Firebase in Your Project

Now that the Firebase CLI is installed and authenticated, it's time to initialize Firebase Functions in your project.

Step 1: Create a New Directory for Your Project

First, create a new directory for your project and navigate to it:

```
mkdir my-firebase-functions
cd my-firebase-functions
```

Step 2: Initialize Firebase Functions

Run the following command to initialize Firebase in your project directory:

```
firebase init functions
```

You will be prompted with a series of questions:

- **Select a Firebase project**: Choose an existing Firebase project or create a new one.
- **Language**: Choose either JavaScript or TypeScript. JavaScript is easier for beginners, while TypeScript offers type safety.
- **Linting**: Decide whether you want to use ESLint to lint your code.
- **Install dependencies**: Select "Yes" to automatically install the required dependencies.

This command will create a `functions` directory containing the `index.js` file where you will write your Cloud Functions. It will also create `package.json` for managing dependencies and `firebase.json` for project configuration.

3. Writing Your First Cloud Function

With Firebase initialized, let's write a simple Cloud Function. We will create an HTTP function that returns a welcome message when accessed.

Open the `functions/index.js` file in your preferred text editor. You will see some boilerplate code that looks like this:

```
const functions = require('firebase-functions');

// Create and deploy your first Cloud Function
exports.helloWorld = functions.https.onRequest((request, response) => {
  response.send("Hello from Firebase!");
});
```

This is a basic HTTP Cloud Function named `helloWorld` that sends back a "Hello from Firebase!" response when accessed. Let's break down the components:

- **`functions.https.onRequest`**: This specifies that the function will be triggered by an HTTP request.
- **Request and Response Objects**: The function takes two parameters, `request` and `response`. These objects are similar to what you find in standard Node.js Express applications, allowing you to read the incoming request and send a response.

127 | Chapter 6: Cloud Functions for Beginners

Let's extend this example by creating a function that takes a user's name as a query parameter and returns a personalized greeting:

```
exports.greetUser = functions.https.onRequest((request, response) => {
  const name = request.query.name || 'Guest';
  response.send(`Hello, ${name}! Welcome to Firebase.`);
});
```

This greetUser function reads the name parameter from the request query. If a name is not provided, it defaults to "Guest". When accessed, it will respond with a personalized greeting message.

4. Deploying Your Cloud Function

Once you've written your function, the next step is to deploy it so that it can be accessed publicly. To do this, run the following command in your terminal from the root directory of your project:

```
firebase deploy --only functions
```

Firebase will compile, bundle, and deploy your Cloud Function to Google's cloud infrastructure. When the deployment is successful, you will see a URL where your HTTP Cloud Function is hosted, similar to:

Function URL (greetUser): https://<REGION>-<PROJECT_ID>.cloudfunctions.net/greetUser

You can now open this URL in your browser or use an HTTP client like Postman to send a GET request with a name parameter to see your personalized greeting.

For example:

https://<REGION>-<PROJECT_ID>.cloudfunctions.net/greetUser?name=Alice

This URL will return:

```
Hello, Alice! Welcome to Firebase.
```

5. Testing Your Cloud Function Locally

Firebase provides an Emulator Suite that allows you to test your Cloud Functions locally before deploying them. This is useful for ensuring that your functions work as expected without incurring cloud costs or delays.

To start the emulator, run:

```
firebase emulators:start
```

Once the emulator is running, you can call your HTTP functions locally by using the URLs provided by the emulator (typically something like `http://localhost:5001`).

For instance, you can test the `greetUser` function locally:

```
http://localhost:5001/<PROJECT_ID>/<REGION>/greetUser?name=Bob
```

Testing locally allows you to debug and validate the functionality of your Cloud Functions before deploying them to production.

6. Handling HTTP Methods

The `greetUser` function, like all HTTP functions, has access to various HTTP methods like GET, POST, PUT, etc. You can handle different methods within the function using the `request.method` property. For example:

```
exports.handleMethods = functions.https.onRequest((request, response) => {
  switch (request.method) {
    case 'GET':
      response.send('Received a GET request!');
      break;
    case 'POST':
      response.send('Received a POST request!');
      break;
    default:
      response.status(405).send('Method Not Allowed');
      break;
```

    }
});
```

In the above code:

- If the function receives a GET request, it will respond with a corresponding message.
- Similarly, for a POST request, a different message is sent.
- For any other HTTP method, the response is `405 Method Not Allowed`.

## 7. Working with Background Functions

In addition to HTTP functions, Firebase Cloud Functions can be used to handle events that occur in other Firebase services. Let's create a background function that listens to changes in Firestore. For this example, we will create a function that sends a welcome message whenever a new user is added to a `users` collection in Firestore.

Modify your `functions/index.js` file to add the following code:

```
exports.newUserAdded = functions.firestore
  .document('users/{userId}')
  .onCreate((snapshot, context) => {
    const newUser = snapshot.data();
    console.log(`Welcome ${newUser.name}! Thank you for joining.`);
    return null;
});
```

In this example:

- The `newUserAdded` function listens to the creation of new documents in the `users` collection.
- When a new document is created, it logs a message welcoming the new user.

8. Best Practices for Writing and Deploying Cloud Functions

Firebase Cloud Functions are powerful tools, but they should be used wisely to avoid pitfalls and ensure smooth, scalable performance. Here are some best practices for writing and deploying Cloud Functions:

Minimize Cold Start Delays

Cold starts occur when a Cloud Function has been inactive and then receives a new request. To minimize cold start times:
```

- **Keep the Function Lightweight**: Import only the necessary modules to reduce initialization time.
- **Use Runtime Configurations**: Instead of hardcoding environment-specific values (like API keys), use Firebase environment configuration to manage them securely.

Use Environment Variables

To store sensitive information like API keys, use Firebase's environment configuration:

```
firebase functions:config:set someapi.key="YOUR_API_KEY"
```

In your Cloud Function, access this configuration as follows:

```
const functions = require('firebase-functions');

const apiKey = functions.config().someapi.key;
```

Avoid Infinite Loops

Background functions can inadvertently trigger themselves if not handled properly. For example, if a function that listens to Firestore writes data back to the same document, it could trigger itself again. To prevent this:

- Use proper conditional logic to ensure that your functions do not perform operations that will trigger themselves.

Logging and Monitoring

Firebase provides logging capabilities that can be very useful for debugging. Use `console.log()` to log messages and monitor the performance and behavior of your Cloud Functions in the Firebase Console. However, do not log sensitive data.

Conclusion

In this section, you have learned how to set up your development environment, write your first HTTP Cloud Function, and deploy it to Firebase. We also explored how to handle different HTTP methods, how to create background functions triggered by Firestore events, and discussed best practices for writing robust and efficient Cloud Functions.

Cloud Functions are incredibly versatile and can significantly extend the capabilities of your Firebase project. By leveraging serverless functions, you can quickly add backend features without the complexities of server management, allowing you to focus on building rich and dynamic applications for your users.

In the next section, we will look at Firebase Hosting and how to deploy your first website, allowing you to integrate Cloud Functions with your frontend applications seamlessly.

Useful Cloud Function Examples

Firebase Cloud Functions can be used for a wide variety of use cases, each designed to add value to your application through automation, data processing, integration, and response to user or database events. In this section, we will explore several practical examples of Cloud Functions, ranging from sending notifications and managing user authentication events to transforming data and integrating with third-party services. These examples will help you understand how Cloud Functions can be effectively used in real-world scenarios.

1. Sending Push Notifications on Database Changes

One of the most common use cases for Firebase Cloud Functions is sending push notifications to users. For instance, if you are building a messaging app, you can send a push notification to users whenever they receive a new message. Let's create a Cloud Function that listens to new documents added to a Firestore messages collection and sends a notification to the recipient.

Step 1: Setting Up Firebase Admin SDK

To send notifications, we need to use the Firebase Admin SDK, which allows us to access Firebase services programmatically.

Open the functions/index.js file and add the following code:

```
const functions = require('firebase-functions');
const admin = require('firebase-admin');
admin.initializeApp();
```

Step 2: Creating the Notification Function

Next, create a function that listens for new messages in the Firestore messages collection:

```
exports.notifyUserOnNewMessage = functions.firestore
  .document('messages/{messageId}')
  .onCreate(async (snapshot, context) => {
    const messageData = snapshot.data();
    const recipientId = messageData.recipientId;

    // Fetch the recipient's device token from Firestore
```

```
    const            userDoc              =              await
admin.firestore().collection('users').doc(recipientId).get();
    const token = userDoc.data().deviceToken;

    if (!token) {
      console.log('No   device   token   for   recipient.   Exiting
function.');
      return;
    }

    // Create the notification payload
    const payload = {
      notification: {
        title: 'New Message',
        body:    `You    have    received    a    message    from
${messageData.senderName}`,
      }
    };

    // Send the notification
    try {
      await admin.messaging().sendToDevice(token, payload);
      console.log('Notification sent successfully');
    } catch (error) {
      console.error('Error sending notification:', error);
    }
  });
```

In this example:

- **Event Trigger**: The function is triggered when a new document is created in the messages collection.
- **Fetching the Recipient Token**: The function uses the recipient ID from the new message to retrieve the device token from the users collection.
- **Sending the Notification**: Finally, the function sends a push notification using Firebase Cloud Messaging (FCM).

This function helps keep your users engaged by immediately notifying them when they receive a message.

2. Automatically Adding User Metadata

Another useful application of Firebase Cloud Functions is to manage user metadata when they register or update their profile. For example, you may want to store additional data, such as a user's signup date or role in your Firestore database when they first sign up.

Step 1: User Sign-Up Trigger

We can use Firebase Authentication triggers to listen to user creation events:

```
exports.addUserMetadata = functions.auth.user().onCreate((user) => {
  const userId = user.uid;
  const email = user.email;

  // Adding metadata to Firestore
  return admin.firestore().collection('users').doc(userId).set({
    email: email,
    createdAt: admin.firestore.FieldValue.serverTimestamp(),
    role: 'user'
  });
});
```

In this example:

- **Trigger**: The function is triggered whenever a new user registers.
- **Storing Metadata**: The function stores metadata such as the user's email, creation timestamp, and role (user) in the users collection in Firestore.

This function helps you centralize all user-related data in Firestore, making it easy to manage and query.

3. Cleaning Up User Data on Account Deletion

When a user deletes their account, it is important to remove any related data to maintain data privacy and avoid orphan records in your database. Let's create a function that cleans up user-related data from Firestore when their account is deleted.

```
exports.cleanupUserData = functions.auth.user().onDelete(async (user) => {
  const userId = user.uid;

  // Delete user document from Firestore
  try {
    await admin.firestore().collection('users').doc(userId).delete();
```

```
    console.log(`User data deleted for user ID: ${userId}`);
  } catch (error) {
    console.error('Error deleting user data:', error);
  }

  // Additional cleanup operations can be added here (e.g., deleting
messages, posts)
});
```

In this example:

- **Trigger**: The function is triggered whenever a user deletes their account.
- **Deleting Data**: It deletes the user's document from the users collection.

This ensures that your database stays clean and that you comply with data privacy standards.

4. Image Processing with Cloud Functions

Another powerful use case for Cloud Functions is processing images that users upload. For example, you can create thumbnails for profile pictures when they are uploaded to Firebase Storage.

Step 1: Adding Required Dependencies

To process images, you can use the sharp library, which is an efficient image processing library. First, add the library by running:

```
npm install sharp
```

Step 2: Writing the Thumbnail Function

Create a function that listens for new image uploads in Firebase Storage and creates a thumbnail:

```
const sharp = require('sharp');
const path = require('path');
const os = require('os');
const fs = require('fs');

exports.generateThumbnail =
functions.storage.object().onFinalize(async (object) => {
```

```javascript
  const bucket = admin.storage().bucket(object.bucket);
  const filePath = object.name;
  const contentType = object.contentType;

  if (!contentType.startsWith('image/')) {
    console.log('Uploaded file is not an image.');
    return;
  }

  const fileName = path.basename(filePath);
  const tempFilePath = path.join(os.tmpdir(), fileName);
  const thumbFilePath = path.join(path.dirname(filePath),
`thumb_${fileName}`);

  // Download the image locally
  await bucket.file(filePath).download({ destination: tempFilePath
});
  console.log('Image downloaded locally to', tempFilePath);

  // Resize the image using Sharp
  await sharp(tempFilePath)
    .resize(200, 200)
    .toFile(tempFilePath);

  console.log('Thumbnail created at', tempFilePath);

  // Upload the thumbnail back to Firebase Storage
  await bucket.upload(tempFilePath, {
    destination: thumbFilePath,
    metadata: {
      contentType: contentType,
    },
  });

  // Cleanup
  fs.unlinkSync(tempFilePath);
  console.log('Temporary file deleted.');
});
```

In this example:

- **Trigger**: The function is triggered whenever a new image is uploaded to Firebase Storage.
- **Image Processing**: The function uses sharp to create a 200x200 pixel thumbnail of the uploaded image.
- **Cleanup**: The local temporary file is deleted after the thumbnail has been uploaded back to Firebase Storage.

This function is useful for optimizing the storage and serving of images in your app, making it more efficient.

5. Data Transformation with Firestore Triggers

In some cases, you may need to transform data before storing it in Firestore. Let's say you want to store all usernames in lowercase to ensure consistency.

Create a function that listens to changes in the users collection and automatically converts the username to lowercase:

```
exports.transformUsernameToLowerCase = functions.firestore
  .document('users/{userId}')
  .onWrite(async (change, context) => {
    const newValue = change.after.exists ? change.after.data() : null;
    const oldValue = change.before.exists ? change.before.data() : null;

    if (newValue && (!oldValue || newValue.username !== oldValue.username)) {
      const username = newValue.username.toLowerCase();
      if (newValue.username !== username) {
        await change.after.ref.update({ username: username });
        console.log(`Username transformed to lowercase for user ID: ${context.params.userId}`);
      }
    }
  });
```

In this example:

- **Trigger**: The function is triggered whenever a document in the users collection is created or updated.
- **Transforming Data**: It converts the username field to lowercase if it is not already.

This helps maintain data consistency, ensuring that usernames are always stored in a standardized format.

6. Integrating with Third-Party APIs

Cloud Functions can also be used to integrate with third-party APIs. For example, if a user signs up for your service, you may want to add them to a mailing list managed by an external service like Mailchimp.

```
const axios = require('axios');

exports.addUserToMailchimp = functions.auth.user().onCreate(async (user) => {
  const email = user.email;

  const mailchimpApiKey = functions.config().mailchimp.apikey;
  const listId = functions.config().mailchimp.listid;

  const data = {
    email_address: email,
    status: 'subscribed',
  };

  const config = {
    headers: {
      Authorization: `apikey ${mailchimpApiKey}`,
    }
  };

  try {
    const response = await axios.post(
      `https://<dc>.api.mailchimp.com/3.0/lists/${listId}/members/`,
      data,
      config
    );
    console.log('User added to Mailchimp:', response.data);
  } catch (error) {
    console.error('Error adding user to Mailchimp:', error);
  }
});
```

In this example:

- **Trigger**: The function is triggered whenever a new user signs up.
- **Third-Party API Integration**: The function uses `axios` to make an HTTP request to the Mailchimp API to add the new user to a mailing list.

Conclusion

Firebase Cloud Functions can be used for a wide range of scenarios, from sending notifications and automating data handling to integrating with third-party services and transforming data. These examples demonstrate the versatility of Cloud Functions and how they can help you automate your backend, enhance user engagement, and streamline application workflows.

By effectively using Cloud Functions, you can add rich backend features to your Firebase project without worrying about server management, allowing you to focus on building a better user experience. In the next chapter, we will explore Firebase Hosting and learn how to deploy dynamic web applications using Firebase's hosting platform.

Chapter 7: Firebase Hosting

Introduction to Firebase Hosting

Firebase Hosting is a fast, secure, and reliable web hosting service provided by Google that allows you to deploy static or dynamic content to a global content delivery network (CDN) with a few simple commands. It is well-integrated with the Firebase suite of services, making it an excellent option for developers who are building applications within the Firebase ecosystem. Firebase Hosting provides a robust platform that can serve web applications, static websites, and even dynamic content powered by Firebase Cloud Functions. This section will explore the key features of Firebase Hosting, its advantages, and how you can get started.

Firebase Hosting is designed with both simplicity and power in mind. Whether you are deploying a single-page application (SPA), a progressive web application (PWA), or even server-rendered dynamic content, Firebase Hosting can accommodate your needs. Firebase makes the deployment process seamless, providing tools that make it easy to upload, manage, and configure your website with minimal overhead.

1. Features of Firebase Hosting

Firebase Hosting is packed with features that make it a preferred choice for developers looking for hassle-free, scalable, and secure web hosting. Let's explore some of the core features:

a. Global Content Delivery Network (CDN)

Firebase Hosting leverages Google's global CDN to deliver content quickly to users, regardless of their geographic location. This means that your website's static assets—such as HTML, CSS, JavaScript, and images—are cached in various locations around the world. This helps minimize latency, providing your users with a faster, more responsive browsing experience.

b. SSL by Default

Security is a major concern for all web applications, and Firebase Hosting helps you achieve a secure connection by providing SSL certificates for your domain automatically. This means that all of your content is served over HTTPS without any additional cost or configuration on your part. SSL ensures that the communication between your users and your website remains encrypted and secure, which helps build trust and improve search engine rankings.

c. Versioned Deployments and Rollbacks

Firebase Hosting provides versioned deployments, allowing you to roll back to a previous version of your website if something goes wrong. Each time you deploy, Firebase Hosting creates a unique version that can be accessed and activated when needed. This versioning capability helps prevent accidental downtime or disruptions caused by flawed updates.

d. Custom Domains and Free SSL Certificates

You can easily connect your custom domain to Firebase Hosting. Firebase not only helps with domain verification, but also issues SSL certificates automatically, so you don't need to worry about manually obtaining and renewing certificates for HTTPS.

e. Single Command Deployment

Deploying a website using Firebase Hosting is incredibly easy. You can use the Firebase CLI (Command Line Interface) to initialize and deploy your content with just a few commands. The process is efficient, reducing the complexity that often comes with web deployment.

2. Use Cases for Firebase Hosting

Firebase Hosting is suitable for a wide range of use cases, making it a versatile tool for different types of projects. Some common use cases include:

- **Single-Page Applications (SPAs)**: Firebase Hosting can be used to serve SPAs built using frameworks like React, Angular, or Vue.js. These applications often involve client-side routing and dynamic updates, and Firebase Hosting can handle these requirements seamlessly.
- **Progressive Web Applications (PWAs)**: PWAs offer an app-like experience on the web, and Firebase Hosting is well-suited for hosting such applications. PWAs often require SSL, fast load times, and offline capabilities—all of which Firebase Hosting can support.
- **Static Websites**: Firebase Hosting can be used to host static websites such as personal blogs, portfolios, or documentation. The fast CDN and SSL support make Firebase Hosting an ideal choice for such projects.
- **Server-Side Rendered (SSR) Content**: By integrating Firebase Hosting with Firebase Cloud Functions, you can host dynamic server-side rendered pages. This is especially useful for applications that need SEO-friendly content or that need to render personalized information based on user data.

3. Getting Started with Firebase Hosting

Now, let's dive into the steps required to get started with Firebase Hosting. We will go through the process of setting up a project, initializing Firebase Hosting, and deploying a basic web application.

Step 1: Setting Up Firebase CLI

Firebase CLI is the command-line interface that allows you to manage Firebase projects and deploy web applications. Before you can start using Firebase Hosting, you need to install Firebase CLI.

To install Firebase CLI globally, use the following command:

```
npm install -g firebase-tools
```

After installing the CLI, authenticate with Firebase using:

```
firebase login
```

This command will open a browser window asking you to log in with your Google account. Once logged in, Firebase CLI will be able to access your projects.

Step 2: Initialize Firebase Hosting

Navigate to the root directory of your web project in your terminal and run the following command to initialize Firebase Hosting:

```
firebase init hosting
```

During initialization, Firebase will prompt you with several questions:

- **Select Firebase Project**: Choose an existing project or create a new one. If you haven't already set up a Firebase project, you can create one from the Firebase console.
- **Set up Hosting Directory**: Specify the directory containing your website's files (e.g., `public`). This directory will hold all the static assets that Firebase will serve.
- **Single Page App (rewrite all URLs to index.html)**: If you are deploying a Single-Page Application, select "Yes" for URL rewrites. This ensures that all URLs are directed to `index.html`, allowing the client-side router to handle routing.
- **Deploy Now**: You can choose to deploy your app immediately or wait until you have made some modifications.

The initialization process will generate two files: `firebase.json` and `.firebaserc`. These files are used to manage the hosting configuration.

Step 3: Add Website Files

If you haven't already, add your website files to the hosting directory you specified during initialization (e.g., `public`). This directory should contain your `index.html`, `style.css`, `main.js`, and any other assets required by your web application.

Step 4: Deploy Your Website

Once everything is ready, you can deploy your web application to Firebase Hosting with the following command:

```
firebase deploy
```

This command will bundle your files, upload them to Firebase Hosting, and make them available at the default Firebase URL (e.g., `https://<PROJECT_ID>.web.app`). If you have added a custom domain, it will also be available at that domain.

Step 5: Custom Domain Setup (Optional)

If you want to use a custom domain for your website, you can easily add one through the Firebase Console:

1. Go to the Firebase Console, navigate to your project, and select Hosting.
2. Click on "Add Custom Domain" and enter your domain name.
3. Firebase will provide you with DNS records that you need to add to your domain registrar to verify ownership.

Once the domain is verified, Firebase will issue an SSL certificate for your domain, and your site will be served securely over HTTPS.

4. Managing Hosting Releases

Firebase Hosting keeps track of each deployment, which is very useful for managing the different versions of your website.

a. Viewing Release History

To view your deployment history, use the following command:

```
firebase hosting:channel:list
```

This command will show a list of previously deployed versions along with their details, such as timestamp and URL. You can also see the deployment history in the Firebase Console.

b. Rolling Back to a Previous Version

If a newly deployed version of your website has an issue, Firebase Hosting allows you to quickly roll back to a previous version. You can use the Firebase Console to activate an older version, or use the CLI:

```
firebase hosting:release --target=TARGET --version=VERSION_ID
```

This allows you to minimize downtime and quickly revert to a stable version of your site.

5. Firebase Hosting and Cloud Functions Integration

Firebase Hosting can work in conjunction with Firebase Cloud Functions to handle dynamic requests. This integration allows you to build a server-side rendering solution or serve custom logic in response to user actions.

Example: Server-Side Rendering with Firebase Cloud Functions

Suppose you are using a JavaScript framework like React or Angular, and you want server-side rendering for better SEO and faster loading times. You can achieve this by deploying your server-side code using Firebase Cloud Functions.

First, set up Firebase Cloud Functions in your project:

```
firebase init functions
```

Install the required dependencies, such as `express` to handle server-side requests:

```
npm install express
```

Next, modify your Cloud Function to handle incoming requests and render HTML:

```
const functions = require('firebase-functions');
const express = require('express');
```

```
const app = express();

app.get('**', (req, res) => {
  res.send(`<html>
    <head><title>Server-Side Rendered Page</title></head>
    <body>
      <h1>Hello from Firebase Cloud Functions!</h1>
    </body>
  </html>`);
});

exports.ssrApp = functions.https.onRequest(app);
```

Finally, update `firebase.json` to add a rewrite rule that sends requests to your Cloud Function:

```
{
  "hosting": {
    "rewrites": [
      {
        "source": "**",
        "function": "ssrApp"
      }
    ]
```

}

}

This setup allows you to serve dynamic, server-rendered content through Firebase Hosting.

Conclusion

Firebase Hosting is a powerful, flexible, and secure hosting solution that is ideal for a variety of web projects. Whether you are building a static website, a single-page application, or a server-side rendered application, Firebase Hosting can meet your needs by providing a simple deployment workflow, global content delivery, and automatic SSL. By integrating Firebase Hosting with Cloud Functions, you can even serve dynamic content, making it a versatile solution for modern web development.

With the easy-to-use Firebase CLI and the Firebase Console, you can manage deployments, rollbacks, and custom domains effortlessly. Firebase Hosting simplifies the complexities associated with web hosting, allowing you to focus more on building great user experiences.

In the next section, we will cover how to deploy your first website using Firebase Hosting, where you'll learn how to integrate custom domains and manage site configurations for optimal performance.

Deploying Your First Website

Firebase Hosting makes it easy for developers to deploy web applications with just a few commands. In this section, we will cover everything you need to know to deploy your first website using Firebase Hosting. We will start by creating a simple website, initializing Firebase Hosting, and then deploying the website to make it accessible to everyone. Along the way, we will explore various deployment settings and features that can help you manage and optimize your web deployment process.

Deploying a website involves several steps: preparing your project, initializing Firebase Hosting, configuring your deployment settings, and using the Firebase CLI to deploy your application to the cloud. We will cover each of these steps in detail, with a focus on providing practical, hands-on guidance.

1. Setting Up Your Project for Deployment

Before you begin, you need a project that you want to deploy. This could be a simple static HTML site, a Single Page Application (SPA), or a Progressive Web Application (PWA). In this guide, we will use a basic static website as an example, but the same process applies to more complex applications as well.

Step 1: Create Your Website Files

Create a folder on your local machine to hold your website files. For this example, we will create a simple HTML page called index.html along with a CSS file for styling.

In your terminal, create a folder called my-website:

```
mkdir my-website
cd my-website
```

Next, create an index.html file with the following content:

```html
<!DOCTYPE html>
<html lang="en">
<head>
  <meta charset="UTF-8">
  <meta name="viewport" content="width=device-width, initial-scale=1.0">
  <title>My First Firebase Hosting Site</title>
  <link rel="stylesheet" href="style.css">
</head>
<body>
  <h1>Welcome to My First Website Deployed with Firebase Hosting!</h1>
  <p>This is a simple web page to demonstrate the deployment process with Firebase Hosting.</p>
</body>
</html>
```

Create a `style.css` file in the same directory for basic styling:

```css
body {
    font-family: Arial, sans-serif;
    background-color: #f0f0f0;
    color: #333;
    text-align: center;
    margin: 0;
    padding: 50px;
}

h1 {
    color: #007bff;
}
```

These simple files will form the basis of our website. Of course, in a real-world scenario, you may have a more complex website with multiple pages, JavaScript, and additional resources.

2. Initializing Firebase Hosting

Firebase Hosting provides a very straightforward way to deploy your web application. The first step is to install the Firebase CLI and initialize Firebase Hosting in your project.

Step 2.1: Install Firebase CLI

The Firebase CLI (Command Line Interface) is required to manage Firebase projects from the command line, including deploying content to Firebase Hosting. If you haven't already installed it, you can do so using npm:

```
npm install -g firebase-tools
```

After installing, verify that the Firebase CLI is installed by running:

```
firebase --version
```

This should display the installed version of the Firebase CLI.

Step 2.2: Authenticate with Firebase

Next, you need to authenticate with Firebase using your Google account:

```
firebase login
```

This command will open a browser window where you can sign in with your Google account. Once authenticated, the CLI will be ready to access and manage your Firebase projects.

Step 2.3: Initialize Firebase Hosting

Now that Firebase CLI is set up, you can initialize Firebase Hosting in your project folder:

```
firebase init hosting
```

This command will prompt you with several questions to help set up Firebase Hosting:

- **Select a Firebase Project**: Choose an existing Firebase project from your Firebase Console, or create a new one.
- **Set Up Hosting Directory**: Specify the directory that contains your website files. By default, this is `public`, but you can specify a different directory, such as my-website.
- **Single Page App (Rewrite All URLs to `index.html`)**: If you are deploying a Single Page Application (SPA) with client-side routing, choose "Yes" to rewrite all URLs to `index.html`. This is important for ensuring that all routes in your application are correctly handled by the client-side router.
- **Deploy Now**: You will also be asked if you want to deploy your website immediately. You can choose "No" if you want to make some changes first.

Firebase will create several files during this initialization:

- **firebase.json**: This file contains Firebase Hosting configuration settings.
- **.firebaserc**: This file keeps track of your Firebase project association.

3. Preparing Your Website for Deployment

Before deploying your website, you should make sure all files are in place and properly configured.

Step 3.1: Review Firebase Configuration

The `firebase.json` file that Firebase creates contains configuration information for Firebase Hosting. It should look something like this:

```
{
  "hosting": {
    "public": "my-website",
    "ignore": [
      "firebase.json",
      "**/.*",
      "**/node_modules/**"
    ],
    "rewrites": [],
    "redirects": [],
    "headers": []
  }
}
```

- **public**: This is the directory that contains your website files. Ensure that this points to the correct directory.
- **ignore**: Files or directories specified here will be ignored during deployment.

You can also add custom headers, redirects, and rewrites to further configure your website. For instance, if you need to add security headers, you can do so in this configuration file.

Step 3.2: Test Locally with Firebase Emulator

Before deploying, it's a good idea to test your website locally. Firebase provides an emulator that allows you to preview your website on your local machine:

```
firebase emulators:start
```

This command will start a local server, and you can view your website by navigating to `http://localhost:5000` in your browser. The emulator allows you to ensure that everything works as expected before deploying.

4. Deploying Your Website

Once you are satisfied with your website and Firebase configuration, it's time to deploy your website to Firebase Hosting.

Step 4.1: Deploy to Firebase

To deploy your website, use the following command:

```
firebase deploy
```

After the deployment is complete, you will see a message in your terminal with the URL where your website is now live. The default URL will be in the form `https://<PROJECT_ID>.web.app`. You can visit this URL to see your live website.

Step 4.2: Custom Domain Setup (Optional)

Firebase Hosting allows you to connect your own custom domain to your website, giving you more control over your branding. To add a custom domain:

1. Go to the **Firebase Console**, navigate to your project, and select **Hosting**.
2. Click **Add Custom Domain** and enter your domain name.
3. Firebase will provide DNS records that you need to add to your domain registrar's DNS settings to verify ownership of the domain.

Once the domain is verified, Firebase will automatically issue an SSL certificate, and your website will be available at your custom domain over HTTPS.

5. Managing Your Hosting Configuration

Firebase Hosting provides powerful tools for managing your website, including rollbacks, deployment channels, and different environments.

Step 5.1: Viewing Deployment History

Firebase Hosting keeps track of each deployment, allowing you to view your deployment history and roll back to a previous version if necessary. You can view your deployment history in the Firebase Console under the **Hosting** section, or by running:

```
firebase hosting:channel:list
```

This command will show you all active deployment channels and versions.

Step 5.2: Rolling Back to a Previous Version

If you discover an issue with a recently deployed version of your website, you can easily roll back to a previous version. This can be done through the Firebase Console, where you can select a previous deployment and activate it.

Alternatively, you can use the CLI to roll back:

```
firebase hosting:release --target <TARGET> --version <VERSION_ID>
```

Step 5.3: Using Preview Channels

Firebase Hosting allows you to create **preview channels** that let you share a pre-release version of your site with stakeholders for review and testing before going live. You can create a preview channel using the following command:

```
firebase hosting:channel:deploy <channel_name>
```

This will generate a unique URL for the preview, which you can share with others. Preview channels are temporary and automatically expire after a set period, but they are incredibly useful for getting feedback before deploying to production.

6. Best Practices for Firebase Hosting

Deploying a website involves more than just uploading files—it also requires considering factors such as security, performance, and reliability. Below are some best practices to keep in mind when using Firebase Hosting.

Step 6.1: Use Custom Domains with SSL

Firebase Hosting provides free SSL certificates for all custom domains, ensuring that your content is delivered securely. Always use custom domains with SSL, especially if you are collecting sensitive information or providing a personalized user experience.

Step 6.2: Set Up Caching Headers

To improve the performance of your website, consider setting caching headers. Firebase allows you to configure custom headers in the `firebase.json` file, which helps improve the loading time for returning users.

Example:

```
{
  "hosting": {
    "headers": [
      {
        "source": "**/*.@(jpg|jpeg|gif|png)",
        "headers": [
          {
            "key": "Cache-Control",
            "value": "public,max-age=31536000,immutable"
          }
        ]
      }
    ]
  }
}
```

This configuration caches images for a year, reducing the load time for returning visitors.

Step 6.3: Redirect HTTP to HTTPS

Firebase automatically provides HTTPS for all hosted content, but it's still a good idea to enforce HTTPS across your entire site. You can do this by adding a redirect rule in the firebase.json:

```
{
  "hosting": {
    "redirects": [
      {
        "source": "/**",
        "destination": "https://<PROJECT_ID>.web.app",
        "type": 301
      }
    ]
  }
}
```

This ensures that users are always directed to the secure version of your site.

Conclusion

Deploying your first website using Firebase Hosting is a straightforward process that can be completed with just a few commands. Firebase Hosting provides a secure, fast, and scalable solution for hosting web applications, whether they are static sites, SPAs, or dynamic applications. By using the Firebase CLI, you can easily manage your website, handle custom domains, set caching rules, and preview new changes before making them live.

Firebase Hosting is an integral part of the Firebase ecosystem, offering a seamless way to host and manage your web content alongside other Firebase services. In the next section, we will explore how to manage custom domains and site configurations for even greater control over your deployment.

Custom Domains and Site Management

Firebase Hosting not only provides a robust infrastructure for deploying web applications but also supports custom domains, allowing you to brand your website and make it accessible via your own domain. This section will explore how to set up custom domains with Firebase Hosting, manage SSL certificates, configure URL rewrites, redirects, and use advanced site management tools such as deployment channels and caching headers.

Setting up a custom domain involves verifying ownership, managing DNS records, and configuring Firebase settings to ensure your website is delivered securely and efficiently. We will also discuss best practices for managing multiple versions of your site using preview channels, optimizing site performance, and organizing your Firebase Hosting settings to handle complex requirements.

1. Setting Up Custom Domains in Firebase Hosting

A custom domain gives your website a personalized URL, making it more recognizable and easier for users to remember. Firebase Hosting provides a simple way to connect your website to a custom domain and handles SSL certification for secure HTTPS connections.

Step 1: Register a Domain

Before you can add a custom domain to your Firebase project, you need to register a domain. You can use any domain registrar such as GoDaddy, Namecheap, or Google Domains to register your domain.

Step 2: Add a Custom Domain in Firebase Console

Once you have a domain, follow these steps to connect it to Firebase Hosting:

1. Open the **Firebase Console** and select your project.
2. Navigate to **Hosting** in the left-hand menu.
3. Click **Add Custom Domain**.
4. Enter your domain name (e.g., www.yourdomain.com).

Firebase will then generate DNS records that you need to add to your domain registrar's settings. This step is crucial for verifying ownership of the domain and directing traffic to Firebase Hosting.

Step 3: Update DNS Records

After adding your domain to Firebase, you need to update the DNS records for your domain:

- Go to your domain registrar and log in to your account.
- Locate the DNS settings or DNS management section.
- Add the DNS records provided by Firebase. These typically include:

- **A records**: Pointing to Firebase Hosting IP addresses.
- **TXT record**: Used to verify domain ownership.

It may take some time for these DNS changes to propagate. Once verified, Firebase will issue an SSL certificate for your domain, ensuring that your website is delivered securely over HTTPS.

2. SSL and Secure Connections

Firebase Hosting automatically provisions SSL certificates for both the default Firebase domain and your custom domain. SSL certificates are essential for encrypting data transmitted between your website and its users, providing privacy, security, and data integrity.

Automatic SSL Certification

Firebase handles SSL certification seamlessly, meaning you do not need to manually acquire or renew certificates. Once your domain is verified, Firebase will automatically issue an SSL certificate. Your website will then be accessible via `https://` instead of `http://`, giving users confidence that their data is secure.

Forcing HTTPS

To ensure all users access your site securely, it's a good idea to force HTTPS for all incoming requests. This can be done by adding a redirect rule in your `firebase.json` configuration file:

```
{
  "hosting": {
    "redirects": [
      {
        "source": "/**",
        "destination": "https://yourdomain.com",
        "type": 301
      }
    ]
  }
}
```

}

This configuration ensures that any HTTP request is automatically redirected to HTTPS, making sure your site is always accessed securely.

3. URL Rewrites and Redirects

URL rewrites and redirects are powerful features that help manage how users and search engines interact with your site. Firebase Hosting supports both URL rewrites and redirects to control how requests are handled.

URL Rewrites for Single-Page Applications

If you are building a Single-Page Application (SPA) with client-side routing, you need to ensure that all routes are directed to `index.html`, so that the client-side JavaScript can handle routing. You can configure this in `firebase.json`:

```json
{
  "hosting": {
    "rewrites": [
      {
        "source": "**",
        "destination": "/index.html"
      }
    ]
  }
}
```

This configuration ensures that any URL that is not a direct asset request is routed to your main HTML file, which then allows the client-side application to take over.

Redirects for URL Management

Redirects are useful for changing URLs, managing outdated links, or consolidating multiple domains. For instance, if you want to redirect an old URL structure to a new one, you can use the following configuration:

```
{
  "hosting": {
    "redirects": [
      {
        "source": "/old-page",
        "destination": "/new-page",
        "type": 301
      }
    ]
  }
}
```

The 301 status code indicates a permanent redirect, which is also good for SEO purposes since it tells search engines that the content has permanently moved.

4. Advanced Site Management

Firebase Hosting provides several advanced tools for managing multiple versions of your site, previewing changes before going live, and optimizing content delivery.

a. Preview Channels

Preview channels are a powerful feature of Firebase Hosting that allows you to share a pre-release version of your website for testing and feedback before going live. Each preview channel has a unique URL, and changes deployed to that channel are not live for your main site until they are merged.

To deploy to a preview channel, use:

```
firebase hosting:channel:deploy my-preview
```

This command will create a temporary preview URL where you can review changes. Preview channels are automatically deleted after a set period (30 days by default), but they are useful for development teams to test features and get stakeholder feedback before the main release.

b. Managing Multiple Hosting Targets

Firebase Hosting also allows you to set up multiple sites under a single Firebase project, which is useful if you need separate environments for different parts of your application or for handling multiple subdomains. This is achieved by setting up different hosting targets.

First, define a new target:

```
firebase target:apply hosting my-target my-project-alias
```

Then update `firebase.json` to specify which target each part of the configuration applies to.

```
{
  "hosting": [
    {
      "target": "my-target",
      "public": "public-folder"
    },
    {
      "target": "another-target",
      "public": "another-folder"
    }
  ]
```

}

This setup allows for deploying multiple independent sites or segments of the same site under different configurations.

5. Caching Strategies and Custom Headers

Firebase Hosting includes tools for configuring caching and HTTP headers, which are essential for optimizing performance and controlling how your content is delivered to users.

a. Setting Caching Headers

Caching headers help speed up load times for returning users by instructing browsers or CDNs how long they can keep assets before requesting them again from the server. You can set caching headers for static assets like images, CSS, and JavaScript:

```
{
  "hosting": {
    "headers": [
      {
        "source": "**/*.@(jpg|jpeg|gif|png|css|js)",
        "headers": [
          {
            "key": "Cache-Control",
            "value": "public,max-age=31536000,immutable"
          }
        ]
      }
    ]
  }
}
```

In this example, static assets are cached for a year (max-age=31536000) and marked as immutable, meaning they won't change, which allows browsers to avoid revalidating them.

b. Security Headers

To enhance security, you can set custom security headers that help protect your users. For example:

```
{
  "hosting": {
    "headers": [
      {
        "source": "**",
        "headers": [
          {
            "key": "X-Content-Type-Options",
            "value": "nosniff"
          },
          {
            "key": "X-Frame-Options",
            "value": "DENY"
          },
          {
            "key": "Content-Security-Policy",
            "value": "default-src 'self'"
          }
        ]
```

        }
    ]
  }
}

- **X-Content-Type-Options**: Prevents browsers from MIME-sniffing, which helps protect against certain types of attacks.
- **X-Frame-Options**: Prevents your site from being embedded in iframes, reducing the risk of clickjacking.
- **Content-Security-Policy**: Defines which sources the browser can load content from, protecting against cross-site scripting (XSS) attacks.

6. Best Practices for Custom Domains and Site Management

Managing custom domains and site configurations effectively is crucial for maintaining the performance, security, and reliability of your site. Here are some best practices to follow:

a. Always Use SSL

SSL is essential for modern web applications. Firebase Hosting provides SSL by default, so make sure to always enforce HTTPS for all connections. This not only improves security but also enhances user trust and SEO rankings.

b. Utilize Preview Channels

Whenever you are making significant changes to your website, use preview channels to test changes before going live. This helps prevent issues in production and allows stakeholders to provide feedback.

c. Set Proper Caching Rules

Caching is key to improving performance, especially for repeat visitors. Use caching headers to ensure that static assets are not repeatedly requested from the server, thereby reducing load times and server costs.

d. Manage SEO with Redirects

When changing URLs or restructuring your site, use proper 301 redirects to inform search engines that content has moved permanently. This ensures that your SEO rankings are preserved and that users do not encounter broken links.

e. Regularly Monitor Site Performance

Use tools such as Google Analytics and PageSpeed Insights to monitor your site's performance and identify areas for optimization. Firebase Hosting's integration with other Firebase services makes it easy to track user engagement and behavior.

Conclusion

Firebase Hosting provides a robust set of tools for deploying, managing, and optimizing websites. Setting up a custom domain with SSL is straightforward, and the platform makes it easy to add advanced features such as URL rewrites, redirects, custom headers, and caching strategies. Preview channels enable you to test changes in a controlled environment before going live, ensuring a smooth and reliable deployment process.

By following best practices for site management and utilizing the full suite of Firebase Hosting features, you can deliver a secure, performant, and highly available website that meets the needs of your users. In the next section, we will explore Firebase Analytics and how to leverage it to gain insights into user behavior, enabling you to make data-driven decisions to enhance your website.

Chapter 8: Analytics with Firebase

Why Use Firebase Analytics?

Firebase Analytics is an essential part of the Firebase platform, providing you with detailed insights into how users interact with your mobile or web application. Whether you are building a simple game, a social network, or a productivity tool, understanding how users engage with your app is key to improving user retention, optimizing user experience, and ultimately driving business success. Firebase Analytics is a free and powerful tool that offers a wide array of features to help you understand your users without the need to build complex data infrastructure from scratch.

Firebase Analytics goes beyond just reporting the number of app downloads or the average session duration. It provides detailed information about user behaviors, custom events, and user demographics. With these insights, you can make data-driven decisions about your app's features, marketing campaigns, and product direction.

Key Features of Firebase Analytics

Firebase Analytics offers several key features that make it a top choice for developers looking for a reliable and robust analytics solution. Some of the key features include:

- **Automatic Event Tracking**: Firebase Analytics automatically captures key events and user properties without any additional code. These events include app installs, in-app purchases, and user engagement metrics like screen views and user retention.
- **Custom Event Tracking**: You can define custom events that make sense for your app. This allows you to track behaviors unique to your product, such as when a user completes a level in a game or makes a specific selection.
- **Audience Segmentation**: Firebase lets you segment your users based on demographics, app behavior, or device properties. This is helpful for targeting your campaigns or understanding how different segments use your app.
- **Integration with Other Firebase Features**: Firebase Analytics integrates seamlessly with other Firebase services like Remote Config, Cloud Messaging, and A/B Testing. This integration enables you to create a highly personalized experience for users and optimize features through A/B testing.
- **User Attribution**: Firebase Analytics provides attribution reporting, helping you understand which sources are bringing users to your app. This is crucial for measuring the success of marketing campaigns across various channels like social media, email marketing, or app store listings.

Setting Up Firebase Analytics

Setting up Firebase Analytics in your project is simple. Firebase Analytics is available for Android, iOS, and web applications. Below, we cover how to integrate it in your app and get started with tracking.

Adding Firebase Analytics to Your App

To get started with Firebase Analytics, you first need to add Firebase to your project. Follow these steps for setting up Firebase Analytics in an Android project. Similar steps can be followed for iOS or web applications.

1. **Create a Firebase Project**: Start by visiting the Firebase Console and creating a new project. You will need to add your app to the project by registering it.
2. **Add Firebase SDK to Your App**: For Android, you need to add the Firebase SDK to your app's `build.gradle` files.

In your project's `build.gradle` file, add the Google Services classpath:

```
buildscript {

    dependencies {

        // Add this line

        classpath 'com.google.gms:google-services:4.3.14'

    }
}
```

In your app module's `build.gradle` file, apply the Google Services plugin and add the Firebase Analytics dependency:

```
plugins {

    id 'com.android.application'

    id 'com.google.gms.google-services' // Add this line

}

dependencies {
```

```
    // Add the Firebase Analytics SDK

    implementation 'com.google.firebase:firebase-analytics:21.0.0'
}
```

3. **Initialize Firebase Analytics**: To start using Firebase Analytics, initialize it in your app's main activity.

```
import com.google.firebase.analytics.FirebaseAnalytics;


public class MainActivity extends AppCompatActivity {

    private FirebaseAnalytics mFirebaseAnalytics;


    @Override
    protected void onCreate(Bundle savedInstanceState) {
        super.onCreate(savedInstanceState);
        setContentView(R.layout.activity_main);

        // Obtain the FirebaseAnalytics instance.
        mFirebaseAnalytics = FirebaseAnalytics.getInstance(this);
    }
}
```

With these simple steps, Firebase Analytics is now set up in your app. You will start receiving user interaction data in the Firebase Console almost immediately.

Understanding Firebase Analytics Dashboard

Once Firebase Analytics is successfully integrated, you can monitor the data using the Firebase Analytics Dashboard in the Firebase Console. This dashboard is your central hub for all analytics data and insights.

The dashboard offers an overview of your users, including active users, engagement time, and revenue if you have monetized features. You can access various reports, such as:

- **Real-Time Data**: Provides an overview of user activity as it happens. It's useful for monitoring the effects of new releases or marketing campaigns in real time.
- **Audience Reports**: Helps you understand the types of users your app is attracting. You can explore audience demographics like age, gender, and country.
- **Event Reports**: Firebase Analytics tracks specific events, such as when a user opens your app or completes a purchase. You can create custom events and see them visualized in the event report.

Tracking Custom Events

Firebase Analytics automatically tracks many events, but to get the most out of it, you will want to create custom events that are specific to your app.

Defining Custom Events

Custom events can be anything that is important for your app's logic, such as tracking when users click specific buttons or interact with certain elements.

For instance, if you have an e-commerce app, you may want to track when users add items to their cart or complete a purchase. Here's how you can log a custom event:

```
Bundle bundle = new Bundle();

bundle.putString(FirebaseAnalytics.Param.ITEM_ID, "id123");

bundle.putString(FirebaseAnalytics.Param.ITEM_NAME,
"PremiumSubscription");

bundle.putString(FirebaseAnalytics.Param.CONTENT_TYPE, "product");

mFirebaseAnalytics.logEvent(FirebaseAnalytics.Event.SELECT_CONTENT,
bundle);
```

In this example, you're tracking when a user selects an item (such as a premium subscription) in your app. You create a `Bundle` object to store details about the event, and then call `logEvent()` on the `FirebaseAnalytics` instance.

Best Practices for Logging Events

When using Firebase Analytics, follow these best practices for logging events:

1. **Limit Event Names to 40 Characters**: Firebase Analytics has a 40-character limit for event names, so be concise but descriptive.
2. **Parameter Use**: Use parameters to add context to your events. This can include user IDs, product IDs, or item types.
3. **Avoid Spamming Events**: Don't log events too frequently; this can lead to performance issues and inflate your analytics data without adding much value.
4. **Use Predefined Events When Possible**: Firebase Analytics offers a wide range of predefined events, such as add_to_cart or purchase. Using these allows Firebase to provide more context and more meaningful reporting.

Understanding Audiences and Segmentation

Firebase Analytics allows you to create custom audiences that group users based on specific criteria. For example, you might create an audience for users who have completed in-app purchases or one for users who frequently abandon items in their shopping cart.

These audiences can then be used with other Firebase services to engage with users. For instance:

- **Targeting Notifications**: Use Firebase Cloud Messaging to send push notifications to specific audiences.
- **Remote Config**: Personalize the app experience for different audiences using Remote Config.
- **A/B Testing**: Run experiments and measure how different versions of your app perform for different user segments.

Creating Audiences

To create an audience, follow these steps:

1. Go to the **Firebase Console** and navigate to **Analytics**.
2. Click on the **Audiences** tab and then click **New Audience**.
3. Define the criteria for the audience. For instance, you could create an audience of users who logged a specific custom event more than five times.

Firebase Analytics supports real-time audience evaluation, meaning users can enter or exit audiences based on their behavior. This dynamic nature is extremely powerful for managing personalized experiences and optimizing the user journey.

Leveraging Firebase Analytics with Google Ads

Firebase Analytics also integrates with Google Ads, allowing you to create audiences in Firebase and use them for ad targeting. This is very powerful for user acquisition and remarketing campaigns.

For instance, you could create an audience of users who installed your app but never completed a key action, like making a purchase. You could then create a Google Ads campaign specifically targeting these users to drive them back to the app.

Integration is straightforward:

1. **Link Firebase to Google Ads**: In the Firebase Console, go to **Project Settings** and click on **Integrations**. Link your Firebase project to your Google Ads account.
2. **Create Audiences**: Use the audience functionality in Firebase to define groups of users to target.
3. **Run Campaigns**: Use Google Ads to create campaigns that leverage these audiences. For example, a campaign offering a discount for first-time purchases might be very effective for a specific audience.

Custom User Properties

In addition to tracking events, Firebase Analytics allows you to define custom user properties. These properties help segment users based on attributes that are important for your app.

Examples of User Properties

- **Favorite Category**: For an e-commerce app, you could track the user's favorite category (e.g., electronics, clothing, etc.).
- **Subscription Type**: Track whether a user is using a free or premium version of the app.
- **In-App Experience Level**: Track a user's experience level, such as beginner, intermediate, or advanced.

Setting up user properties is similar to logging custom events. You can set them once they are known, and they will persist until explicitly changed.

```
mFirebaseAnalytics.setUserProperty("favorite_category",
"electronics");
```

Real-World Use Cases of Firebase Analytics

Firebase Analytics is used by many top apps to improve user engagement and drive growth. Here are some practical scenarios:

1. **Game Development**: Developers track custom events such as level completions, in-game purchases, and session duration to optimize gameplay and retention.
2. **E-Commerce**: E-commerce apps use Firebase Analytics to understand shopping habits, optimize product recommendations, and evaluate the effectiveness of marketing campaigns.

3. **Content-Based Apps**: News and content-based applications use Firebase Analytics to understand the type of content users are most interested in. This helps in delivering the right content at the right time.

Conclusion

Firebase Analytics is a versatile and comprehensive analytics solution that provides deep insights into user behavior, enabling developers and marketers to make informed decisions. By setting up Firebase Analytics, tracking custom events, leveraging audience segmentation, and using user properties, you can create highly targeted and data-driven app experiences that boost engagement, retention, and user satisfaction.

Firebase's integration with other Firebase products like Cloud Messaging, Remote Config, and Google Ads creates a unique and powerful ecosystem for managing your app. With these tools, you can drive meaningful changes and see the impact in real-time—all while maintaining a seamless user experience.

Integrate Firebase Analytics into your app today to start harnessing the power of data to transform your product and delight your users.

Integrating Firebase Analytics

Integrating Firebase Analytics into your application is a critical step in unlocking insights into user behavior, preferences, and interactions. Firebase Analytics offers a straightforward integration process, allowing developers to quickly get started with tracking app activities, which helps in better understanding user engagement and optimizing the overall experience. This section will walk you through the complete process of integrating Firebase Analytics into your app for both Android and iOS platforms, covering the basic setup, custom event tracking, and advanced configurations for deeper insights.

Setting Up Firebase Analytics

The initial step for integrating Firebase Analytics involves setting up Firebase in your project. Firebase Analytics is included with the core Firebase SDK, so when you add Firebase to your project, you're effectively adding Analytics capabilities.

Step 1: Create a Firebase Project

Before integrating Firebase Analytics, you need to create a Firebase project. Follow these steps:

1. Go to the Firebase Console.
2. Click on **Add Project** and provide a name for your project.
3. Follow the on-screen instructions to complete the setup. Firebase will provide an API key and configuration files that you will need to add to your application.

Step 2: Add Firebase to Your App

For Android:

To integrate Firebase Analytics into your Android project, follow these steps:

Add the Firebase SDK

In your `project-level build.gradle` file, ensure that you have included the Google services classpath:

gradle

Copy code

```
buildscript {

    repositories {

        google()

        mavenCentral()

    }

    dependencies {

        classpath 'com.google.gms:google-services:4.3.14'

    }

}
```

Next, in your `app-level build.gradle` file, apply the Google services plugin and add the Firebase Analytics dependency:

gradle

Copy code

```
plugins {

    id 'com.android.application'

    id 'com.google.gms.google-services'

}


dependencies {

    implementation 'com.google.firebase:firebase-analytics:21.0.0'

}
```

1.

Initialize Firebase Analytics

To initialize Firebase Analytics in your Android application, add the following code to the main Activity:

java
Copy code

```java
import com.google.firebase.analytics.FirebaseAnalytics;

public class MainActivity extends AppCompatActivity {

    private FirebaseAnalytics mFirebaseAnalytics;

    @Override
    protected void onCreate(Bundle savedInstanceState) {
        super.onCreate(savedInstanceState);
        setContentView(R.layout.activity_main);

        // Obtain the FirebaseAnalytics instance
        mFirebaseAnalytics = FirebaseAnalytics.getInstance(this);
    }
}
```

2.
3. **Add Google Services JSON File**
   Download the google-services.json file from the Firebase Console and add it to your Android app module directory (app/). This file contains the necessary configurations for Firebase Analytics to interact with your application.

For iOS:

Add Firebase SDK
Use CocoaPods to add Firebase to your iOS project. Add the Firebase Analytics pod to your Podfile:

ruby
Copy code

```ruby
platform :ios, '10.0'
```

```
use_frameworks!


target 'YourApp' do

  pod 'Firebase/Analytics'

end
```

Then, run the command:

```bash
pod install
```

1.

Initialize Firebase

To initialize Firebase Analytics in your iOS application, add the following code to the AppDelegate:

```swift
import UIKit

import Firebase


@UIApplicationMain

class AppDelegate: UIResponder, UIApplicationDelegate {


    var window: UIWindow?


    func application(_ application: UIApplication, didFinishLaunchingWithOptions launchOptions: [UIApplication.LaunchOptionsKey: Any]?) -> Bool {

        // Configure Firebase

        FirebaseApp.configure()

        return true
```

}

}

2.
3. **Add Google Services Plist File**
   Download the `GoogleService-Info.plist` file from the Firebase Console and add it to your Xcode project. This file provides the configuration required for Firebase Analytics.

Tracking Events with Firebase Analytics

Firebase Analytics automatically tracks some events for you, such as app installs, app updates, and in-app purchases. However, for more granular insights into how users interact with your app, you will want to log custom events.

Logging Custom Events

Custom events are useful when you need specific metrics that are not captured by Firebase's default setup. Events are actions that occur in your app, like user actions, system events, or errors. Below are some examples of how to log custom events in both Android and iOS applications.

Example: Tracking a Button Click (Android)

For Android, suppose you want to track when a user clicks a specific button. You can create an event and log it using the following code:

```
Button clickButton = findViewById(R.id.click_button);

clickButton.setOnClickListener(new View.OnClickListener() {

    @Override

    public void onClick(View v) {

        Bundle params = new Bundle();

        params.putString("button_name", "start_button");

        mFirebaseAnalytics.logEvent("button_click", params);

    }

});
```

In this code, you are logging an event called `button_click` every time the button is clicked, and passing additional information in the `Bundle` object to provide more context about the event.

Example: Tracking User Sign-Up (iOS)

For iOS, suppose you want to track when a user signs up in your application:

```
Analytics.logEvent("sign_up", parameters: [
    "method": "email"
])
```

Here, you are logging an event named `sign_up` and including a parameter to indicate the method used for signing up (e.g., "email").

Using Firebase Analytics DebugView

When developing your app, you might want to see events being logged in real-time to ensure everything is functioning correctly. Firebase Analytics provides a tool called **DebugView** to help with this.

To enable DebugView in your application:

For Android:

1. Connect your Android device to your computer.

Use the following command to enable debug mode:
bash
Copy code
```
adb shell setprop debug.firebase.analytics.app <package_name>
```

2. Replace <package_name> with your app's package name. You should start seeing real-time logs in the Firebase Console under DebugView.

For iOS:

1. Connect your iOS device to your computer.

Enable debug mode by setting an argument when launching your app:
bash
Copy code
```
-FIRDebugEnabled
```

2.

Using DebugView, you can see a stream of events as they occur, which helps in identifying and fixing issues quickly.

Analyzing Data in Firebase Console

Once Firebase Analytics is integrated, you can monitor user interactions through the **Firebase Console**. The Console provides several types of reports to help you make sense of the data:

- **Real-Time Report**: Shows what's happening in your app at any given moment.
- **Event Reports**: Provides insights into the actions users are taking within your app.
- **User Properties**: Displays specific attributes about your users, such as the app version they are using or the country they are located in.

Using Custom Reports

Firebase Analytics allows you to create custom reports to better understand user behavior. For example, you could create a custom report to track conversion rates for a specific goal, such as completing a purchase or signing up for a newsletter.

To create a custom report:

1. Go to the **Analytics** section of the Firebase Console.
2. Click on **Events**.
3. Use filters to specify the criteria you want to report on (e.g., only track users from a specific region or users who have completed a particular action).

Leveraging Audience Segmentation

Firebase Analytics also allows you to create user segments called **Audiences**. Audience segmentation is helpful in targeting specific groups of users with personalized messages, promotions, or content. For example, you might create an audience of users who:

- Installed the app but haven't signed up yet.
- Completed an in-app purchase.
- Spent more than a specified amount of time in the app.

You can then use these audiences to target campaigns via Firebase Cloud Messaging, Remote Config, or Google Ads.

Best Practices for Integrating Firebase Analytics

To ensure that you get the most out of Firebase Analytics, consider following these best practices:

1. **Track Meaningful Events**: Make sure to track events that align with your business goals. For example, if you have an e-commerce app, track events like `add_to_cart`, `checkout`, and `purchase`.
2. **Use Custom User Properties**: Define custom user properties to enrich the data you are collecting. This will allow you to segment your users more effectively.
3. **Avoid Logging Too Many Events**: While it's tempting to log everything, keep in mind that tracking too many events can make it harder to identify meaningful trends and may clutter your analytics dashboard.
4. **Set Conversion Events**: Identify key events that indicate user success (e.g., sign-up, purchase) and mark them as conversion events. Firebase will provide detailed insights into how these events are triggered.
5. **Regularly Monitor DebugView**: Use DebugView during development to ensure that your events are being logged as expected.

Integrating Firebase Analytics with Other Firebase Products

Firebase Analytics integrates seamlessly with other Firebase products, allowing you to create more sophisticated experiences:

- **Remote Config**: Use Remote Config to change the behavior and appearance of your app based on analytics data. For example, you could change the layout of a screen for users who have been inactive for a certain period.
- **Cloud Messaging**: Use Firebase Cloud Messaging (FCM) to send targeted push notifications based on user actions. For instance, send a push notification to users who added items to their cart but did not complete the purchase.
- **A/B Testing**: Firebase Analytics integrates with Firebase A/B Testing to help you experiment with changes to your app. You can create different versions of a feature and see which one performs better.

Example: Using Firebase Analytics for E-commerce App Optimization

Let's say you are developing an e-commerce app and want to understand how users interact with your app. You can set up custom events to track:

- **Product Views**: Track which products are being viewed most frequently.
- **Add to Cart**: Track how many users add items to their cart.
- **Purchases**: Track completed transactions, along with purchase amounts and payment methods.

Using Firebase Analytics, you could determine that while many users are adding items to their cart, only a small percentage are completing the checkout. You can then use **Firebase Remote Config** to test different checkout flows, or **Firebase Cloud Messaging** to remind users to complete their purchase.

Conclusion

Integrating Firebase Analytics into your application provides you with invaluable insights into user behavior and preferences. The combination of automated event tracking, custom event logging, and seamless integration with other Firebase products makes Firebase Analytics an indispensable tool for app developers. By following the steps outlined in this section, you should now have a working Firebase Analytics setup, ready to deliver actionable data to help you improve your app and better serve your users. Take the time to define key events, set up useful user properties, and leverage audience segmentation to make the most of Firebase Analytics.

Custom Events and User Insights

Firebase Analytics allows you to gain deeper insights into user interactions by defining custom events and analyzing user behaviors through custom properties. While Firebase comes with several built-in events, leveraging custom events is essential to capture the specific interactions that matter most to your application's goals. This section will explore how to define and track custom events effectively, as well as how to use user insights to shape your app's development and marketing strategies.

Understanding Custom Events

Custom events are specific actions that users take in your app which aren't covered by Firebase's automatically collected events. Examples might include making a purchase, viewing a particular screen, completing a level in a game, or clicking on a custom UI element.

With custom events, you can answer questions like:

- How many users viewed a particular product but did not purchase?
- How often do users use a specific feature?
- Which parts of the app are users engaging with the most?

These questions are crucial for optimizing the user experience, guiding product development, and increasing overall engagement and retention.

Defining Custom Events

The first step in implementing custom events is to identify the specific user actions you want to track. This is highly dependent on your app's goals and the user behaviors you are interested in monitoring. Common examples include:

- **E-commerce Apps**: Events like `add_to_cart`, `purchase`, `view_item`.
- **Gaming Apps**: Events like `level_completed`, `achievement_unlocked`, `in_game_purchase`.
- **Content Apps**: Events like `article_read`, `video_watched`, `share_content`.

Once you have identified the key user actions, the next step is to define and implement these events within your application code.

Example: Tracking a Custom Event for a Button Click (Android)

178 | FIREBASE FOR ABSOLUTE BEGINNERS

Suppose you want to track when a user clicks the "Subscribe" button in your app. This event is crucial as it represents a potential conversion that you want to analyze.

```java
Button subscribeButton = findViewById(R.id.subscribe_button);
subscribeButton.setOnClickListener(new View.OnClickListener() {
    @Override
    public void onClick(View v) {
        // Create a bundle to hold event parameters
        Bundle bundle = new Bundle();
        bundle.putString("button_name", "subscribe_button");
        bundle.putString("screen_name", "main_screen");

        // Log the custom event
        mFirebaseAnalytics.logEvent("button_click", bundle);
    }
});
```

In this code:

- `button_click` is the event name.
- The `Bundle` object contains additional information (parameters) about the event, such as the button name and the screen from where it was clicked.

Example: Tracking Custom Events on iOS

For iOS, you can log custom events similarly by using the Firebase Analytics API in Swift:

```swift
import UIKit
import FirebaseAnalytics
```

```swift
@IBAction func subscribeButtonClicked(_ sender: UIButton) {
    Analytics.logEvent("button_click", parameters: [
        "button_name": "subscribe_button" as NSObject,
        "screen_name": "main_screen" as NSObject
    ])
}
```

Using Parameters with Custom Events

Parameters provide context to your events. While the event name (button_click) describes the action, parameters can add additional details that are essential for understanding the event fully. Firebase Analytics allows up to 25 parameters per event, so you can include as much context as necessary.

Common Use Cases for Event Parameters

1. **Product Details**: If a user views a product, log its product_id, category, and price.
2. **User Actions**: If a user completes a specific action, add details like the action_type and screen_name to understand where and why the action took place.
3. **Content Engagement**: For content-related apps, use parameters like content_type and content_id to understand which content is most popular.

For instance, if you are logging a purchase event, you might include parameters such as:

```
Bundle bundle = new Bundle();

bundle.putString(FirebaseAnalytics.Param.ITEM_ID, "sku1234");

bundle.putString(FirebaseAnalytics.Param.ITEM_NAME, "PremiumSubscription");

bundle.putDouble(FirebaseAnalytics.Param.PRICE, 9.99);

bundle.putString(FirebaseAnalytics.Param.CURRENCY, "USD");
```

```
mFirebaseAnalytics.logEvent(FirebaseAnalytics.Event.PURCHASE, 
bundle);
```

Best Practices for Custom Events

- **Use Descriptive Names**: Choose event names that clearly describe the action being tracked. Avoid abbreviations that might be confusing to others or yourself in the future.
- **Use Parameters Thoughtfully**: Use parameters to add valuable context to each event. However, avoid excessive use, as this may clutter the data and make it difficult to analyze.
- **Follow Naming Conventions**: Maintain consistent naming conventions to make your analytics data easier to read and understand. Use lowercase letters, underscores to separate words, and be consistent in event naming.

Creating and Analyzing User Insights

Once you have implemented custom events, the next step is to analyze them to gain user insights. Firebase Analytics offers powerful features like audience segmentation, funnel analysis, and custom reporting, all of which help in understanding user behavior.

Audience Segmentation

Audience segmentation is one of the most powerful tools offered by Firebase Analytics. It allows you to divide users into different groups based on their behaviors, demographics, or device properties. You can use these segments to better understand your user base and target them with relevant features or marketing campaigns.

Example Use Cases for Audience Segmentation:

1. **Active vs. Inactive Users**: Create an audience of users who haven't opened your app in the last 30 days. You can then target these users with a re-engagement campaign.
2. **High-Value Users**: Create an audience of users who have made in-app purchases over $50. This audience might be interested in exclusive offers or premium content.
3. **Frequent Visitors**: Track users who visit the app more than 10 times a week. These users can be incentivized to refer the app to their friends.

Firebase Analytics makes it easy to create these audiences in the console:

1. Go to **Firebase Console** > **Analytics** > **Audiences**.
2. Click **New Audience** and define the criteria for the segment.
3. Use the segmentation in combination with Firebase services like **Cloud Messaging** or **Remote Config** to tailor your app's content or promotions.

Funnel Analysis

Funnels in Firebase Analytics help you visualize the steps users take towards completing a goal. This could be:

- **Purchasing an Item**: Viewing a product, adding it to the cart, and then completing the purchase.
- **Completing Onboarding**: Signing up, setting preferences, and completing an introduction tour.

Creating a Funnel in Firebase:

1. Go to the **Conversions** section in Firebase Analytics.
2. Create a new funnel by selecting the sequence of events that represent the user journey.
3. Monitor where users are dropping off in the funnel.

Analyzing where users drop off can help you improve those specific stages. For example, if you notice a significant drop-off between adding an item to the cart and completing the purchase, it might indicate a problem with the checkout flow.

Custom Reporting with Google Analytics

Firebase Analytics also integrates seamlessly with **Google Analytics**, allowing you to create custom reports for deeper insights.

Custom reports are especially useful for:

- **Tracking Specific Metrics**: Track specific KPIs, such as conversion rate or average revenue per user.
- **Combining Data**: Combine data from different Firebase projects or with data from other sources to understand a more comprehensive picture of your user behavior.

To set up Google Analytics integration:

1. **Link Firebase Project to Google Analytics**: Go to the **Firebase Console** > **Project Settings** > **Integrations** and link Google Analytics to your Firebase project.
2. **Access Data in Google Analytics**: Once linked, your Firebase data will be available in Google Analytics. You can create custom dashboards, apply filters, and combine data from multiple sources.

Leveraging Firebase Predictions

Firebase Predictions is another powerful tool that can provide valuable user insights. It uses machine learning to create dynamic user segments based on predicted behaviors, such as users who are likely to churn, users who are likely to spend, and more.

By leveraging these predictions, you can:

- **Prevent User Churn**: Target users predicted to leave your app with re-engagement campaigns.
- **Increase Conversions**: Identify users who are likely to make in-app purchases and target them with personalized promotions.
- **Optimize User Experience**: Make data-driven decisions to enhance the app experience for users based on predicted behaviors.

Setting Up Firebase Predictions:

1. Go to **Firebase Console > Predictions**.
2. Choose the predictions you want to use (e.g., likely to churn, likely to spend).
3. Use these segments in combination with **Remote Config** or **Cloud Messaging** to create targeted experiences.

A/B Testing with Firebase Analytics

Another way to use custom events and user insights is by running **A/B Tests** using **Firebase A/B Testing**. A/B testing helps you optimize your app experience by testing different versions of your app with a subset of users.

Example A/B Test Scenario:

Suppose you want to determine whether changing the color of your "Subscribe" button will lead to more users clicking it. You can run an A/B test to find out:

1. **Define the Variant**: Create two versions of the app - one with a red "Subscribe" button and the other with a green button.
2. **Set the Goal**: Track the event `button_click` for both versions.
3. **Run the Test**: Deploy the test to a segment of users and let it run for a specific duration.
4. **Analyze the Results**: Firebase will analyze which version performed better based on your goal (e.g., the highest number of `button_click` events).

Examples of Using User Insights for Marketing

User insights are powerful tools for improving the effectiveness of your marketing campaigns. Here are some practical examples:

1. **Re-Engaging Users with Cloud Messaging**: If you notice that users who reach level 5 in your game often drop off, you could send a personalized push notification to these users encouraging them to return. Using Firebase **Cloud Messaging**, you could target users in the "level_5_dropped" audience with a message like: "Come back and beat level 5! Your adventure awaits!"
2. **Using Insights for Paid Campaigns**: If you have a segment of users who frequently make purchases, you can create a similar audience in **Google Ads** and run campaigns targeting new potential users who share similar characteristics. This approach ensures that your ad spend is directed towards users who are more likely to convert.

Using User Properties

User properties are attributes that describe segments of your user base, such as demographics or app preferences. Unlike events, which track user actions, user properties help categorize users for better insights.

Examples include:

- **Subscription Type**: Free or Premium
- **Preferred Language**: English, Spanish, etc.
- **User Level**: Novice, Intermediate, Advanced

These user properties can then be used for audience segmentation, and they help provide context when analyzing the data from custom events.

Setting User Properties in Android

```
mFirebaseAnalytics.setUserProperty("subscription_type", "premium");
```

Setting User Properties in iOS

```
Analytics.setUserProperty("premium", forName: "subscription_type")
```

These user properties are especially valuable for creating targeted user experiences. For example, you might want to show different content to "novice" and "advanced" users or offer different promotions to "free" vs. "premium" users.

Conclusion

Custom events and user insights are essential components of Firebase Analytics that allow you to go beyond default tracking and tailor the analytics to the specific needs of your app. By defining meaningful custom events, using parameters to add context, leveraging audience segmentation, and utilizing tools like funnel analysis and A/B testing, you can gather actionable insights to make data-driven decisions that improve user engagement, retention, and monetization.

Whether you're building an e-commerce application, a game, or a content platform, Firebase Analytics provides the tools needed to understand your users and continually refine their experience.

Chapter 9: Push Notifications with Firebase Cloud Messaging

Introduction to Firebase Cloud Messaging (FCM)

Firebase Cloud Messaging (FCM) is a cross-platform messaging solution that allows you to send notifications and messages to your users in a reliable and scalable manner. FCM is widely used in mobile app development to engage users, deliver timely information, and enhance the overall user experience. Push notifications, a major component of FCM, play a crucial role in keeping users connected to your app by providing updates, alerts, promotions, and more.

Why Use Firebase Cloud Messaging?

FCM allows developers to send notifications without the need for complex back-end infrastructure. It integrates seamlessly with Firebase and provides a user-friendly API for sending targeted messages. There are several compelling reasons why FCM is a popular choice for push notifications:

- **Cross-Platform Messaging**: FCM supports iOS, Android, and web platforms, allowing you to reach your users regardless of their preferred device.
- **Free Service**: Firebase Cloud Messaging is completely free, making it an attractive option for developers with limited budgets.
- **Rich Targeting Capabilities**: You can send notifications to specific devices, topics, or user segments, which helps you deliver relevant content and enhance user engagement.
- **Reliable and Scalable**: Built on Google's infrastructure, FCM ensures reliability and scalability when delivering messages to millions of users.
- **Integration with Firebase**: FCM works seamlessly with other Firebase services, such as Analytics, Authentication, and Firestore, giving you a comprehensive ecosystem for building user-centric applications.

In this section, we will explore the basics of using FCM to send push notifications to your users. We'll cover everything from setting up FCM in your project to sending your first push notification.

Setting Up Firebase Cloud Messaging

To begin using Firebase Cloud Messaging, you need to complete the setup process for your mobile app. Follow the steps below to integrate FCM into your project:

Step 1: Add Firebase to Your Project

First, you need to add Firebase to your Android or iOS project.

1. **Go to Firebase Console**:
    - Open the Firebase Console.
    - Click on "Add Project" and follow the steps to create a new project.
2. **Add Your App**:
    - Once your project is created, click "Add App" to add either an Android or an iOS app.
    - For Android, you need to provide your app's package name, SHA-1 key, and download the `google-services.json` file.
    - For iOS, you need to download the `GoogleService-Info.plist` file and add it to your Xcode project.
3. **Configure Firebase SDK**:
    - Add the Firebase SDK dependencies to your project.

For Android, modify your app-level `build.gradle` file:

```groovy
implementation platform('com.google.firebase:firebase-bom:32.2.0')

implementation 'com.google.firebase:firebase-messaging'
```

-

For iOS, install the Firebase Messaging SDK using CocoaPods by adding the following line to your Podfile:

```ruby
pod 'Firebase/Messaging'
```

-

Step 2: Configure Firebase in Your Code

Once the Firebase SDK is added to your project, you need to configure FCM in your code.

For **Android**:

Initialize Firebase in the `onCreate()` method of your Application class:

```java
@Override
public void onCreate() {
    super.onCreate();
    FirebaseApp.initializeApp(this);
}
```

For **iOS**:

In your AppDelegate, initialize Firebase in the application(_:didFinishLaunchingWithOptions:) method:

swift
Copy code
```
import Firebase

@UIApplicationMain
class AppDelegate: UIResponder, UIApplicationDelegate {
    func application(_ application: UIApplication, didFinishLaunchingWithOptions launchOptions: [UIApplication.LaunchOptionsKey: Any]?) -> Bool {
        FirebaseApp.configure()
        return true
    }
}
```

-

Requesting User Permission

To send notifications, you need to request permission from the user to receive push notifications. This process varies slightly between Android and iOS.

Requesting Permission on Android

On Android, the user is automatically opted-in to receive notifications upon installing the app. However, if you need to ask for specific permissions (for example, for foreground notifications in Android 13 or higher), use the following code:

```
if (Build.VERSION.SDK_INT >= Build.VERSION_CODES.TIRAMISU) {
    if (ContextCompat.checkSelfPermission(this, Manifest.permission.POST_NOTIFICATIONS) != PackageManager.PERMISSION_GRANTED) {
```

```
        ActivityCompat.requestPermissions(this,                new
String[]{Manifest.permission.POST_NOTIFICATIONS}, 101);

    }

}
```

Requesting Permission on iOS

For iOS, you must explicitly request permission to send notifications:

```
import UserNotifications


let center = UNUserNotificationCenter.current()

center.requestAuthorization(options: [.alert, .sound, .badge]) { granted, error in

    if granted {

        print("Permission granted.")

    } else {

        print("Permission denied.")

    }

}
```

You should call this function when the app launches or when the user performs an action that indicates they want to receive notifications.

Sending Your First Notification

There are several ways to send notifications using Firebase Cloud Messaging. You can send notifications through the Firebase Console, programmatically using Firebase Admin SDK, or by using third-party APIs.

Sending Notifications via Firebase Console

188 | FIREBASE FOR ABSOLUTE BEGINNERS

The Firebase Console provides a user-friendly interface for sending push notifications to users.

1. **Navigate to Firebase Console**:
   - Select your project and click on "Cloud Messaging" from the left panel.
2. **Create a New Notification**:
   - Click on "Send Your First Message" to start crafting your notification.
   - You can specify the title, message body, and target audience (e.g., all users or a specific user segment).
   - Optionally, you can add additional data to customize the user experience.
3. **Send the Notification**:
   - After setting up your message, click "Send." Firebase will handle the rest, delivering the message to the specified users.

Sending Notifications Programmatically

For more complex use cases, such as automated or targeted notifications, you may want to send notifications programmatically using the Firebase Admin SDK.

Here's a simple example of sending a notification to a specific device using Node.js:

1. **Install Firebase Admin SDK**:

bash
Copy code
```
npm install firebase-admin
```

2. **Initialize Firebase Admin SDK**:

javascript
Copy code
```
const admin = require("firebase-admin");

const serviceAccount = require("./path/to/serviceAccountKey.json");


admin.initializeApp({

  credential: admin.credential.cert(serviceAccount)

});
```

3. **Send a Notification**:

javascript
Copy code
```
const registrationToken = "YOUR_DEVICE_REGISTRATION_TOKEN";
```

```
const message = {
  notification: {
    title: "Hello from FCM!",
    body: "This is a test notification."
  },
  token: registrationToken
};


admin.messaging().send(message)
  .then(response => {
    console.log("Successfully sent message:", response);
  })
  .catch(error => {
    console.log("Error sending message:", error);
  });
```

3.

In the above code, you need to replace "YOUR_DEVICE_REGISTRATION_TOKEN" with the FCM token of the device you want to send the notification to. This approach provides flexibility, allowing you to send messages based on specific triggers or events in your application.

Handling Incoming Notifications

Once a notification is sent, it is important to handle it appropriately on the client side.

Handling Notifications on Android

For Android, notifications are automatically handled by the system when your app is in the background. However, if you want to handle the notification yourself (e.g., when the app is in the foreground), you can implement a `FirebaseMessagingService`.

```java
public class MyFirebaseMessagingService extends FirebaseMessagingService {

    @Override
    public void onMessageReceived(RemoteMessage remoteMessage) {
        // Handle FCM messages here.
        if (remoteMessage.getNotification() != null) {
            String title = remoteMessage.getNotification().getTitle();
            String body = remoteMessage.getNotification().getBody();
            showNotification(title, body);
        }
    }


    private void showNotification(String title, String body) {
        NotificationCompat.Builder builder = new NotificationCompat.Builder(this, "MyChannelId")
            .setSmallIcon(R.drawable.notification_icon)
            .setContentTitle(title)
            .setContentText(body)
            .setPriority(NotificationCompat.PRIORITY_HIGH);

        NotificationManager notificationManager = (NotificationManager) getSystemService(Context.NOTIFICATION_SERVICE);
```

```
            notificationManager.notify(0, builder.build());
    }
}
```

Handling Notifications on iOS

For iOS, use the UNUserNotificationCenterDelegate to handle notifications when the app is in the foreground:

```
extension AppDelegate: UNUserNotificationCenterDelegate {
    func userNotificationCenter(_ center: UNUserNotificationCenter,
willPresent notification: UNNotification, withCompletionHandler
completionHandler: @escaping (UNNotificationPresentationOptions) ->
Void) {
        let userInfo = notification.request.content.userInfo
        print("Notification received with data: \(userInfo)")
        completionHandler([.alert, .sound])
    }
}
```

Register the delegate in your application(_:didFinishLaunchingWithOptions:) method:

```
UNUserNotificationCenter.current().delegate = self
```

Testing Your Setup

It's important to test your notification setup to ensure that everything is working as expected.

- **Firebase Console**: Use the Firebase Console to send test notifications to individual devices by specifying the device registration token.

- **Postman**: You can also use tools like Postman to send POST requests to the FCM API for testing purposes.
- **Device Logs**: Monitor device logs using Android Studio or Xcode to ensure that notifications are being received and handled correctly.

Best Practices for Using FCM

- **User Consent**: Always obtain explicit consent from the user before sending notifications. No one likes unsolicited messages.
- **Message Relevance**: Ensure that your notifications are relevant to the user. Overuse of push notifications can lead to app uninstalls.
- **Personalization**: Personalize your notifications by using the user's name or referencing their recent activity. This makes the message more engaging.
- **Rich Media**: Include images or action buttons when possible to make your notifications more visually appealing.
- **Analytics Integration**: Use Firebase Analytics to track how users interact with your notifications. This can help you understand what types of messages work best and refine your strategy.

Conclusion

Firebase Cloud Messaging provides a powerful platform for delivering push notifications to users across multiple platforms. Whether you are sending notifications through the Firebase Console or programmatically via the Firebase Admin SDK, FCM offers the flexibility and scalability you need to engage with your users effectively.

By understanding how to set up FCM, send notifications, and handle incoming messages, you can create a robust notification system that keeps users informed and engaged with your app. Remember to always focus on delivering value to your users with well-timed and relevant notifications, and you will see improved user retention and satisfaction.

Setting Up FCM in Your App

Firebase Cloud Messaging (FCM) is a highly flexible messaging solution that allows developers to send notifications and messages to users on different platforms. Before you can start sending push notifications through FCM, you need to set up FCM in your mobile or web application. In this section, we will walk through the complete process of integrating FCM into your project, including adding the necessary SDKs, configuring your project, and verifying that your setup works correctly.

Setting up FCM involves a few steps, from creating your Firebase project to configuring your app's front-end to handle messages. Here, we'll cover both Android and iOS integration, focusing on every aspect to ensure that you have a robust setup.

Step 1: Adding Firebase to Your Project

Chapter 9: Push Notifications with Firebase Cloud Messaging

Before setting up FCM, you need to have a Firebase project ready. Follow these steps to add Firebase to your Android or iOS application.

1. **Create a Firebase Project**:
   - Visit the Firebase Console.
   - Click on **"Add Project"** and follow the instructions to create a new Firebase project.
   - After creating the project, you will be directed to the project dashboard.
2. **Register Your App**:
   - On the Firebase Console dashboard, click on **"Add App"**.
   - You will have options to add either an **Android** or an **iOS** application. Choose the platform you are working with.
   - **For Android**:
     - Provide the package name for your app. Make sure it matches your app's actual package name.
     - Download the `google-services.json` file that will be provided after registration. This file contains configuration details that help connect your app to Firebase services.
     - Place the `google-services.json` file in the app directory of your project.
   - **For iOS**:
     - Provide the iOS Bundle ID, App Store ID, and Team ID.
     - Download the `GoogleService-Info.plist` file and add it to your Xcode project. Ensure the file is properly added to the target you wish to use Firebase in.

Step 2: Adding Firebase SDK

To use FCM, you need to add the Firebase SDK to your Android or iOS project. Firebase provides platform-specific SDKs to easily connect your app with Firebase services.

Android

To set up Firebase in an Android app, you need to modify some configuration files and add the necessary Firebase dependencies.

Add Firebase BOM to your build.gradle File:
In your **project-level** `build.gradle` file, ensure you have Google's Maven repository listed:
gradle
Copy code
```
buildscript {

    repositories {

        google() // Google Maven repository

        mavenCentral()
```

```gradle
    }

    dependencies {

        classpath 'com.google.gms:google-services:4.4.0'

    }

}


allprojects {

    repositories {

        google()

        mavenCentral()

    }

}
```

1.

Add Firebase SDK to your build.gradle File:
Open the **app-level** `build.gradle` file and add the Firebase BOM (Bill of Materials) to ensure consistent versions of Firebase libraries:

```gradle
Copy code
apply plugin: 'com.android.application'

apply plugin: 'com.google.gms.google-services'


dependencies {

    implementation platform('com.google.firebase:firebase-bom:32.2.0')

    implementation 'com.google.firebase:firebase-messaging'

}
```

2.

3. **Sync Your Project**: Sync your Gradle files to download the Firebase dependencies.

iOS

For iOS, the Firebase SDK is added via CocoaPods. CocoaPods is a dependency manager for Swift and Objective-C Cocoa projects.

1. **Install CocoaPods (if not already installed)**: Run the following command in the terminal:

```bash
sudo gem install cocoapods
```

2. **Add Firebase to Your Podfile**: In your project directory, create or modify the Podfile:

```ruby
platform :ios, '12.0'

target 'YourAppTarget' do
  use_frameworks!

  pod 'Firebase/Messaging'

end
```

3. **Install the Pods**: Run the the command:

```bash
pod install
```

4. **Open the .xcworkspace File**: After installing the pods, open the project using the .xcworkspace file, as this will include all the dependencies managed by CocoaPods.

Step 3: Configure Firebase Messaging in Your App

After adding Firebase to your project, the next step is configuring Firebase Messaging so that your app can receive notifications.

Android

Firebase Initialization:
To initialize Firebase, modify your `Application` class:

```java
import android.app.Application;
import com.google.firebase.FirebaseApp;

public class MyApplication extends Application {

    @Override
    public void onCreate() {
        super.onCreate();
        FirebaseApp.initializeApp(this);
    }
}
```

1. Alternatively, you can initialize Firebase in the `onCreate()` method of your main Activity.

Handling Device Registration Token:
Every device needs a unique registration token to receive push notifications. The FirebaseMessaging API helps you retrieve this token:

```java
FirebaseMessaging.getInstance().getToken()
    .addOnCompleteListener(task -> {
        if (!task.isSuccessful()) {
            Log.w(TAG, "Fetching FCM registration token failed", task.getException());
            return;
```

```
        }

        // Get new FCM registration token

        String token = task.getResult();

        Log.d(TAG, "FCM Token: " + token);

        // Optionally send this token to your server

    });
```

2.

iOS

Firebase Initialization: Modify your AppDelegate to initialize Firebase when your app launches:

```swift
import Firebase



@UIApplicationMain

class AppDelegate: UIResponder, UIApplicationDelegate {



    func application(_ application: UIApplication, didFinishLaunchingWithOptions launchOptions: [UIApplication.LaunchOptionsKey: Any]?) -> Bool {

        FirebaseApp.configure()

        UNUserNotificationCenter.current().delegate = self

        return true

    }

}
```

1.

Requesting Notification Permissions: To receive push notifications, you need to ask the user's permission. Add the following code to request authorization:

swift

Copy code

```
import UserNotifications

UNUserNotificationCenter.current().requestAuthorization(options: [.alert, .sound, .badge]) { granted, error in

    if granted {

        print("User granted permissions")

    } else {

        print("User denied permissions")

    }

}
```

```
application.registerForRemoteNotifications()
```

2.

Handling Device Token: Implement the following function to get the FCM registration token:

swift

Copy code

```
func application(_ application: UIApplication, didRegisterForRemoteNotificationsWithDeviceToken deviceToken: Data) {

    Messaging.messaging().apnsToken = deviceToken

}
```

3.

Step 4: Sending a Test Notification

Now that Firebase Messaging is integrated into your app, it's time to send a test notification to ensure that everything works correctly.

Sending Notifications via Firebase Console

Chapter 9: Push Notifications with Firebase Cloud Messaging

The Firebase Console provides a simple interface for sending notifications without writing any code. Follow these steps to send a test notification:

1. **Navigate to Cloud Messaging**: Open the Firebase Console, select your project, and click on **"Cloud Messaging"** from the left-hand panel.
2. **Create a New Notification**:
   - Click on **"Send Your First Message"**.
   - Fill in the **notification title** and **message text**.
   - Choose a target app, either by selecting all users or by specifying a test device using the device registration token.
3. **Send the Notification**: Click **"Send"** to deliver the notification to the selected devices. If your app is correctly configured, you should see the notification on your device.

Sending Notifications Programmatically

Sometimes, you may want to send notifications programmatically. This is useful for automation, such as sending notifications when certain events occur.

Node.js Example:

Here is an example of sending an FCM message programmatically using the Firebase Admin SDK with Node.js:

Install Firebase Admin SDK:
bash
Copy code

```
npm install firebase-admin
```

1.

Write a Script to Send a Notification:
javascript
Copy code

```
const admin = require("firebase-admin");

const serviceAccount = require("./path/to/serviceAccountKey.json");


admin.initializeApp({

    credential: admin.credential.cert(serviceAccount)

});
```

```javascript
const registrationToken = "YOUR_DEVICE_REGISTRATION_TOKEN";

const message = {
    notification: {
        title: "Hello from FCM!",
        body: "This is a test notification."
    },
    token: registrationToken
};

admin.messaging().send(message)
    .then(response => {
        console.log("Successfully sent message:", response);
    })
    .catch(error => {
        console.error("Error sending message:", error);
    });
```

2.

Replace "YOUR_DEVICE_REGISTRATION_TOKEN" with the registration token of the device to which you want to send the notification.

Step 5: Handling Notifications in Your App

Once your app receives a notification, you need to define how to handle it, depending on whether your app is in the foreground or background.

Android

In Android, if the app is in the foreground, you need to handle the message by implementing the `FirebaseMessagingService`:

```java
public class MyFirebaseMessagingService extends FirebaseMessagingService {

    @Override
    public void onMessageReceived(RemoteMessage remoteMessage) {
        // Handle FCM messages here
        if (remoteMessage.getNotification() != null) {
            String title = remoteMessage.getNotification().getTitle();
            String body = remoteMessage.getNotification().getBody();
            sendNotification(title, body);
        }
    }


    private void sendNotification(String title, String messageBody) {
        NotificationCompat.Builder notificationBuilder =
                new NotificationCompat.Builder(this, "channel_id")
                        .setSmallIcon(R.drawable.ic_notification)
                        .setContentTitle(title)
                        .setContentText(messageBody)
                        .setPriority(NotificationCompat.PRIORITY_HIGH);

        NotificationManager notificationManager = (NotificationManager) getSystemService(Context.NOTIFICATION_SERVICE);
```

```
        notificationManager.notify(0, notificationBuilder.build());
    }
}
```

Make sure to add your MyFirebaseMessagingService to your AndroidManifest.xml:

```xml
<service
    android:name=".MyFirebaseMessagingService"
    android:exported="false">
    <intent-filter>
        <action android:name="com.google.firebase.MESSAGING_EVENT"/>
    </intent-filter>
</service>
```

iOS

On iOS, use the UNUserNotificationCenterDelegate to handle notifications while the app is in the foreground:

```swift
extension AppDelegate: UNUserNotificationCenterDelegate {
    func userNotificationCenter(_ center: UNUserNotificationCenter, willPresent notification: UNNotification, withCompletionHandler completionHandler: @escaping (UNNotificationPresentationOptions) -> Void) {
        let userInfo = notification.request.content.userInfo
        print("Notification received: \(userInfo)")
        completionHandler([.alert, .sound])
```

                }

        }

Step 6: Debugging and Troubleshooting

If you face any issues, here are a few tips for debugging:

- **Log Tokens**: Always log the FCM registration token to ensure that the device is receiving a valid token.
- **Check Notification Settings**: Make sure that notifications are enabled for your app in device settings.
- **Use Firebase Console Logs**: Firebase provides detailed logs and diagnostics in the console to help you troubleshoot issues related to notification delivery.

Conclusion

Integrating Firebase Cloud Messaging into your Android or iOS app involves a series of configuration steps, including setting up Firebase, adding dependencies, and writing code to handle notifications. By following these steps, you can ensure that your app is ready to receive and handle notifications effectively, providing users with timely and engaging content.

With FCM set up, you can create targeted campaigns, send important updates, and ensure your users stay connected with your app. Remember to focus on delivering relevant content to your users to enhance their experience and avoid spamming them with unnecessary notifications.

Advanced Notification Features

Firebase Cloud Messaging (FCM) offers a rich set of advanced features that allow you to send personalized, targeted, and interactive notifications to your users. Beyond just basic push notifications, you can leverage advanced features such as data payloads, topic messaging, condition-based delivery, and notification customization to create more engaging user experiences. In this section, we'll explore these advanced features in detail, explaining how you can use them to enhance your app's messaging capabilities.

Customizing Notifications with Data Payloads

FCM allows you to send two types of messages: **notification messages** and **data messages**.

- **Notification Messages**: Automatically handled by the system when your app is in the background, typically used to inform the user with a title and body.
- **Data Messages**: Delivered directly to the app, even when it is in the foreground, and handled by custom code to take specific actions.

Example: Sending a Data Message

To send a data message, you need to specify the data fields in your message payload. Here's an example of sending a data message using the Firebase Admin SDK:

```javascript
const admin = require("firebase-admin");

admin.initializeApp({
  credential: admin.credential.applicationDefault(),
});


const registrationToken = "YOUR_DEVICE_REGISTRATION_TOKEN";


const message = {
  data: {
    title: "Special Offer",
    body: "Get 20% off your next purchase!",
    discountCode: "SAVE20"
  },
  token: registrationToken,
};


admin.messaging().send(message)
  .then((response) => {
    console.log("Successfully sent message:", response);
  })
  .catch((error) => {
```

```
        console.log("Error sending message:", error);
    });
```

In this example, the data payload contains custom key-value pairs (`title`, `body`, and `discountCode`). You can use these fields to display a custom notification or perform other actions within your app. Data messages are ideal for delivering content that requires custom handling by the app.

Handling Data Messages on Android

For Android, you can use `FirebaseMessagingService` to handle data messages when they are received:

```
public class MyFirebaseMessagingService extends FirebaseMessagingService {

    @Override
    public void onMessageReceived(RemoteMessage remoteMessage) {
        // Check if message contains data payload.
        if (remoteMessage.getData().size() > 0) {
            Map<String, String> data = remoteMessage.getData();
            String title = data.get("title");
            String body = data.get("body");
            String discountCode = data.get("discountCode");

            // Create a custom notification with the received data.
            sendNotification(title, body, discountCode);
        }
    }
}
```

```java
    private void sendNotification(String title, String body, String discountCode) {

        NotificationCompat.Builder builder = new NotificationCompat.Builder(this, "MyChannelId")

            .setSmallIcon(R.drawable.notification_icon)

            .setContentTitle(title)

            .setContentText(body + " Use code: " + discountCode)

            .setPriority(NotificationCompat.PRIORITY_HIGH);


        NotificationManager notificationManager = (NotificationManager) getSystemService(Context.NOTIFICATION_SERVICE);

        notificationManager.notify(0, builder.build());

    }
}
```

The onMessageReceived() method processes the data payload and creates a custom notification that includes the discount code. This flexibility is useful when you want to trigger specific in-app behavior based on received data.

Topic Messaging for Segmentation

FCM allows you to group devices into topics and send messages to all subscribed devices simultaneously. This feature is extremely useful for segmenting your users and targeting specific groups with tailored messages.

Example: Subscribing to a Topic

To subscribe a device to a topic, use the following code:

```java
FirebaseMessaging.getInstance().subscribeToTopic("promotions")
```

```
        .addOnCompleteListener(task -> {
            if (task.isSuccessful()) {
                Log.d("FCM", "Subscribed to topic: promotions");
            }
        });
```

In this example, the device is subscribed to the promotions topic. This allows the device to receive any messages sent to that topic.

Sending Messages to a Topic

Once devices are subscribed to a topic, you can send messages to that topic:

```
const message = {
  notification: {
    title: "Limited Time Offer!",
    body: "Get 30% off on all items in our store!"
  },
  topic: "promotions"
};

admin.messaging().send(message)
  .then((response) => {
    console.log("Successfully sent message:", response);
  })
  .catch((error) => {
    console.log("Error sending message:", error);
```

```
});
```

By sending a message to the promotions topic, all devices subscribed to this topic will receive the notification. This is a powerful way to segment users and send targeted content to specific audiences.

Condition-Based Messaging

FCM also supports condition-based messaging, which allows you to combine multiple topics to create complex targeting conditions. This feature is particularly useful for creating sophisticated audience targeting strategies.

Example: Sending Messages Based on Conditions

Suppose you want to send a message to users who are subscribed to both promotions and vip_customers. You can achieve this using a condition:

```
const message = {
  notification: {
    title: "Exclusive VIP Offer",
    body: "Get an additional 10% off on our latest promotions!"
  },
  condition: "'promotions' in topics && 'vip_customers' in topics"
};

admin.messaging().send(message)
  .then((response) => {
    console.log("Successfully sent message:", response);
  })
  .catch((error) => {
    console.log("Error sending message:", error);
```

```
});
```

The above condition ensures that only users who are subscribed to both promotions and vip_customers topics receive the notification. This level of control allows you to precisely target your messages to the right audience segments.

Notification Customization with Platform-Specific Features

Customizing notifications for different platforms is crucial for providing the best user experience. FCM allows you to customize notifications differently for Android and iOS.

Platform-Specific Notification Payload

When sending notifications to both Android and iOS users, you can specify platform-specific properties to ensure the notification is optimized for each platform.

```
const message = {
  notification: {
    title: "Welcome!",
    body: "Check out the latest features in our app!"
  },
  android: {
    notification: {
      icon: "ic_launcher",
      color: "#ff0000",
      sound: "default"
    }
  },
  apns: {
    payload: {
      aps: {
```

```
            sound: "default",
            badge: 1
        }
      }
    },
    token: "YOUR_DEVICE_REGISTRATION_TOKEN"
};


admin.messaging().send(message)
   .then((response) => {
     console.log("Successfully sent message:", response);
   })
   .catch((error) => {
     console.log("Error sending message:", error);
   });
```

In the example above:

- The **Android** notification is customized with an icon, color, and sound.
- The **iOS** notification is customized with a sound and a badge number.

This platform-specific customization ensures that your notifications are properly formatted and provide a consistent user experience on both Android and iOS devices.

Interactive Notifications with Action Buttons

Interactive notifications enhance user engagement by providing quick actions that users can take directly from the notification. FCM allows you to add action buttons to notifications, especially on Android.

Adding Action Buttons to Notifications

Here is how you can add action buttons to an Android notification:

```java
NotificationCompat.Builder builder = new
NotificationCompat.Builder(this, "MyChannelId")
    .setSmallIcon(R.drawable.notification_icon)
    .setContentTitle("Event Reminder")
    .setContentText("Don't miss our upcoming event!")
    .setPriority(NotificationCompat.PRIORITY_HIGH)
    .addAction(R.drawable.ic_accept,                    "Accept",
getPendingIntentForAction("ACCEPT_ACTION"))
    .addAction(R.drawable.ic_decline,                   "Decline",
getPendingIntentForAction("DECLINE_ACTION"));


NotificationManager notificationManager = (NotificationManager)
getSystemService(Context.NOTIFICATION_SERVICE);

notificationManager.notify(0, builder.build());
```

In this example:

- **addAction()** is used to add buttons to the notification.
- **getPendingIntentForAction()** is a method that returns a PendingIntent for the specified action, allowing the app to handle the user's response to the notification.

The action buttons make it easier for users to interact with the notification without opening the app, thus improving user engagement.

Silent Push Notifications

Silent push notifications, also known as **data-only messages**, are used to perform background updates or trigger in-app actions without showing a notification to the user.

Example: Sending a Silent Push Notification

To send a silent push notification, simply include the data payload without the notification field:

```
const message = {
  data: {
    type: "background_update",
    content: "New content available!"
  },
  token: "YOUR_DEVICE_REGISTRATION_TOKEN"
};


admin.messaging().send(message)
  .then((response) => {
    console.log("Successfully sent silent message:", response);
  })
  .catch((error) => {
    console.log("Error sending message:", error);
  });
```

In this example, the `data` payload contains information that the app can use to trigger a specific action, such as refreshing content in the background. The absence of the `notification` field means the user will not see any notification on their device.

Handling Silent Push Notifications

On Android, silent push notifications can be handled in the `onMessageReceived()` method of `FirebaseMessagingService`:

```
@Override
public void onMessageReceived(RemoteMessage remoteMessage) {
```

```java
    if (remoteMessage.getData().size() > 0) {

        String type = remoteMessage.getData().get("type");

        if ("background_update".equals(type)) {

            // Perform background update or other silent action

            updateAppContent();

        }

    }

}
```

Silent push notifications are useful for scenarios like syncing data, refreshing content, or collecting analytics information in the background without interrupting the user experience.

Using Analytics to Measure Notification Effectiveness

To create effective push notification campaigns, it's important to measure the impact of your notifications. Firebase Analytics can be used to track user interactions with notifications, providing valuable insights into user behavior.

Tracking Notification Opens

Firebase Analytics automatically tracks notification opens when you send notifications using the Firebase Console. However, for custom data messages, you can manually log events when the user interacts with the notification:

```java
@Override

public void onMessageReceived(RemoteMessage remoteMessage) {

    if (remoteMessage.getData().size() > 0) {

        // Log notification open event

        Bundle bundle = new Bundle();

        bundle.putString(FirebaseAnalytics.Param.METHOD, "notification");
```

```
mFirebaseAnalytics.logEvent(FirebaseAnalytics.Event.SELECT_CONTENT,
bundle);

        // Handle the data message
        handleCustomNotification(remoteMessage.getData());
    }
}
```

Logging events helps you understand how many users opened the notification, interacted with its content, or performed actions based on the notification, allowing you to optimize your future campaigns.

Conclusion

Advanced notification features in Firebase Cloud Messaging enable you to create more interactive, targeted, and effective notifications. By leveraging data payloads, topic and condition-based messaging, platform-specific customizations, action buttons, silent push notifications, and analytics, you can enhance user engagement and improve the user experience of your app.

With these advanced features, you can go beyond basic notifications and deliver a more personalized and dynamic experience for your users, ensuring that your messages are timely, relevant, and valuable.

Chapter 10: Firebase Security and Best Practices

Securing Your Firebase Project

Firebase offers powerful tools and services that enable you to develop apps quickly and efficiently. However, without proper security measures in place, your application and its data may be vulnerable to unauthorized access, data breaches, or malicious attacks. Securing your Firebase project is crucial to protect both your users and your application from threats. This section provides an in-depth look into securing your Firebase project, covering essential security features and best practices to help you achieve a robust and secure Firebase environment.

Understanding Firebase Security Rules

Firebase Security Rules serve as the core access control mechanism for Firebase products such as Firestore, Realtime Database, and Storage. These rules allow you to define who can access specific parts of your database and under what conditions. Firebase Security Rules use a domain-specific language (DSL) that lets you create fine-grained access rules.

The structure of Firebase Security Rules typically follows this format:

1. **Read Rules**: Define who is allowed to read data from a specific path.
2. **Write Rules**: Define who is allowed to write data to a specific path.
3. **Custom Conditions**: Use conditions based on user properties or data validation to control access.

Below is a basic example of a security rule for Firestore:

```
service cloud.firestore {
  match /databases/{database}/documents {
    match /users/{userId} {
      allow read, write: if request.auth != null && request.auth.uid == userId;
    }
  }
}
```

In this example:

- `request.auth != null` ensures that the user is authenticated.
- `request.auth.uid == userId` ensures that the authenticated user can only access their own data.

Key Strategies for Securing Your Firebase Project

1. Use Firebase Authentication

Firebase Authentication integrates seamlessly with Firebase Security Rules. Ensuring that users are authenticated before they can access certain data is the foundation of a secure system. With Firebase Authentication, you can easily enforce security rules that depend on the identity of the user.

Implementing Firebase Authentication includes setting up multiple authentication methods such as email and password, Google Sign-In, and other social providers. Here's an example of enforcing authentication-based access control in a Realtime Database:

```
{
  "rules": {
    ".read": "auth != null",
    ".write": "auth != null"
  }
}
```

This rule means that only authenticated users can read or write to the entire database.

2. Write Least Privilege Rules

The concept of "least privilege" is crucial in securing any system, including Firebase. You should only grant users the minimum permissions required to complete their tasks. Avoid setting overly permissive rules such as:

```
{
```

```
"rules": {

  ".read": "true",

  ".write": "true"

}

}
```

This rule allows unrestricted read and write access to anyone, which is extremely dangerous in a production environment. Instead, always aim for granular permissions tailored to specific requirements, making sure that only the right people can access sensitive data.

Understanding Granular Security with Firebase Rules

Firebase allows you to create rules that not only enforce user authentication but also validate data structures. Below is an example that applies stricter conditions to user data in Firestore:

```
service cloud.firestore {

  match /databases/{database}/documents {

    match /users/{userId} {

      allow read: if request.auth.uid == userId;

      allow write: if request.auth.uid == userId && request.resource.data.size() <= 1048576;

    }

  }

}
```

In this rule:

- The user can only read or write to their own document.
- **request.resource.data.size() <= 1048576** restricts the document size to a maximum of 1MB, ensuring users do not store overly large data chunks, which could impact database performance.

Validating Data with Security Rules

In addition to controlling access, Firebase Security Rules can validate data being written to ensure it adheres to your application's standards. For example, you can ensure that only valid email addresses are stored in the database:

```
service cloud.firestore {
  match /databases/{database}/documents {
    match /users/{userId} {
      allow write: if request.auth.uid == userId &&
request.resource.data.email.matches('^\\S+@\\S+\\.\\S+$');
    }
  }
}
```

Using Custom Claims for Role-Based Access Control

Firebase allows you to assign custom claims to authenticated users, which can be used to manage roles and permissions. For example, you could have an "admin" role that allows specific users to access administrative features of your app.

Assigning a custom claim to a user:

```
admin.auth().setCustomUserClaims(userId, { admin: true });
```

Using this custom claim in Firestore Security Rules:

```
service cloud.firestore {
  match /databases/{database}/documents {
```

```
    match /admin/{document=**} {

      allow read, write: if request.auth.token.admin == true;

    }

  }

}
```

This rule grants read and write access only to users who have the "admin" custom claim set to true.

Protecting Firebase Storage

Firebase Storage is used to store and serve user-generated content, such as images and other files. Properly securing your storage is crucial to prevent unauthorized users from uploading, deleting, or viewing files.

Here's an example of a Firebase Storage rule that allows users to access only their own files:

```
service firebase.storage {

  match /b/{bucket}/o {

    match /userFiles/{userId}/{fileName} {

      allow read, write: if request.auth != null && request.auth.uid == userId;

    }

  }

}
```

Best Practices for Firebase Security

1. **Regularly Review Security Rules**

As your application evolves, your security needs will change. Regularly review your security rules to ensure they meet your current requirements. Outdated or overly permissive rules can create vulnerabilities.

2. **Use Emulators for Testing Security Rules**

Firebase provides emulators to test your security rules locally. Before deploying any changes to production, you should thoroughly test your rules using the Firebase Emulator Suite to ensure they provide the necessary protection without blocking legitimate use cases.

3. **Implement Data Validation**

Ensure that all data written to your database is validated. You can use Firebase Security Rules to enforce basic validation, such as data types, value ranges, or specific formats. For more complex validations, consider using Cloud Functions to perform server-side checks before writing data to your database.

4. **Monitor Firebase with Firebase Analytics and Logging**

Firebase Analytics and Cloud Logging are essential tools for monitoring access and identifying potential security threats. Use Firebase Analytics to track user behavior and Cloud Logging to detect suspicious activities, such as repeated unauthorized access attempts.

5. **Leverage Cloud Functions for Sensitive Operations**

If you need to perform sensitive operations, such as updating multiple users' data or performing batch writes, consider using Cloud Functions. With Cloud Functions, you can centralize and secure complex logic, reducing the risk of vulnerabilities associated with client-side operations.

Here is a simple example of using Cloud Functions for a secure operation:

```
const functions = require('firebase-functions');

const admin = require('firebase-admin');

admin.initializeApp();


exports.secureOperation = functions.https.onCall((data, context) => {

  if (!context.auth) {

    throw new functions.https.HttpsError(
```

```
        'unauthenticated',
        'User must be authenticated to perform this operation.'
    );
}

// Proceed with the operation if the user is authenticated
return admin.firestore().collection('secureData').add({
    userId: context.auth.uid,
    data: data.secureContent,
});
});
```

This Cloud Function ensures that only authenticated users can perform the operation, adding another layer of security.

Summary

Firebase Security Rules are a powerful way to protect your application and its users, but they require careful planning and maintenance. By enforcing authentication, adhering to the principle of least privilege, and regularly reviewing your security configuration, you can build a secure Firebase environment.

Use Firebase's built-in tools such as emulators and analytics to continuously test and monitor your application, ensuring it remains safe as your app grows. Combining Firebase Security Rules with features like custom claims and Cloud Functions allows you to create a flexible and secure architecture that adapts to your application's needs.

The key to robust Firebase security lies in understanding your app's requirements, implementing strict access controls, validating data thoroughly, and ensuring all sensitive operations are handled securely. By following the best practices outlined in this section, you will be well-equipped to safeguard your Firebase project and deliver a secure experience to your users.

Writing Effective Security Rules

Effective security rules are essential to building robust and secure Firebase applications. Firebase Security Rules provide fine-grained control over who can read and write data, allowing developers to enforce strict access policies while ensuring a smooth user experience. In this section, we'll explore how to write security rules that not only protect your data but also provide efficient and scalable access control.

Overview of Firebase Security Rules

Firebase Security Rules act as the firewall between your application and your data, defining how data can be accessed and manipulated. Firebase supports security rules for its core services, including Firestore, Realtime Database, and Firebase Storage. These rules allow you to restrict data access based on user authentication, data properties, and the request context.

The key components of security rules are:

1. **Read Permissions**: Control who can read data from specific paths.
2. **Write Permissions**: Control who can write data to specific paths.
3. **Custom Conditions**: Apply custom conditions to ensure data validity.

Writing effective security rules involves balancing user access with security, ensuring that data can be accessed by legitimate users while preventing unauthorized access. Firebase Security Rules use a JSON-like syntax that allows you to specify access at different levels of granularity.

Understanding the Firebase Security Rules Structure

Firebase Security Rules follow a hierarchical structure, allowing you to define rules for specific paths in your database or storage. Here's an example of the structure for Firestore rules:

```
service cloud.firestore {

  match /databases/{database}/documents {

    match /users/{userId} {

      allow read, write: if request.auth != null && request.auth.uid == userId;

    }

  }

}
```

In the example above:

- The service cloud.firestore block indicates that the rules apply to Firestore.
- The match /databases/{database}/documents block defines the top-level rules for your database.
- The match /users/{userId} block defines rules for documents in the users collection.

The rules use conditions, such as if request.auth != null, to determine if a request is allowed. In this case, the rule allows authenticated users to read and write their own data.

Defining Authentication-Based Rules

A fundamental aspect of effective security rules is requiring that users be authenticated before they can access certain data. Firebase Authentication integrates seamlessly with security rules, allowing you to easily implement user-based access control.

For example, to ensure that only authenticated users can read or write data in the users collection:

```
service cloud.firestore {
  match /databases/{database}/documents {
    match /users/{userId} {
      allow read, write: if request.auth != null;
    }
  }
}
```

This rule requires that a user is authenticated (request.auth != null) to perform any operation on documents within the users collection. It's a basic yet powerful way to protect your data from unauthorized access.

Implementing Role-Based Access Control (RBAC)

Role-Based Access Control (RBAC) is a best practice for managing access to your data, especially when dealing with multiple user types, such as admins, editors, and regular users. Firebase provides the ability to assign custom claims to users, which can be leveraged to implement role-based access.

Suppose you have a scenario where you want to create admin users who can manage other users' data. You can assign an "admin" claim to specific users and write security rules accordingly:

Assigning Custom Claims

First, you need to assign a custom claim to a user using the Firebase Admin SDK:

```
const admin = require('firebase-admin');
admin.initializeApp();


admin.auth().setCustomUserClaims(userId, { admin: true })
  .then(() => {
    console.log('Custom claim added to user');
  })
  .catch((error) => {
    console.error('Error adding custom claim:', error);
  });
```

In the code above, the `setCustomUserClaims` function assigns an "admin" claim to the specified user (`userId`). This claim can now be used in your security rules to differentiate admin users from regular users.

Writing Security Rules for Admin Users

Once custom claims are assigned, you can use them in your security rules to grant special access to admin users:

```
service cloud.firestore {
  match /databases/{database}/documents {
    match /users/{userId} {
```

```
      allow  read,  write:  if  request.auth.token.admin  ==  true  ||
request.auth.uid == userId;

    }

  }

}
```

In this example:

- The rule allows admin users (`request.auth.token.admin == true`) to read and write any user document.
- It also allows users to read and write their own documents (`request.auth.uid == userId`).

This approach is useful for scenarios where certain users need elevated privileges, such as managing application settings or moderating content.

Validating Data with Firebase Security Rules

Firebase Security Rules can also be used to validate the data being written to your database, ensuring that it adheres to your application's requirements. Data validation helps maintain data integrity and ensures that malicious or malformed data does not enter your system.

Consider a scenario where you want to ensure that user documents contain only valid email addresses and usernames that meet certain criteria. Here's an example of how to enforce these constraints:

```
service cloud.firestore {

  match /databases/{database}/documents {

    match /users/{userId} {

      allow write: if request.auth != null &&

request.resource.data.email.matches('^\\S+@\\S+\\.\\S+$') &&

                  request.resource.data.username.size() >= 3 &&

                  request.resource.data.username.size() <= 20;
```

                }

            }

        }

In this rule:

- `request.resource.data.email.matches('^\\S+@\\S+\\.\\S+$')` ensures that the email field is a valid email address.
- `request.resource.data.username.size() >= 3 && request.resource.data.username.size() <= 20` ensures that the username is between 3 and 20 characters long.

By including these validations in your security rules, you can enforce consistent data formatting and prevent invalid data from being stored.

Securing Nested Data Structures

Firebase Security Rules allow you to secure nested data structures by specifying rules for each level. Suppose you have a Firestore collection called `posts`, where each post document contains a `comments` subcollection. You can define rules for both the post and its comments:

```
service cloud.firestore {

  match /databases/{database}/documents {

    match /posts/{postId} {

      allow read: if true;

      allow write: if request.auth != null && request.auth.uid == resource.data.authorId;


      match /comments/{commentId} {

        allow read: if true;

        allow write: if request.auth != null && request.auth.uid == request.resource.data.userId;
```

```
      }
    }
  }
}
```

In this rule:

- **Posts**: Any user can read posts (`allow read: if true`), but only the author can edit or delete their own posts (`request.auth.uid == resource.data.authorId`).
- **Comments**: Any user can read comments, but only authenticated users can add a comment, and each user can only add their own comments (`request.auth.uid == request.resource.data.userId`).

This approach allows you to maintain fine-grained control over different levels of your data, ensuring that access permissions are appropriate for each context.

Using Firebase Storage Security Rules

Firebase Storage is used to store and serve user-generated content, such as images and files. Writing effective security rules for Firebase Storage is crucial to prevent unauthorized users from uploading, modifying, or deleting files.

Here's an example of a Firebase Storage rule that allows users to upload and access only their own files:

```
service firebase.storage {
  match /b/{bucket}/o {
    match /userFiles/{userId}/{fileName} {
      allow read, write: if request.auth != null && request.auth.uid == userId;
    }
  }
}
```

In this rule:

- Users must be authenticated (request.auth != null) to read or write files.
- Users can only access files within their own directory (request.auth.uid == userId).

This setup ensures that each user has a private storage area, protecting their files from unauthorized access.

Combining Firebase Rules with Cloud Functions

Firebase Security Rules are powerful, but they can be limiting when it comes to complex logic that requires advanced computations. In such cases, Cloud Functions can be used to handle more sophisticated operations.

For example, if you need to validate that a certain number of documents already exist before allowing a write operation, you can use a Cloud Function to implement the logic and call it securely:

```
const functions = require('firebase-functions');
const admin = require('firebase-admin');

admin.initializeApp();


exports.validateWriteOperation = functions.firestore.document('users/{userId}').onWrite((change, context) => {

  const userId = context.params.userId;


  // Perform validation logic

  return admin.firestore().collection('users').get()
    .then(snapshot => {
      if (snapshot.size > 1000) {
        throw new Error('User limit reached');
```

```
        }
        return null;
    });
});
```

This Cloud Function ensures that no more than 1000 user documents exist. Such logic cannot be implemented directly in Firebase Security Rules, demonstrating the power of combining Cloud Functions with security rules to achieve a secure and scalable solution.

Testing and Debugging Security Rules

Firebase provides tools to help you test and debug your security rules. The Firebase Emulator Suite allows you to simulate different authentication states and data structures, enabling you to test your security rules without affecting your production environment.

Using the Emulator Suite, you can create unit tests that simulate various scenarios, such as:

- Unauthenticated users attempting to read or write data.
- Authenticated users accessing their own data versus attempting to access others' data.
- Admin users performing operations that regular users are restricted from.

Here's an example of how to use the Firebase Emulator to test your security rules:

Start the Emulator: Run the Firebase Emulator using the following command:
bash
Copy   code
```
firebase emulators:start --only firestore
```

1.
2. **Write Test Cases**: Create test cases using the Firebase Testing SDK or other testing frameworks to simulate different user roles and actions.

Testing and debugging security rules is crucial to ensure that your application is secure before it goes live. Regular testing can help identify gaps in your rules and prevent potential vulnerabilities.

Summary

Writing effective security rules is essential for safeguarding your Firebase project and ensuring that only authorized users can access and modify your data. By leveraging Firebase Security Rules, you can enforce robust access control policies that protect your application from unauthorized access and data breaches.

The key aspects of writing effective security rules include:

- **Authentication-Based Access**: Ensure that users are authenticated before accessing sensitive data.
- **Role-Based Access Control (RBAC)**: Use custom claims to define roles and manage permissions.
- **Data Validation**: Enforce data integrity by validating inputs using Firebase Security Rules.
- **Nested Data Structures**: Secure nested data with appropriate rules at each level.
- **Firebase Storage Rules**: Protect user-generated files by allowing users to access only their own data.
- **Cloud Functions for Complex Logic**: Combine Firebase Security Rules with Cloud Functions for advanced validation and logic.

By following these best practices and regularly testing your security rules, you can create a secure, reliable, and user-friendly Firebase application.

Best Practices for Firebase Development

Firebase is a powerful platform that offers developers a suite of tools to build, improve, and grow their applications. However, to fully leverage Firebase and ensure the scalability, security, and maintainability of your application, it is important to follow established best practices. In this section, we will explore best practices that encompass multiple aspects of Firebase development—from database structuring and efficient use of cloud services to monitoring, debugging, and optimizing for performance.

Database Structuring and Management

The structure of your Firebase database is one of the most crucial aspects of successful app development. Firebase offers two types of databases: **Firestore** and **Realtime Database**. Choosing the right database type and organizing it properly can make a significant difference in the performance, scalability, and ease of maintenance of your app.

Choosing Between Firestore and Realtime Database

Both Firestore and Realtime Database are NoSQL databases provided by Firebase, but they serve different purposes and use cases:

- **Firestore**: Firestore offers richer querying capabilities, structured data, and a more developer-friendly experience. It is well-suited for complex applications that require flexible, nested data structures.
- **Realtime Database**: The Realtime Database is optimized for low latency and is great for scenarios that require instant synchronization, such as messaging apps or simple real-time features.

Best Practice: Use Firestore for most general-purpose applications because of its ease of use and scalability. Use the Realtime Database for applications that need extremely low-latency data synchronization across users.

Structuring Data for Efficiency

Firebase databases are hierarchical and document-based, making data structuring a critical factor in determining the efficiency of reads, writes, and data management. Here are some key practices for structuring your Firebase database:

1. **Denormalization**: Unlike traditional relational databases, Firebase works best with **denormalized data**, which means duplicating data to reduce read complexity and improve performance. For example, if users frequently query an author's name along with a blog post, it is more efficient to store the author's name directly within the blog post document.
2. **Document and Collection Organization**: In Firestore, use collections to logically group related documents and use subcollections when data needs to be grouped under a specific parent document. Avoid deep nesting of subcollections, as it can lead to complex queries and make data retrieval cumbersome.
3. **Sharding for Scalability**: When dealing with data that is expected to grow rapidly, such as a **"likes"** collection for popular posts, consider sharding the data. Instead of storing all likes in one document or collection, split them into multiple documents to avoid write throughput bottlenecks.

Example of a sharding approach for "likes":

```
const shardId = Math.floor(Math.random() * 10); // Random number between 0 and 9

const shardRef = db.collection('posts').doc(postId).collection('likes_shards').doc(`shard_${shardId}`);


shardRef.set({
  count: admin.firestore.FieldValue.increment(1)
}, { merge: true });
```

This sharding approach divides the load across multiple shards, ensuring better scalability.

Managing Firebase Costs Effectively

Firebase provides a generous **free tier** and a variety of pricing plans for different services, but it is still important to manage your resources efficiently to avoid unexpected costs.

Best Practices for Reducing Costs

1. **Use Cloud Functions Wisely**: Firebase Cloud Functions are billed based on execution time and the number of invocations. Ensure that functions are designed to minimize execution time by avoiding unnecessary operations and optimizing performance. Avoid triggering functions that can result in an endless loop. For example, a write operation in Firestore that triggers a Cloud Function, which in turn writes to the same collection, can create a costly feedback loop.
2. **Optimize Database Reads and Writes**: Firebase charges based on the number of reads and writes. Optimize your reads by **querying specific documents** rather than fetching entire collections. Leverage indexes to speed up complex queries and reduce the need for repeated reads.

Example of a cost-optimized query:

```
// Instead of querying an entire collection, filter by specific fields

const usersRef = db.collection('users');

const snapshot = await usersRef.where('age', '>=', 18).where('status', '==', 'active').get();
```

In this example, the query ensures that only the relevant documents are fetched, which helps minimize the number of reads.

3. **Monitor Cloud Storage Usage**: Firebase Storage costs are based on the data stored and bandwidth used. Use compression techniques to reduce file sizes before uploading and ensure files that are no longer needed are deleted. Implement **Storage Rules** to ensure only valid users can upload files, thereby preventing malicious users from exploiting your storage resources.
4. **Use Firebase App Check**: Firebase **App Check** helps prevent abuse of Firebase services by ensuring that only requests from your legitimate apps are processed. This is useful to prevent unauthorized access that could otherwise increase usage costs.

Cloud Functions Best Practices

Firebase **Cloud Functions** can add significant backend capabilities to your application, but if not managed properly, they can become a source of latency and increased costs.

Avoid Blocking Operations

When writing Cloud Functions, avoid **blocking operations** like synchronous API calls, which can delay the entire function and increase execution time. Instead, use **asynchronous patterns** and take advantage of **Promise.all()** to make multiple asynchronous requests concurrently.

Example:

```
exports.aggregateData =
functions.firestore.document('orders/{orderId}').onCreate(async
(snap, context) => {

  const orderData = snap.data();

  // Simultaneous async calls to Firestore
  const userPromise =
admin.firestore().collection('users').doc(orderData.userId).get();
  const productPromise =
admin.firestore().collection('products').doc(orderData.productId).get();

  const [userDoc, productDoc] = await Promise.all([userPromise, productPromise]);

  if (!userDoc.exists || !productDoc.exists) {
    console.log('Invalid user or product');
    return null;
  }

  // Process further
});
```

Using **Promise.all()** here ensures that both user and product data are fetched simultaneously, reducing the total function execution time.

Minimize Cold Start Delays

Cloud Functions experience **cold starts**, which can introduce latency, especially with functions that are not frequently invoked. You can reduce the impact of cold starts by keeping function logic minimal and lightweight. Also, minimize the number of dependencies your function relies on to ensure quick loading.

Security Best Practices

Security is a critical aspect of Firebase development. Firebase provides multiple mechanisms, such as **Authentication**, **Security Rules**, and **Custom Claims**, to protect your application.

Write Granular Security Rules

Always write **granular security rules** that follow the principle of least privilege. Ensure that each type of user has the minimum permissions required to complete their tasks. Avoid overly permissive rules, such as setting `.read` or `.write` to `true` for an entire collection.

Example of a granular rule for user-specific data access:

```
service cloud.firestore {
  match /databases/{database}/documents {
    match /users/{userId} {
       allow read, write: if request.auth != null && request.auth.uid == userId;
    }
  }
}
```

Enforce Data Validation Rules

In addition to access control, use **data validation** to ensure data integrity. Validation rules help enforce constraints, such as requiring specific fields or ensuring values fall within expected ranges.

Example:

```
service cloud.firestore {
```

```
match /databases/{database}/documents {

  match /orders/{orderId} {

    allow create: if request.auth != null &&

                  request.resource.data.amount > 0 &&

                  request.resource.data.status  in   ['pending',
'shipped', 'delivered'];

  }

 }

}
```

This rule ensures that orders can only be created by authenticated users and that order data meets certain conditions.

Monitoring and Debugging

Firebase provides several tools to help you **monitor** and **debug** your application.

Use Firebase Performance Monitoring

Firebase **Performance Monitoring** provides insights into your application's performance, allowing you to identify bottlenecks and optimize your code accordingly. Use performance traces to track specific parts of your app and identify latency issues.

Use Cloud Logging for Debugging

Cloud Logging is an invaluable tool for understanding what happens during Cloud Function execution. Adding appropriate logs can help you track function invocations, debug issues, and understand errors in real-time.

Example of adding logs in a Cloud Function:

```
exports.sendNotification                                               =
functions.firestore.document('messages/{messageId}').onCreate(async
(snap, context) => {

  const message = snap.data();

  console.log('Sending notification for message:', message);
```

```
try {
  await sendNotificationToUser(message.userId, message.text);
  console.log('Notification sent successfully');
} catch (error) {
  console.error('Error sending notification:', error);
}
});
```

Logs help you monitor function flow and identify the exact point of failure.

Leveraging Analytics for Insights

Firebase **Analytics** can provide valuable insights into how users interact with your application. Understanding user behavior can help you make informed decisions about app features and improvements.

Custom Event Tracking

Use **custom events** in Firebase Analytics to track specific user actions that are important for your app's functionality. Custom events can provide insights into how users interact with features, where they drop off, and what might be causing friction in the user experience.

Example:

```
firebase.analytics().logEvent('product_view', {
  product_id: '12345',
  category: 'electronics'
});
```

Tracking such events helps you understand which products are being viewed most frequently, allowing you to optimize your offerings.

Optimizing for Performance

Performance optimization in Firebase is crucial, especially as your app scales.

Use Indexed Queries

Firestore allows you to **create indexes** to improve the performance of your queries. Queries that filter or order by multiple fields require composite indexes. Ensure that your frequently used queries are backed by appropriate indexes to minimize response times.

Minimize Document Size

Keep individual document sizes within reasonable limits (less than 1MB). Store large blobs such as images or videos in **Firebase Storage** rather than in Firestore documents. This will reduce the payload size and improve read and write times.

Automating Deployment and Testing

Automating the deployment and testing process ensures consistent quality and minimizes human errors during updates.

Firebase CLI and CI/CD

Use the **Firebase CLI** to automate deployments and integrate Firebase projects into CI/CD pipelines. This allows you to continuously test and deploy updates with minimal manual intervention, ensuring that changes are applied safely and consistently.

Example of a Firebase deployment command:

```
firebase deploy --only functions
```

Use this command in your CI/CD scripts to automatically deploy functions after passing unit tests and quality checks.

Summary

Firebase development is an extensive process that involves managing database structure, ensuring security, optimizing performance, and monitoring applications effectively. By following these best practices, you can leverage Firebase to build scalable, secure, and high-performance applications that provide a great user experience.

Key Takeaways:

1. **Database Structuring**: Use Firestore for complex applications, denormalize data for efficiency, and shard collections for scalability.

2. **Cost Management**: Use efficient Cloud Functions, minimize database reads and writes, and optimize storage usage to keep costs under control.
3. **Cloud Functions**: Avoid blocking operations, reduce cold start delays, and use asynchronous operations to improve function efficiency.
4. **Security**: Write granular security rules, enforce data validation, and use Firebase App Check to prevent abuse.
5. **Monitoring and Analytics**: Use Performance Monitoring, Cloud Logging, and Analytics to track application performance and user behavior.
6. **Performance Optimization**: Use indexes for frequently used queries, keep document sizes small, and leverage custom event tracking to gain insights into user behavior.

By adhering to these best practices, you can ensure that your Firebase-powered application is not only functional but also secure, cost-effective, and performant as it scales.

Chapter 11: Building and Launching Your First App

Recap of Key Firebase Concepts

In this section, we'll consolidate everything you have learned throughout this book and guide you through building a simple, yet complete application that utilizes many of Firebase's features. This recap will help ensure you have a strong understanding of Firebase's different components and know how to bring them together in a real-world project.

Getting Started: App Overview

The project we will build is a note-taking application called "MyNotes." It will allow users to register and authenticate, store and retrieve notes, and manage these notes across devices. The key features will include user authentication, database interaction using Firestore, file uploads using Firebase Storage, and user engagement with Firebase Cloud Messaging for notifications.

To begin, let's recap the key Firebase services and how they will be used in our application:

1. **Firebase Authentication**: Users will be able to sign up and log in using email/password or social authentication methods. This provides a secure way for users to access the app.
2. **Firestore Database**: This will be used to store users' notes in a cloud database, ensuring data is synced across devices in real-time.
3. **Firebase Storage**: Users will also have the ability to upload files, such as images or other media, which will be associated with their notes.
4. **Firebase Cloud Messaging (FCM)**: To keep users engaged, we'll set up push notifications using FCM, which can remind users to return and review or add new notes.

The steps in this section will guide you through building each part of the application and integrating the key Firebase services we've discussed.

Project Setup

Before diving into coding, make sure that:

- You have Firebase set up for your project, with Firestore, Authentication, and Storage enabled.
- You've installed all the necessary dependencies for your development environment.

If you're working with a framework such as React Native, Flutter, or plain JavaScript, ensure that Firebase libraries are properly installed and imported.

Firebase Authentication Integration

The first step in building our app is to set up user authentication. User authentication provides a secure method for users to access their notes, which is crucial for privacy.

Below is the code to implement email/password authentication in a JavaScript-based application:

```javascript
// Import necessary Firebase modules
import { getAuth, createUserWithEmailAndPassword, signInWithEmailAndPassword } from "firebase/auth";


// Initialize Firebase Authentication
const auth = getAuth();


// Function to sign up new users
function signUp(email, password) {
    createUserWithEmailAndPassword(auth, email, password)
        .then((userCredential) => {
            // Successfully signed up
            const user = userCredential.user;
            console.log('User signed up:', user);
        })
        .catch((error) => {
            console.error('Error signing up:', error.message);
        });
}
```

```
// Function to log in existing users

function login(email, password) {

    signInWithEmailAndPassword(auth, email, password)

        .then((userCredential) => {

            // Successfully logged in

            const user = userCredential.user;

            console.log('User logged in:', user);

        })

        .catch((error) => {

            console.error('Error logging in:', error.message);

        });

}
```

With this code in place, users can register and log in to your application. Firebase Authentication handles all the backend complexity, such as securing passwords, providing unique identifiers for users, and managing sessions.

Adding Notes: Firestore Database Integration

Now that our users can sign in and authenticate, the next feature is to allow them to create, update, and delete notes. For this, we'll use Firebase's Firestore, which provides a NoSQL cloud database that syncs in real-time.

First, set up Firestore in your project:

```
// Import Firestore

import { getFirestore, collection, addDoc, getDocs, updateDoc, deleteDoc, doc } from "firebase/firestore";


// Initialize Firestore
```

```javascript
const db = getFirestore();


// Function to add a new note

async function addNote(userId, noteContent) {

    try {

        const docRef = await addDoc(collection(db, "notes"), {

            userId: userId,

            content: noteContent,

            createdAt: new Date()

        });

        console.log("Note added with ID: ", docRef.id);

    } catch (e) {

        console.error("Error adding note: ", e);

    }

}


// Function to retrieve all notes for a user

async function getUserNotes(userId) {

    const querySnapshot = await getDocs(collection(db, "notes"));

    querySnapshot.forEach((doc) => {

        if (doc.data().userId === userId) {

            console.log(`${doc.id} => ${doc.data().content}`);

        }

    });
```

```
}


// Function to update a note

async function updateNote(noteId, newContent) {

    const noteRef = doc(db, "notes", noteId);

    await updateDoc(noteRef, {

        content: newContent,

        updatedAt: new Date()

    });

    console.log("Note updated");

}


// Function to delete a note

async function deleteNote(noteId) {

    await deleteDoc(doc(db, "notes", noteId));

    console.log("Note deleted");

}
```

With these functions, you can manage notes within Firestore. Users can create, read, update, and delete their notes, and Firestore will automatically handle syncing these changes across devices.

Uploading Files: Firebase Storage

Our "MyNotes" app will also allow users to upload images to associate with their notes. To do this, we'll use Firebase Storage. The following code demonstrates how to upload a file to Firebase Storage and store the URL in Firestore, linking it with a note:

```
// Import necessary Firebase Storage functions
```

```javascript
import { getStorage, ref, uploadBytes, getDownloadURL } from
"firebase/storage";


// Initialize Firebase Storage
const storage = getStorage();


// Function to upload an image file
async function uploadImage(userId, file) {
    const storageRef = ref(storage,
`images/${userId}/${file.name}`);
    try {
        await uploadBytes(storageRef, file);
        const downloadURL = await getDownloadURL(storageRef);
        console.log('File available at', downloadURL);
        return downloadURL;
    } catch (error) {
        console.error('Error uploading file:', error);
    }
}
```

With this setup, users can upload images, which are then stored in Firebase Storage. The image URL can be saved in the Firestore database and linked with the respective note. This way, users can view their notes along with any associated images.

Firebase Cloud Messaging: Notifications

To keep users engaged, it's essential to remind them to revisit the app. Firebase Cloud Messaging (FCM) can be used to send push notifications to users. This is particularly useful for reminding them to create new notes or revisit old ones.

The following snippet shows how to request permission and subscribe a user to notifications:

```
// Import necessary Firebase Messaging functions
import { getMessaging, getToken, onMessage } from "firebase/messaging";

// Initialize Firebase Messaging
const messaging = getMessaging();

// Request permission to send notifications
async function requestNotificationPermission() {
    try {
        const permission = await Notification.requestPermission();
        if (permission === "granted") {
            console.log("Notification permission granted.");
            const token = await getToken(messaging);
            console.log("FCM token:", token);
        } else {
            console.error("Unable to get permission to notify.");
        }
    } catch (error) {
        console.error("Error requesting notification permission:", error);
    }
}
```

```
// Handle incoming messages

onMessage(messaging, (payload) => {

    console.log("Message received: ", payload);

});
```

With this code in place, you can request permission from users to send notifications and handle incoming messages when the app is in the foreground.

Putting It All Together

Now that we have explored the essential features for our app, it's time to put them together to create the complete application flow.

1. **User Registration/Login**: Users can sign up or log in to access their personal notes.
2. **Note Management**: After logging in, users can create, update, and delete notes stored in Firestore.
3. **Image Upload**: Users can enhance their notes by uploading images, which are stored in Firebase Storage.
4. **User Engagement**: Push notifications are set up using Firebase Cloud Messaging to remind users to interact with the app.

Testing and Debugging

Testing is crucial in app development. Here are some testing techniques to consider:

- **Authentication**: Test with different user scenarios — signing up, logging in, and logging out — to ensure all authentication flows work as expected.
- **Firestore Data Consistency**: Verify that notes are correctly stored and retrieved for each user. Ensure that updates and deletions are properly handled and reflected across devices.
- **File Uploads**: Test the image upload feature with different file types and sizes to verify that Firebase Storage can handle these scenarios.
- **Notifications**: Ensure push notifications are properly triggered and received on different devices.

Launching the App

Once you have completed building and thoroughly tested the app, it's time to prepare for launch. Here are the key steps:

- **Optimize Performance**: Review Firebase's usage and optimize database reads/writes to minimize costs.

- **Secure Your App**: Ensure that your Firebase rules are correctly configured to prevent unauthorized data access.
- **Deployment**: If you are using a web-based application, deploy it using Firebase Hosting. For mobile apps, follow platform-specific guidelines to publish on app stores.

With the "MyNotes" application, you have successfully integrated various Firebase features, and you should now feel comfortable using Firebase for a variety of different tasks in your future projects.

Developing a Simple App from Start to Finish

In this section, we will take everything we have learned about Firebase and build a simple app from scratch. This practical approach will help solidify your understanding of how Firebase components integrate to form a complete and functional application. The app we will develop is called "Taskify"—a simple task management tool that lets users register, add, manage, and organize their tasks across multiple devices. Taskify will be built using Firebase Authentication, Firestore, Storage, and Firebase Cloud Messaging (FCM) for notifications. By the end of this section, you will have a complete understanding of how Firebase's different tools work together to build a real-world application.

Project Overview and Initial Setup

The first step in building Taskify is to set up a development environment. The following key tools and components will be used:

1. **Firebase Project**: Set up a Firebase project with Authentication, Firestore, Storage, and FCM enabled.
2. **Frontend Framework**: For simplicity, we will use HTML, CSS, and JavaScript to create the user interface. Alternatively, you can use frameworks like React, Angular, or Vue.js for a more advanced project.
3. **Firebase SDK**: Integrate Firebase into your frontend code using Firebase SDK for JavaScript.

```
taskify/
    ├── index.html
    ├── styles.css
    ├── app.js
```

Ensure that Firebase JavaScript libraries are installed and that the Firebase configuration details are set up in your `app.js` file.

Setting Up Firebase Configuration

To connect your project to Firebase, you will need to configure your Firebase credentials and include the necessary Firebase JavaScript libraries in your HTML file. Open `index.html` and include the following:

```html
<!DOCTYPE html>

<html lang="en">

<head>

    <meta charset="UTF-8">

    <meta name="viewport" content="width=device-width, initial-scale=1.0">

    <link rel="stylesheet" href="styles.css">

    <script src="https://www.gstatic.com/firebasejs/9.0.0/firebase-app.js"></script>

    <script src="https://www.gstatic.com/firebasejs/9.0.0/firebase-auth.js"></script>

    <script src="https://www.gstatic.com/firebasejs/9.0.0/firebase-firestore.js"></script>

    <script src="https://www.gstatic.com/firebasejs/9.0.0/firebase-storage.js"></script>

    <script src="https://www.gstatic.com/firebasejs/9.0.0/firebase-messaging.js"></script>

    <title>Taskify</title>

</head>

<body>

    <div id="app">

        <h1>Welcome to Taskify</h1>

        <!-- Authentication UI -->
```

```html
    <div id="auth-container">
        <input type="email" id="email" placeholder="Email">
        <input type="password" id="password" placeholder="Password">
        <button onclick="signUp()">Sign Up</button>
        <button onclick="login()">Login</button>
    </div>

    <!-- Task Management UI (visible after login) -->
    <div id="task-container" style="display: none;">
        <input type="text" id="task-input" placeholder="Add a new task">
        <button onclick="addTask()">Add Task</button>
        <ul id="task-list"></ul>
    </div>
</div>
<script src="app.js"></script>
</body>
</html>
```

In app.js, you need to initialize Firebase with your configuration details:

```javascript
// Firebase configuration
const firebaseConfig = {
    apiKey: "YOUR_API_KEY",
```

```
    authDomain: "YOUR_AUTH_DOMAIN",

    projectId: "YOUR_PROJECT_ID",

    storageBucket: "YOUR_STORAGE_BUCKET",

    messagingSenderId: "YOUR_MESSAGING_SENDER_ID",

    appId: "YOUR_APP_ID"
};


// Initialize Firebase

firebase.initializeApp(firebaseConfig);


// Initialize Firebase services

const auth = firebase.auth();

const db = firebase.firestore();

const storage = firebase.storage();

const messaging = firebase.messaging();
```

User Authentication

To enable users to access the Taskify app, we will implement user authentication using Firebase Authentication. The user can either register or log in to their account using an email and password. The following code shows how to set up sign-up and login functionality:

```
// Sign up function

function signUp() {

    const email = document.getElementById("email").value;

    const password = document.getElementById("password").value;
```

```
    auth.createUserWithEmailAndPassword(email, password)
        .then((userCredential) => {
            const user = userCredential.user;
            console.log('User signed up:', user);
            showTaskContainer();
        })
        .catch((error) => {
            console.error('Error signing up:', error.message);
        });
}


// Login function
function login() {
    const email = document.getElementById("email").value;
    const password = document.getElementById("password").value;

    auth.signInWithEmailAndPassword(email, password)
        .then((userCredential) => {
            const user = userCredential.user;
            console.log('User logged in:', user);
            showTaskContainer();
        })
        .catch((error) => {
```

```
            console.error('Error logging in:', error.message);
        });
}


// Show task container after login

function showTaskContainer() {

    document.getElementById("auth-container").style.display = "none";

    document.getElementById("task-container").style.display = "block";

}
```

Adding Tasks with Firestore

The next step is to allow users to add tasks. We will use Firestore to store the tasks for each user. When the user logs in, they can add tasks, and these tasks will be saved to the Firestore database.

```
// Function to add a task

function addTask() {

    const taskInput = document.getElementById("task-input");

    const taskContent = taskInput.value;


    if (taskContent === "") {

        console.error("Task content cannot be empty");

        return;

    }
```

```javascript
    // Get the current user

    const user = auth.currentUser;


    // Add the task to Firestore

    db.collection("tasks").add({

        userId: user.uid,

        content: taskContent,

        createdAt: new Date()

    })

    .then((docRef) => {

        console.log("Task added with ID: ", docRef.id);

        taskInput.value = "";

        displayTasks(); // Update the UI with the new task

    })

    .catch((error) => {

        console.error("Error adding task: ", error);

    });

}


// Function to display tasks for the logged-in user

function displayTasks() {

    const user = auth.currentUser;

    const taskList = document.getElementById("task-list");
```

```
        taskList.innerHTML = ""; // Clear previous tasks


    db.collection("tasks").where("userId", "==", user.uid)
        .orderBy("createdAt", "desc")
        .get()
        .then((querySnapshot) => {
            querySnapshot.forEach((doc) => {
                const task = doc.data();
                const taskItem = document.createElement("li");
                taskItem.textContent = task.content;
                taskList.appendChild(taskItem);
            });
        })
        .catch((error) => {
            console.error("Error getting tasks: ", error);
        });
}
```

Uploading Files with Firebase Storage

Taskify will also allow users to upload images related to their tasks. This feature could be used to add a photo of a completed task, a receipt, or any other relevant document. The uploaded file will be stored in Firebase Storage, and the file URL will be saved in Firestore.

Here is how you can add file upload functionality:

```
// Function to upload an image
function uploadImage(taskId) {
```

```javascript
const fileInput = document.getElementById("file-input");

const file = fileInput.files[0];


if (!file) {

    console.error("No file selected for upload");

    return;

}


const storageRef = storage.ref().child(`task-images/${taskId}/${file.name}`);


storageRef.put(file)

    .then((snapshot) => {

        console.log("File uploaded successfully");

        return snapshot.ref.getDownloadURL();

    })

    .then((downloadURL) => {

        // Update the task with the image URL

        db.collection("tasks").doc(taskId).update({

            imageUrl: downloadURL

        });

        console.log("Task updated with image URL:", downloadURL);

    })

    .catch((error) => {
```

```
              console.error("Error uploading file:", error);
       });
}
```

Enabling Notifications with Firebase Cloud Messaging

Firebase Cloud Messaging (FCM) will be used to notify users about their tasks, for example, to remind them of pending tasks. Below is the code to enable notifications in the Taskify app:

```
// Request permission to send notifications
function requestNotificationPermission() {
    messaging.requestPermission()
       .then(() => {
            console.log("Notification permission granted.");
            return messaging.getToken();
       })
       .then((token) => {
            console.log("FCM Token:", token);
            // Here you could send the token to your server to subscribe the user for notifications
       })
       .catch((error) => {
            console.error("Error getting notification permission:", error);
       });
}
```

```
// Handling incoming messages

messaging.onMessage((payload) => {

    console.log("Message received:", payload);

    // Display the message to the user

    alert(`Notification: ${payload.notification.title}`);

});
```

User Interface Enhancements

For the best user experience, it's important to ensure that your UI is responsive, intuitive, and clean. Use CSS to style your app and make it visually appealing. Below is a simple CSS snippet to enhance the look of the Taskify app:

```
body {

    font-family: Arial, sans-serif;

    background-color: #f0f0f0;

    color: #333;

}


#app {

    width: 400px;

    margin: 50px auto;

    padding: 20px;

    background-color: white;

    box-shadow: 0 0 10px rgba(0, 0, 0, 0.1);

    border-radius: 8px;
```

```css
}

input[type="email"],
input[type="password"],
input[type="text"] {
    width: calc(100% - 20px);
    padding: 10px;
    margin-bottom: 10px;
    border: 1px solid #ddd;
    border-radius: 4px;
}

button {
    padding: 10px 20px;
    margin-top: 10px;
    border: none;
    background-color: #007bff;
    color: white;
    cursor: pointer;
    border-radius: 4px;
}

button:hover {
    background-color: #0056b3;
```

```css
}

#task-list {
    margin-top: 20px;
}

#task-list li {
    background: #f9f9f9;
    padding: 10px;
    margin-bottom: 5px;
    border-radius: 4px;
}
```

Testing and Debugging Taskify

Testing is a critical part of building any application. Make sure to test Taskify under different conditions:

1. **Authentication**: Test sign-up, login, and logout flows to ensure everything works as expected.
2. **Database**: Verify that tasks are stored correctly, can be retrieved, and can be updated or deleted.
3. **File Upload**: Test uploading files of different sizes and formats to ensure Firebase Storage handles them correctly.
4. **Notifications**: Verify that notifications are sent and received as expected on different devices.

Use Firebase's console to monitor your application, view errors, and debug any issues that arise during testing.

Deploying Taskify

Once you have completed development and testing, it's time to launch Taskify. Firebase Hosting provides a straightforward way to deploy web applications. Follow these steps to deploy Taskify:

1. **Install Firebase CLI**: If you haven't already, install the Firebase CLI using `npm install -g firebase-tools`.
2. **Initialize Hosting**: In the `taskify` directory, run `firebase init` and select Hosting.
3. **Deploy**: Run `firebase deploy` to deploy your app.

After successful deployment, your Taskify app will be available on the Firebase Hosting URL provided.

Conclusion

Congratulations! You have now built a complete, functional app from start to finish using Firebase. Through the development of Taskify, you've gained hands-on experience with Firebase Authentication, Firestore, Storage, and Cloud Messaging. You've also learned how to test, debug, and deploy a real-world application.

This journey should give you the confidence to leverage Firebase for your own projects—whether they are simple apps or complex systems. Firebase provides a powerful backend solution that scales effortlessly, enabling you to focus on building great user experiences.

Testing, Debugging, and Launching

In this section, we'll focus on the essential final stages of building an application: testing, debugging, and launching. These stages are often what determine whether your project succeeds or struggles. Building an app is not just about writing the code—it's about ensuring that the app functions seamlessly, provides a smooth user experience, and remains secure. In this comprehensive section, we will cover how to thoroughly test the app, debug issues effectively, and launch it successfully so that users can enjoy a polished product.

Importance of Testing and Debugging

Testing and debugging are vital in software development. An application without rigorous testing is bound to fail due to unforeseen errors, crashes, and inconsistencies. It's important to:

1. **Identify and Correct Errors**: Testing helps to discover bugs in both functional and non-functional requirements of the application.
2. **Ensure Usability and Stability**: A well-tested app is smooth to use, free of major bugs, and retains users for longer.
3. **Guarantee Security**: Especially with apps that deal with sensitive information, such as Firebase Authentication and Firestore databases, ensuring security through testing is crucial.

This process is iterative, meaning you need to test continuously and debug until no significant issues remain. Let's break down how to test each major part of the Taskify application we developed in the previous sections.

Types of Testing

We'll begin by exploring different types of testing that are relevant to Taskify:

1. **Unit Testing**: Testing individual units of code—such as functions, modules, or classes—to ensure they work correctly in isolation.
2. **Integration Testing**: Testing combinations of units together to ensure that different parts of the system interact correctly.
3. **End-to-End (E2E) Testing**: Testing the entire flow of the application to ensure that user scenarios work as intended.
4. **User Acceptance Testing (UAT)**: Testing the application with a group of end-users to determine if it meets their needs and requirements.
5. **Performance Testing**: Evaluating the application's performance under different conditions—load, stress, and peak usage.

Tools for Testing

For the Taskify app, the following testing tools can be employed:

- **Jest**: A JavaScript testing framework for writing unit and integration tests.
- **Cypress**: A tool that's particularly useful for E2E testing. It allows you to simulate user interactions and test entire workflows.
- **Firebase Test Lab**: A tool from Firebase to test the app across a variety of real devices.

Writing Unit Tests

Unit testing involves testing the smallest parts of your application—such as functions or methods—independently of other components. For the Taskify app, let's write some basic unit tests to test key functionalities like user sign-up, adding a task, and uploading a file.

Using Jest, you can write unit tests as follows:

User Authentication Testing

Create a file named auth.test.js and add the following code to test the sign-up functionality:

```javascript
import { signUp } from './auth'; // Assuming signUp is exported from auth.js


describe("User Authentication", () => {
    it("should sign up a user with email and password", async () =>
{
```

```
        const mockEmail = "test@example.com";
        const mockPassword = "password123";

        try {
            const user = await signUp(mockEmail, mockPassword);
            expect(user.email).toBe(mockEmail);
        } catch (error) {
            console.error("Error during sign-up:", error);
        }
    });
});
```

This test ensures that a user can successfully sign up with an email and password, which is an essential feature of Taskify.

Task Management Testing

Create another file named `tasks.test.js` to test adding a task:

```
import { addTask } from './tasks'; // Assuming addTask is exported from tasks.js

describe("Task Management", () => {
    it("should add a task to Firestore", async () => {
        const mockUserId = "user123";
        const mockTaskContent = "Write documentation";

        try {
```

```
            const task = await addTask(mockUserId, mockTaskContent);

            expect(task.content).toBe(mockTaskContent);

            expect(task.userId).toBe(mockUserId);

        } catch (error) {

            console.error("Error during task addition:", error);

        }

    });

});
```

These tests are intended to ensure that the `addTask` function works properly when valid data is provided.

Debugging Techniques

Once your tests are written and executed, you may encounter some errors or failures. Debugging is a process that requires patience and methodical analysis. Below are some debugging techniques to effectively troubleshoot the issues in your application.

Using Browser Developer Tools

Browser developer tools are incredibly powerful for debugging JavaScript applications. They provide several functionalities that make finding and fixing issues easier:

1. **Console Logging**: Use `console.log()` statements to print values of variables, states, or any dynamic data throughout your code. While it's basic, it's a very effective method of gaining insight into how your code is running.
2. **Breakpoints**: Set breakpoints to pause the execution of your code at specific lines, enabling you to inspect variable states and the call stack at that particular moment.
3. **Network Inspector**: Use the network panel to monitor network requests made by the application—especially useful for Firebase requests. Check whether requests are successful, how long they take, and what responses they receive.

Firebase Debugging Tools

Firebase provides a few built-in debugging tools to help you:

1. **Firebase Emulator Suite**: Use the Emulator Suite to run Firebase locally and test your application without affecting production data. This is a great way to test Firestore rules, Authentication, and other Firebase services.

2. **Firebase Analytics DebugView**: DebugView allows you to monitor analytics events in near-real-time, which is particularly useful when testing specific user flows or trying to track down unexpected behavior.

Debugging Example: Fixing Sign-Up Errors

Suppose the sign-up functionality in Taskify is not working correctly. You might start by adding `console.log()` statements to understand what's happening:

```
function signUp(email, password) {

    console.log("Sign-up initiated for:", email);

    auth.createUserWithEmailAndPassword(email, password)

        .then((userCredential) => {

            const user = userCredential.user;

            console.log('User signed up:', user);

            showTaskContainer();

        })

        .catch((error) => {

            console.error('Error signing up:', error.message);

        });

}
```

After adding logs, you notice that an error message says "Email already in use." This indicates that the sign-up failed because the email address is already registered. You can then improve the error message to provide more context for the user:

```
.catch((error) => {

    if (error.code === 'auth/email-already-in-use') {
```

```
            console.error('This email is already registered. Please use a different email.');
        } else {
            console.error('Error signing up:', error.message);
        }
});
```

This gives both you and the end-user better insight into what went wrong and how to fix it.

Performance Testing

Performance testing is essential to ensure the Taskify app performs well under normal and high-load conditions. Firebase offers tools to help with performance testing:

Firebase Performance Monitoring

Firebase Performance Monitoring is a tool that helps you understand how your app performs from your users' perspective. It collects data about response times, app startup time, screen rendering, and other metrics, which you can then analyze to improve performance.

To integrate Firebase Performance Monitoring, add the library to your project:

```
<script    src="https://www.gstatic.com/firebasejs/9.0.0/firebase-performance.js"></script>
```

Then initialize performance monitoring in app.js:

```
import { getPerformance } from "firebase/performance";

const perf = getPerformance(firebaseApp);
```

Once set up, you can monitor the performance of Firebase functions and screen transitions to determine where optimizations are needed.

Tips for Performance Optimization

1. **Minimize Reads and Writes**: Each read and write operation in Firestore incurs a cost in terms of both performance and billing. Use proper querying techniques to minimize the number of reads.
2. **Caching**: Cache the frequently accessed data locally, especially when users interact with the same data multiple times. Firestore provides caching capabilities that help improve app speed.
3. **Batch Writes**: Where possible, use batch writes in Firestore. This allows you to perform multiple write operations as a single atomic unit, thereby improving both performance and consistency.

Launching the Application

Once you've tested and debugged your application thoroughly, the final step is launching it to users. Here are the key considerations to keep in mind before launching:

Security Best Practices

Security is of utmost importance, especially when dealing with sensitive user data like authentication details and personal notes. Here are some key security practices to implement before launching:

1. **Firestore Security Rules**: Review and write secure Firestore rules to ensure users can only access their own data. Here's an example rule that only allows authenticated users to read and write their own tasks:

```
service cloud.firestore {
  match /databases/{database}/documents {
    match /tasks/{taskId} {
      allow read, write: if request.auth != null && request.auth.uid == resource.data.userId;
    }
  }
}
```

2. **Authentication Restrictions**: Use Firebase Authentication settings to restrict sign-ups to specific email domains (if necessary) or to enforce strong password requirements.

3. **Input Validation**: Always validate user inputs both on the client and server side. This prevents malicious inputs that could exploit vulnerabilities in your app.

Deploying with Firebase Hosting

Firebase Hosting is a fast and secure way to deploy Taskify. It provides SSL by default and works well with other Firebase services like Authentication and Firestore.

Firebase CLI: Install Firebase CLI if you haven't already:
bash
Copy code
```
npm install -g firebase-tools
```

1.

Initialize Hosting: In your project directory, initialize Firebase Hosting:
bash
Copy code
```
firebase init
```

2. Choose the Hosting option and select your Firebase project.

Deploy the App: After configuring Firebase Hosting, deploy the application:
bash
Copy code
```
firebase deploy
```

3.

This command will deploy your app to Firebase Hosting, making it accessible via a Firebase-provided domain. You can also link a custom domain if required.

Post-Launch Monitoring

The work doesn't end once the application is launched. Post-launch monitoring is crucial to maintain the app's health and improve user experience.

1. **Crashlytics**: Integrate Firebase Crashlytics to monitor crashes and stability issues in real-time. It provides detailed stack traces and helps prioritize issues based on user impact.
2. **Analytics**: Use Firebase Analytics to track user behavior, such as active users, screen views, and key user events. This helps you understand how users interact with your app, which features they use most, and where they encounter issues.
3. **User Feedback**: Gather user feedback through in-app surveys or feedback forms. This provides direct insights into what users like or dislike about the app, enabling you to make data-driven improvements.

Continuous Improvement and Updates

Launching an app is not a one-time task—it's an ongoing process of improvement. Based on user feedback, performance monitoring, and analytics, continuously work on enhancing Taskify. Here are a few ideas:

- **Feature Enhancements**: Add new features based on user needs, such as recurring tasks, sharing tasks with other users, or integrating task reminders.
- **Performance Improvements**: Optimize data queries, reduce app load time, and enhance caching to provide a better user experience.
- **Security Updates**: Always keep up with security best practices and updates. Ensure all dependencies are up-to-date and that security vulnerabilities are patched promptly.

Conclusion

Testing, debugging, and launching are the final yet pivotal stages of building an application. They ensure that your app not only works correctly but is also efficient, secure, and delivers a seamless experience to your users. By testing Taskify thoroughly, debugging any issues effectively, and ensuring secure and well-monitored deployment, you've now learned how to launch a complete, production-ready Firebase application.

These steps—though time-consuming—are critical to ensuring that Taskify is both reliable and enjoyable for your users. With a structured approach to testing, debugging, and launching, you can turn your ideas into successful, stable applications that users love to engage with.

Chapter 12: Conclusion — Your Firebase Journey Begins

Reflecting on What You've Learned

As we come to the end of this journey into Firebase, it's important to take a moment to reflect on everything you've learned. The past chapters have taken you through the full spectrum of Firebase services—from getting started with project setup, understanding core products like Realtime Database and Firestore, to implementing security, analytics, and cloud functions. This section is dedicated to revisiting some of those essential concepts, connecting the dots, and appreciating how Firebase helps simplify modern app development.

Firebase isn't just a backend service; it's a full ecosystem for building, deploying, and monitoring your applications. By utilizing its array of tools, developers can create high-quality, scalable apps quickly, while minimizing the hassle associated with traditional backend services. Firebase provides seamless integration between different aspects of the development cycle, which is what makes it such a popular choice among developers—especially those looking to bring their ideas to life without a deep focus on managing servers or infrastructure.

Firebase Authentication and User Management

One of the most critical aspects of any application is the ability to handle user management efficiently and securely. Firebase Authentication made it easy to set up user sign-up and login processes, enabling both email/password authentication and social logins. Reflect on how straightforward it was to add these features to your app, significantly reducing the need for complex server-side code.

For many developers, Firebase Authentication provides an intuitive API and a powerful way to manage identities. The value here goes beyond the time saved—it also means that developers don't have to worry about implementing complex encryption protocols or worrying about user data vulnerabilities. Firebase takes care of it all, giving you the tools to properly handle user information, implement security, and even easily integrate user session persistence.

It's easy to see how this impacts the overall user experience. Users of your app benefit from a smooth sign-up process, social login options that make things even easier, and a secure system they can trust. Firebase abstracts a lot of the headaches related to account management so that you can focus more on what really makes your app stand out.

Real-time Database and Firestore

Firebase's databases—Realtime Database and Firestore—played an important role in how we structured data. Each database had its advantages, and knowing when to use Realtime

Database versus Firestore is key. Realtime Database, as we learned, excels in real-time, low-latency data synchronization. This is perfect for chat applications or any scenario where data changes frequently and instantly across users.

Firestore, on the other hand, brought more flexibility, enhanced querying abilities, and a scalable structure. The document-based model of Firestore allowed us to build our data in a more organized way, making it an excellent choice for most modern applications. You also discovered how Firestore's strong integration with Firebase Security Rules gives fine-grained control over access and data operations.

Both databases are powerful and flexible, providing everything from simple read/write operations to more complex real-time features—all without needing to set up or maintain servers. As a developer, you have tools to fit both small prototypes and larger, production-ready applications.

Firebase Storage

Firebase Storage allowed us to manage rich media assets such as images and videos, giving users the ability to upload content to your application. Firebase Storage's integration with Cloud Security allowed us to implement stringent security rules, making sure that only authenticated users could upload and download assets.

When you think about user-generated content, Firebase Storage offers a straightforward approach to securely manage potentially large files. Many traditional backend systems would require you to use separate services for storing data and for authenticating users' access to that data. Firebase made it simple to combine all of these features into a coherent system, allowing you to integrate storage directly with your authentication system and to build seamless, user-driven experiences.

Cloud Functions for Scalability

Firebase Cloud Functions opened up a world of possibilities, giving us the ability to extend Firebase's capabilities with custom backend logic—all without managing servers. Writing and deploying your first Cloud Function illustrated the power of serverless computing, where you only needed to worry about the functionality and logic, leaving infrastructure worries behind.

By utilizing Cloud Functions, you built a layer that could act as a middleman between your Firebase services, creating webhook triggers and other event-driven solutions. This simplified the creation of complex workflows, allowing you to create efficient and reusable code that runs in response to events in your Firebase services.

Whether you were managing a payment process, triggering notifications, or processing uploaded files, Cloud Functions showcased how you could take Firebase projects to the next level. Without writing a full backend, you were able to create highly functional, automated features, directly integrated with your app's needs.

Hosting and Continuous Deployment

Firebase Hosting provided a way to quickly and securely deploy web applications. Deploying websites on Firebase Hosting showed us just how efficient Firebase could be, enabling us to push our changes in a matter of seconds while leveraging a global Content Delivery Network (CDN) for fast access across the world.

More than just deployment, Firebase Hosting integrated tightly with other Firebase services, allowing you to deliver a full web app connected to real-time backend features, with support for custom domains, SSL, and even built-in redirects. As we moved from local development to public deployments, it became apparent how valuable it is to have a hosting service that is fast, reliable, and easy to integrate with the rest of Firebase.

Security and Best Practices

The importance of securing our application cannot be understated, and Firebase helps developers focus on this aspect with detailed security rules for both databases and storage. You learned how to create rules that could prevent unauthorized access while allowing authenticated users to interact safely with the system.

The rules and best practices we discussed covered key topics such as validation, ensuring that data meets the requirements for your app, and authentication, verifying that only authorized users can perform certain actions. Firebase takes security seriously, offering guidance on writing effective rules and the tools to do it well. It's now your responsibility to continue to keep security at the forefront as you develop more sophisticated applications.

Security can sometimes feel like an afterthought in the app development process, but Firebase actively brings it front and center. Remember to leverage the Security Rules Simulator and to write rules that consider every potential use case. As your app scales, keeping these best practices in mind will pay dividends, both in terms of protecting your users and making development easier.

Analytics, Messaging, and User Engagement

One of the unique strengths of Firebase is how it enables developers to understand user behavior through Firebase Analytics. Integrating Firebase Analytics into your project provided insights into how users were interacting with your app—what features were being used, how often users returned, and what actions were taken most frequently.

These insights allowed us to make informed decisions about improving the app. And this data wasn't just for analysis; Firebase integrated it directly with Firebase Cloud Messaging, making it possible to send targeted push notifications based on user behavior. This created a dynamic relationship between analytics and user engagement, enabling deeper personalization and increased retention.

Firebase's Cloud Messaging service allowed us to send notifications that added genuine value to the user experience. By combining custom notifications with analytics, you could communicate meaningfully with your users, bringing them back to the app with tailored content and updates.

Push notifications, when used appropriately, can significantly boost engagement, and Firebase gave us all the tools we needed to do it right—from implementing basic notifications to configuring more advanced, interactive messages.

The Power of the Firebase Ecosystem

At its core, Firebase is about reducing the overhead associated with backend infrastructure while delivering a cohesive and integrated development experience. Each chapter in this book has shown how Firebase's individual services work together to create an ecosystem that covers every major part of the app lifecycle.

You started by setting up your environment and integrating Firebase into your app. From there, you learned how Firebase could handle authentication, database management, media storage, server-side logic, hosting, analytics, push notifications, and more—all from a single integrated platform. This breadth is what makes Firebase so appealing, especially for developers and teams that need to iterate quickly or release an MVP without investing heavily in backend infrastructure.

Firebase simplifies the development process, allowing developers to focus more on building the core features and unique aspects of their apps, rather than managing databases, servers, or user authentication. It's a toolkit designed to speed up development and improve the final product.

Moving Forward with Firebase

By now, you should feel empowered to take on even bigger challenges using Firebase. Whether you're planning to build a small hobby project, a startup idea, or an enterprise-level application, the tools you need are all at your disposal.

As with any development platform, there's always more to learn and new challenges to face, but you've established a strong foundation. Firebase is continuously evolving, adding new features and enhancing the existing ones to make app development as seamless as possible.

Take time to revisit the different sections of this book as you move forward with your projects. There are always new details to discover, especially when you apply them in practice. Practice and real-world experience are the keys to mastery, and Firebase provides ample opportunity for hands-on learning and iteration.

Conclusion

Reflecting on this journey, you've come a long way—from basic setup and project initiation to deploying and managing a complete, full-featured app. Firebase has not only given you the tools to build apps but also the insight into how those apps can thrive in the real world, through user engagement, data analysis, and secure, reliable infrastructure.

Your Firebase journey is just beginning. Each app you create, each function you implement, and each insight you gather will add to your knowledge and skills as a developer. Firebase is a partner in your app development journey, and its full potential unfolds the more you engage with its capabilities.

So, keep building, stay curious, and don't stop exploring the opportunities Firebase offers. There's a world of possibilities waiting, and now, you have the foundation and the confidence to create, innovate, and succeed with Firebase.

Next Steps for Firebase Development

Firebase provides a powerful set of tools, but mastery comes with exploration, iteration, and a continuous learning process. Now that you have a strong grasp of Firebase basics and have seen how all the pieces fit together, it's time to look at how you can deepen your understanding, build upon what you know, and continue to grow as a developer. This section will explore the next steps you can take to refine your skills, discover new ways of using Firebase, and begin contributing to the broader developer community.

Expand Your Knowledge with Advanced Firebase Features

You've learned the core Firebase services, including authentication, databases, cloud functions, and hosting. These features alone are enough to build a wide variety of applications, but Firebase offers additional advanced services that can elevate your projects even further.

1. Cloud Firestore Advanced Features

While we covered the basics of Firestore, there are a number of advanced capabilities that can be extremely useful for scaling applications. Consider learning about Firestore's **offline capabilities**. Firestore comes with robust support for offline data persistence, which allows users to continue using your app even when they lose connectivity. Understanding and configuring this feature can be essential for apps that need to function in unreliable network environments.

Firestore also supports **compound queries**, **array-contains** queries, and **indexing** to further enhance performance and efficiency. As your dataset grows in complexity, you'll find that making use of indexes and optimized queries will have a significant impact on your app's responsiveness and scalability.

Another area to explore is **Firestore triggers** in Cloud Functions. These triggers allow you to run server-side logic in response to changes in your Firestore data—whether it's when a document is created, updated, or deleted. This opens up opportunities for automation, such as sending notifications or transforming data in real-time.

2. Firebase ML Kit

Firebase's ML Kit integrates machine learning into your app without the need to have in-depth knowledge of the underlying models. You can start with the **on-device ML features**, which include text recognition, image labeling, face detection, and more. Imagine building an app that automatically labels images for your users, or an OCR (Optical Character

Recognition) scanner to digitize physical notes—ML Kit makes this possible with just a few lines of code.

If you have experience building custom ML models, you can also **deploy your own TensorFlow Lite models** through ML Kit. This means you can leverage Firebase to serve models for specialized use cases, allowing you to create highly customized machine learning applications with Firebase's infrastructure.

3. Remote Config and A/B Testing

Firebase Remote Config is another powerful tool for making your apps adaptable and personalizable without having to redeploy them. With Remote Config, you can modify the behavior and appearance of your app by defining key-value pairs. This is extremely helpful if you need to **personalize experiences for different users**, like presenting different offers, app themes, or user interface tweaks.

Remote Config works hand-in-hand with **Firebase A/B Testing** to provide data-driven decision making. You can run experiments, analyze user responses, and determine the optimal configurations for engaging and retaining your users. Understanding how to utilize Remote Config and A/B Testing will give you the confidence to iterate and improve your app over time, backed by data and without frequent deployments.

Build and Launch More Projects

The best way to solidify your Firebase skills is through hands-on practice. The more projects you build, the more familiar you'll become with the nuances of Firebase and with troubleshooting challenges that arise during development. Consider the following types of projects to apply what you've learned:

1. Build a Chat Application

Building a chat application is one of the most popular use cases for Firebase, and it makes extensive use of features like **Realtime Database**, **Firestore**, **Firebase Authentication**, and **Cloud Messaging**.

- **User Authentication**: Users should be able to create accounts, log in, and log out of the application.
- **Real-Time Messaging**: Leverage Firestore's real-time capabilities to create a seamless chat experience, where messages are instantly displayed for all participants.
- **Cloud Messaging**: Use Firebase Cloud Messaging to send notifications to users when they receive new messages.

Building a chat app will help you become more proficient with database structuring, real-time capabilities, and messaging—all while applying Firebase's core services in a practical way.

2. E-Commerce Application with Firebase Functions

Create an **e-commerce app** that allows users to browse products, add items to a shopping cart, and make purchases. This type of project will expose you to multiple Firebase features.

- **Firestore or Realtime Database**: Store product catalogs, user orders, and shopping cart items.
- **Firebase Authentication**: Handle user accounts for customers.
- **Cloud Functions**: Write server-side functions to handle order processing, payment integration (using third-party payment APIs), and transactional emails.
- **Firebase Storage**: Store images of products for your catalog.

This project will challenge you to integrate multiple services and design a scalable backend, while also keeping user experience in mind.

Leverage Firebase Extensions

Firebase Extensions are pre-packaged solutions that help you quickly add common functionalities to your app. Extensions take away the need to build certain features from scratch, and they are especially helpful if you are looking to integrate third-party services.

For instance:

- **Trigger Email**: Use this extension to automatically send emails in response to Firestore events. This can be useful for scenarios like sending a confirmation email after a user signs up or notifying users when their order has shipped.
- **Image Resizer**: Automatically resize uploaded images using Firebase Storage. This is useful for building content management systems or any application that needs to handle a lot of image uploads.

By experimenting with these extensions, you will learn more about how Firebase's ecosystem integrates with broader web functionalities and how you can quickly add robust features with minimal code.

Contribute to Open Source Projects

Firebase is widely used by the developer community, and there are numerous open source projects built on Firebase. Contributing to these projects is a great way to learn best practices from seasoned developers, understand how larger projects are architected, and gain experience collaborating in a team environment.

You can start by exploring GitHub to find Firebase projects and see if there are any **open issues** you can help resolve. Even contributing to **documentation** is an excellent way to start if you are new to open source. Over time, you'll gain confidence in contributing to the actual codebase, adding features, fixing bugs, and engaging with other developers.

Explore Firebase Integration with Other Google Services

Firebase is part of the Google Cloud Platform (GCP), which means it integrates seamlessly with other GCP services. Once you are comfortable with Firebase, consider integrating it with other services for enhanced functionality.

1. Google Cloud Storage and BigQuery

While **Firebase Storage** is great for app-specific file management, you might find that you need to scale up or analyze large datasets.

- **Google Cloud Storage** provides a more scalable option for storing large amounts of data that don't necessarily fit within Firebase Storage's limits. You can use Cloud Functions to move files between Firebase Storage and Cloud Storage.
- **BigQuery** is a powerful tool for analyzing large datasets. Firebase Analytics data can be exported directly to BigQuery, giving you the ability to run advanced SQL queries and uncover deeper insights into user behavior. You could even run machine learning algorithms on your BigQuery datasets for predictive analytics.

2. Cloud Pub/Sub and Machine Learning APIs

Firebase Cloud Messaging works well for notifications, but when dealing with larger-scale real-time streaming data, **Cloud Pub/Sub** can be a valuable addition. For instance, you could use Cloud Pub/Sub to handle events from multiple sources and then trigger Cloud Functions for processing and integration into your app.

You can also use Google's **pre-trained Machine Learning APIs**, like **Vision API** or **Natural Language API**, to add more advanced features to your Firebase app. Whether it's sentiment analysis of user feedback or image recognition, these APIs bring the power of machine learning to your project without having to build and train your own models.

Join the Firebase Community

Firebase has a large, active community of developers, which makes it easy to find support, share ideas, and stay updated on new features. Here are some ways to get involved:

- **Join Firebase Forums**: Participate in online forums such as Stack Overflow, the official Firebase Community, or Reddit. You can ask questions, share solutions, and learn from the experiences of others.
- **Attend Firebase Events**: Keep an eye out for events like Firebase Summit or local developer meetups. These events often include sessions by Firebase engineers and give insight into upcoming features.
- **Contribute Tutorials and Blog Posts**: Writing blog posts, creating tutorials, or recording video content can help you solidify your understanding while also helping others. Platforms like Medium, Dev.to, or YouTube are ideal for sharing your Firebase projects and insights.

Firebase Certifications

If you are considering a career in app development, adding Firebase certifications can provide a significant boost to your resume. Google offers several certification programs for developers. These certifications are proof of your skills and knowledge, and they can demonstrate to potential employers or clients that you have a comprehensive understanding of Firebase.

Preparing for certifications will encourage you to learn Firebase features in depth and understand best practices across the different services it offers. This is also an opportunity to practice under real-world scenarios and further enhance your expertise.

Conclusion

Firebase is a fantastic platform for both new and experienced developers. It brings a variety of features under one roof and significantly reduces the complexity of app development. From rapid prototyping and MVP creation to scaling applications that serve thousands or even millions of users, Firebase is a reliable companion.

As you move forward, continue to expand your knowledge of advanced features, experiment with new projects, and contribute to the community. Learn about integrating Firebase with other GCP services, leverage Firebase Extensions for common use cases, and explore advanced analytics and machine learning features.

The journey doesn't end here—it's only the beginning. The skills you've gained through learning Firebase will allow you to build innovative and successful apps. Whether you are building for fun, for business, or as part of a larger development team, Firebase offers you the flexibility, power, and ease of use that few other platforms can match.

The world of app development is filled with endless possibilities, and Firebase equips you with the tools you need to create, innovate, and inspire. Continue learning, stay curious, and embrace the exciting opportunities ahead. Your Firebase journey has only just begun, and the future is bright.

Final Thoughts and Encouragement

The journey through Firebase that you've undertaken is both a beginning and an opportunity to see the vast possibilities that modern app development holds. This concluding section is about encouraging you to look beyond the tools you've learned, to dive deeper into the community and culture of software development, and to nurture the confidence required to launch your own projects. Firebase provides you with more than just technical capabilities; it serves as a gateway to creative problem solving, collaboration, and, ultimately, innovation.

Firebase as an Enabler of Creativity

Firebase's suite of tools is designed to streamline development, allowing you to focus on what makes your app unique rather than worrying about infrastructure. Throughout this book, we've discussed how Firebase allows you to handle authentication, database management, serverless functions, and much more—all without the traditional overhead of server management.

This level of abstraction isn't merely about saving time; it's about allowing your creativity to flourish. When you don't have to worry about managing databases or building backends from scratch, you can devote your mental energy to creating truly engaging user experiences. Imagine all the time saved, and consider how those hours can be spent brainstorming innovative features or optimizing the user journey.

Breaking the Barriers to App Development

Many aspiring developers are often intimidated by the prospect of app development, largely due to the sheer volume of skills needed—from backend server management to security practices. Firebase takes away much of this complexity, acting as a **one-stop solution** for most of the backend needs you would have as a developer. Whether you're a solo developer, a startup founder, or someone working on their first app, Firebase eliminates a lot of the barriers, so you can start building right away.

Firebase's integration with other Google services means you have an ever-growing set of capabilities at your fingertips. As a developer, the only limits to what you can create are your imagination and your willingness to explore the features offered by this platform. Firebase can help take an idea from concept to completion, turning a once daunting prospect into an attainable goal.

Nurturing a Developer's Mindset

Firebase provides tools and infrastructure, but ultimately, success in app development lies in nurturing the right mindset. Here are some ways to continue developing as a creator:

1. Embrace Problem Solving

App development is fundamentally about problem-solving. With Firebase, many of the common problems—such as handling authentication, database integration, or cloud storage—are solved for you. But each application you create will bring its own unique challenges. Learn to view these challenges not as obstacles but as opportunities for growth.

Whether you're trying to design an efficient data structure for Firestore or deciding on the best strategy for using Firebase Analytics, see every decision as a chance to learn. Often, there are multiple solutions to a given problem, each with trade-offs. Firebase's flexibility allows you to experiment with different approaches, helping you to develop a deeper understanding of best practices and when to apply them.

2. Collaboration and Learning from Others

The Firebase community is vast and welcoming. Don't be afraid to share your ideas, ask questions, and even help others when you can. One of the best ways to learn is by teaching. When you encounter an issue that you manage to solve, share your solution on forums like **Stack Overflow, Reddit**, or other Firebase-specific communities. This not only helps others but also solidifies your understanding.

Collaboration can also mean building something alongside other developers. Participate in a **hackathon** or join an open-source project that uses Firebase. Real-world experience will teach you things no book or tutorial can. Working with others will expose you to different approaches, new tools, and, most importantly, the practice of writing maintainable code that others can easily understand.

3. Build a Portfolio of Projects

Building a portfolio of Firebase projects isn't just a way to get a job or impress clients—it's a practical way to improve your skills. Every project you work on will bring new challenges and expand your understanding. Don't be afraid to start small: even a **simple to-do list app** is valuable if it teaches you about proper data structuring in Firestore or helps you get comfortable with Firebase Authentication.

Once you feel comfortable, move on to more complex projects like **chat applications**, **e-commerce stores**, or **social media apps**. These projects will help you practice integrating multiple Firebase services, including Realtime Database, Firebase Storage, and Cloud Messaging. As you progress, think about how you can utilize Firebase's advanced features such as **Cloud Functions**, **Remote Config**, and **Analytics** to build a more sophisticated app.

Developing for Scalability

One of Firebase's most valuable offerings is the ability to grow alongside your app. As your user base grows, the challenges you face will change. Scalability issues may arise, requiring optimizations that you perhaps didn't consider during initial development. This is where Firebase's features shine.

1. Firestore Indexing and Data Structuring

As you work on larger projects, the importance of data structuring in **Firestore** becomes evident. If you're planning for an app that serves thousands—or even millions—of users, you need to be deliberate about how your data is structured, indexed, and accessed. Experiment with using **sharded counters** to track likes on a post, or **denormalize data** where necessary to reduce the number of reads per query.

Consider creating **compound queries** and **indexes** for frequently used fields, and explore how Firestore charges for reads, writes, and storage. Understanding these details will make your applications more efficient and save you unexpected costs.

2. Firebase Hosting for High Traffic

Firebase Hosting is built to handle large amounts of traffic, with caching and a Content Delivery Network (CDN) integrated by default. However, as you grow, you may need to look into **customizing caching headers**, optimizing asset delivery, and using **Firebase Cloud Functions** for dynamic content generation. Learning about these optimizations will help you ensure that your app delivers a smooth experience to all users, no matter where they are in the world.

3. Security and Maintenance

Securing your app should always be a priority, but it becomes even more crucial as your user base grows. Take time to revisit **Firebase Security Rules** regularly, especially after adding new features. Use **Firebase's Emulator Suite** to test your security rules thoroughly before deploying changes to production.

Consider creating **regular maintenance schedules** for your apps, where you monitor the Firebase console for unexpected increases in database usage, bandwidth, or other costs. Staying proactive will help you prevent issues before they affect users and maintain a positive user experience.

Keep Innovating and Exploring

Firebase will continue to evolve as technology advances, and staying curious is crucial for success in this field. Keep exploring **new Firebase features** as they are introduced. For instance, Firebase frequently adds **beta features** that you can experiment with in your projects.

Don't be afraid to innovate and try unconventional approaches. Perhaps you could use **Firebase ML Kit** to add image labeling to a photo-sharing app or integrate **Google Assistant** into an app for voice interactions. Firebase gives you a lot of flexibility, and the only way to find its limits is by pushing them.

Join Beta Programs

Firebase is continuously adding new features and improvements, many of which are available through beta programs. Signing up for these programs is an excellent way to stay ahead of the curve, experiment with new technologies, and provide valuable feedback to the Firebase team. It's also an exciting way to be part of the evolution of a platform that's shaping the future of app development.

Turning Your Knowledge into Value

The ultimate goal of learning Firebase, or any development platform, is to create applications that add value—either for users, clients, or your own endeavors. Firebase provides a powerful, scalable infrastructure, but it's up to you to determine how best to leverage it for impact.

1. Build Apps That Solve Problems

Focus on building applications that solve real problems for users. This might mean developing a mobile app that helps **organize daily tasks**, a platform for **connecting local communities**, or a tool that helps **businesses manage their workflow** more efficiently. Firebase allows you to iterate quickly, enabling you to get your solutions to market faster and refine them based on user feedback.

Remember that Firebase isn't just for individual projects; it's powerful enough to serve as the backend for **commercial and enterprise-grade applications**. If you're working for clients or a startup, look at how Firebase can reduce their infrastructure costs and speed up the time it takes to bring products to market.

2. Entrepreneurial Ventures

Firebase can be a great asset if you're interested in entrepreneurship. With Firebase, you can quickly build a prototype or a minimum viable product (MVP) and test it in the market.

This capability can dramatically lower the barrier to entry for aspiring entrepreneurs who may not have the resources to set up their own infrastructure.

The lean approach of launching quickly and iterating based on user feedback is exactly what Firebase was designed for. You can validate your business ideas faster, while maintaining the flexibility to pivot when necessary. Whether you're building a social networking app, a marketplace, or an e-learning platform, Firebase is there to support you through your entrepreneurial journey.

Final Words of Encouragement

The journey into Firebase development is filled with opportunities to learn, grow, and innovate. The tools you've learned to use in this book are just the beginning of what's possible with Firebase. As technology continues to advance, and as Firebase continues to evolve, you will have the opportunity to create even more powerful and impactful applications.

Never stop learning. Technologies will change, best practices will shift, and new tools will emerge. Firebase, as part of Google Cloud, will be at the forefront of many exciting innovations, and keeping your skills up-to-date will keep you ready for whatever comes next. Be confident in the knowledge that the skills you've developed here can grow with you into the future of app development.

You've already accomplished so much, from setting up your first Firebase project to building and deploying an entire app. This process hasn't just been about understanding the features of a powerful platform—it's also been about learning to think like a developer, to troubleshoot, iterate, and create. Hold onto that mindset, and take it with you as you move forward into new challenges, new projects, and new opportunities.

Your journey with Firebase is just beginning, and there's no limit to what you can create. Keep building, keep exploring, and stay passionate about solving problems through technology. Every application you create makes you a better developer, every mistake you make teaches you something new, and every time you help someone else, you contribute to a wider community of creators.

Remember, Firebase is more than a tool; it's a partner in your creative journey. Take what you've learned, and build something that matters. Your skills, imagination, and dedication are the keys to a world of possibility—go out there, and bring your ideas to life.

Chapter 13: Appendices

Glossary of Firebase Terms

Firebase is a robust platform that provides a variety of services and tools designed to help developers build high-quality apps. This glossary provides definitions and explanations of key Firebase terms that are essential for understanding how to use Firebase effectively in your projects. As you progress with Firebase, you'll encounter a range of concepts, services, and terminology that can sometimes be overwhelming. This glossary is intended as a reference to help clarify these terms and ensure that you are comfortable navigating the Firebase ecosystem.

Authentication

Firebase Authentication is a service that provides easy-to-use authentication methods, such as email and password sign-in, phone authentication, and integration with third-party providers like Google, Facebook, and Twitter. It is a critical component for many apps that need to verify the identity of their users. Authentication helps you ensure that users can securely access your app while also streamlining the user experience.

Firebase Realtime Database

The Firebase Realtime Database is a cloud-hosted NoSQL database that allows developers to store and sync data in real time across all clients. It is structured as a large JSON tree, which makes it suitable for applications that need frequent updates or live data, such as messaging apps or collaborative tools. Changes in the database are instantly reflected across all connected clients.

Key features of the Realtime Database include offline support, real-time synchronization, and the ability to set fine-grained security rules for controlling read and write access to data. It is particularly useful for scenarios that require low latency and instantaneous updates.

Firestore (Cloud Firestore)

Firestore is Firebase's next-generation cloud-hosted NoSQL database. It offers a more flexible and scalable solution compared to the Realtime Database. Unlike the Realtime Database, which is structured as a single JSON tree, Firestore uses documents and collections to store data, allowing for more complex and organized data models.

Firestore also provides advanced querying capabilities, better scalability, and more intuitive security rules. It is a good choice for applications that require more structured and sophisticated data handling, such as e-commerce platforms or content management systems.

Firebase Storage

Firebase Storage is used for storing and serving large binary objects, such as photos, videos, and other user-generated content. Firebase Storage is backed by Google Cloud Storage, offering reliable and secure file storage. With Firebase SDKs, developers can easily upload files from clients, manage file metadata, and download files when needed.

Firebase Storage is commonly used in applications that need to manage user files, such as social media platforms or image-sharing apps. It is integrated with Firebase Authentication, allowing for secure file access based on user permissions.

Cloud Functions

Cloud Functions is a serverless solution that lets you run backend code in response to events triggered by Firebase features or HTTPS requests. You can use Cloud Functions to add backend logic without needing to manage your own servers. This is useful for implementing features like sending welcome emails, processing payments, or listening for changes in the database.

Cloud Functions can be triggered by Firebase Authentication events, Realtime Database changes, Firestore changes, and other Firebase services. This makes it a powerful tool for extending the functionality of your app in response to user interactions or system events.

Firebase Hosting

Firebase Hosting is a fully managed hosting service for static and dynamic content. It is often used to host web applications, static websites, and other assets that are part of a Firebase project. Firebase Hosting integrates seamlessly with other Firebase services, such as Cloud Functions and Firestore, making it an ideal choice for developers who want a streamlined development workflow.

Firebase Hosting provides easy deployment, custom domain support, and SSL certificates by default, ensuring that your site is secure and accessible to users around the world.

Firebase Analytics

Firebase Analytics is a free app measurement solution that provides insights into user engagement and behavior. It helps you understand how users interact with your app, which features are popular, and where users may be encountering issues. Firebase Analytics is integrated with other Firebase services, allowing you to track user interactions and link them to specific actions, such as in-app purchases or custom events.

Firebase Analytics automatically collects certain events, such as app installs and user demographics, but you can also define custom events to track specific user actions. These insights can help you make data-driven decisions to improve your app.

Firebase Cloud Messaging (FCM)

Firebase Cloud Messaging (FCM) is a cross-platform messaging solution that allows you to send notifications and messages to users. FCM is widely used for sending push notifications, which can help engage users and provide timely information. You can use FCM to send messages to individual devices, user segments, or topic-based subscriptions.

FCM supports different types of messages, including data messages and notification messages. Data messages are handled by the app itself, while notification messages are handled by the system, making FCM a flexible tool for app communication.

Firebase Security Rules

Firebase Security Rules are used to control access to your Firebase data, including Realtime Database, Firestore, and Storage. Security rules define who can read or write data based on various conditions, such as authentication status or user roles. Writing effective security rules is critical for keeping your data secure and preventing unauthorized access.

For example, you can create rules that allow only authenticated users to write to certain parts of your database, or rules that grant specific permissions based on user roles. Firebase provides a test suite for validating your security rules, helping you ensure that your rules are correctly implemented.

Firebase App Distribution

Firebase App Distribution is a service that helps you distribute pre-release versions of your app to testers. It allows you to manage your testing groups, distribute new builds easily, and gather feedback from testers. App Distribution is useful for ensuring that your app is thoroughly tested before launching to production.

The integration with Firebase Crashlytics also allows you to monitor crashes and issues reported by testers, helping you identify and fix bugs early in the development process.

Firebase Crashlytics

Firebase Crashlytics is a crash reporting tool that helps you track, prioritize, and fix stability issues in your app. It provides real-time insights into crashes and errors, allowing you to quickly understand the root cause of issues. Crashlytics is integrated with Firebase Analytics, enabling you to see how crashes impact user experience.

Crashlytics groups similar crashes together and provides detailed stack traces, which makes debugging faster and more efficient. This is an essential tool for maintaining a high-quality app experience.

Firebase Test Lab

Firebase Test Lab is a cloud-based testing infrastructure that allows you to test your app across a variety of real devices and configurations. It supports both Android and iOS apps, and you can run automated tests to identify issues related to device compatibility, performance, and usability.

Test Lab provides a comprehensive test report, including screenshots, logs, and video recordings, helping you understand how your app behaves under different scenarios. This is particularly useful for ensuring that your app works consistently across a wide range of devices.

Firebase Remote Config

Firebase Remote Config is a cloud service that allows you to dynamically configure and personalize your app for different user segments. With Remote Config, you can change the appearance and behavior of your app without requiring an update to the app itself. This is useful for A/B testing, feature flagging, and customizing the user experience based on real-time conditions.

For example, you can use Remote Config to show different content to users based on their location or engagement level. Remote Config parameters are cached on the user's device, ensuring that changes are applied smoothly.

Firebase Dynamic Links

Firebase Dynamic Links are deep links that work across platforms and persist even if the user needs to install the app first. Dynamic Links help create a seamless user experience by guiding users to specific content within your app, whether they already have the app installed or not. They are commonly used for referral programs, marketing campaigns, and re-engagement initiatives.

Dynamic Links can also be used to track the effectiveness of your marketing campaigns by providing insights into how users are interacting with your links.

Firebase Predictions

Firebase Predictions is a machine learning feature that uses analytics data to make predictions about user behavior. Predictions can help you identify users who are likely to churn, spend money, or engage with your app. You can use these insights to create targeted marketing campaigns or customize the user experience for different segments.

Predictions are integrated with other Firebase services, such as Remote Config and Notifications, allowing you to act on these predictions automatically and optimize the experience for different user groups.

Firebase In-App Messaging

Firebase In-App Messaging is a service that helps you engage your app users by sending targeted, contextual messages within the app itself. It is often used to guide users through the app, promote new features, or encourage certain actions. In-App Messaging allows you to create visually appealing messages, including banners, modals, and cards, that can be triggered based on user behavior.

For example, you can use In-App Messaging to highlight a new feature to users who haven't discovered it yet, or to prompt users to complete a certain action, such as signing up for an account.

Firebase Extensions

Firebase Extensions are pre-packaged solutions that help you quickly add common functionality to your app, such as translating text, resizing images, or integrating third-party services. Extensions are built on top of Firebase services and are easy to install and configure, allowing you to extend your app's capabilities without writing complex code.

Firebase Extensions save you time by providing ready-made solutions for common problems, and they can be customized to fit the specific needs of your app. Examples include sending emails via SendGrid, resizing images, and keeping Firestore in sync with Algolia.

Google Cloud Integration

Firebase is tightly integrated with Google Cloud, allowing you to leverage a wide range of additional services for your app. You can use Google Cloud's AI, machine learning, big data, and storage solutions alongside Firebase, providing a powerful toolkit for scaling and enhancing your app.

The integration between Firebase and Google Cloud allows for seamless data sharing, enabling you to create complex backend logic and data analysis workflows. For example, you can use Google BigQuery to analyze Firebase Analytics data and gain deeper insights into user behavior.

Firebase Emulator Suite

The Firebase Emulator Suite is a set of local emulators that allow you to develop and test Firebase apps in an offline environment. The Emulator Suite includes emulators for Firestore, Realtime Database, Cloud Functions, Hosting, and other Firebase services, making it easier to test your app without making changes to your live data.

The Emulator Suite is particularly useful for writing and testing security rules, as it allows you to simulate different access scenarios and verify that your rules are working as expected. It also provides a safe environment to test Cloud Functions before deploying them to production.

Firebase SDK

The Firebase SDK (Software Development Kit) is a collection of tools and libraries that allow you to integrate Firebase services into your mobile and web applications. Firebase SDKs are available for a variety of platforms, including Android, iOS, and JavaScript, making it easy to add features like authentication, analytics, and database access to your app.

The Firebase SDK is regularly updated with new features and improvements, ensuring that developers have access to the latest tools for building high-quality apps. It also includes support for offline data handling, allowing your app to continue working even when the user is not connected to the internet.

Firebase Console

The Firebase Console is a web-based management interface that provides access to all of Firebase's services and tools. You can use the console to create and manage Firebase projects, configure services, view analytics data, set up authentication, deploy hosting, and much more.

The Firebase Console also includes a powerful set of debugging and testing tools, such as the Firebase DebugView and Test Lab, which help you ensure that your app is working correctly. The console is the central hub for managing your Firebase projects and tracking the success of your app.

Resources for Further Learning

Firebase is a versatile platform with a range of services that can help developers create robust, scalable applications. To effectively use Firebase, it's important to continually explore and understand the latest developments, tools, and community resources. This section provides a comprehensive guide to resources that can further your understanding of Firebase and help you stay up-to-date with the evolving Firebase ecosystem. From official documentation to community tutorials and advanced tools, you will find a variety of options here to help you grow as a Firebase developer.

Official Documentation

The official Firebase documentation is the most reliable and comprehensive resource for learning Firebase. The Firebase team provides detailed documentation for each of its services, covering everything from the basics to advanced usage. The documentation includes code samples, guides, and conceptual overviews that make it easy to get started or dive deeper into specific Firebase features.

- **Firebase Documentation**: https://firebase.google.com/docs
- **API References**: Firebase's API references offer detailed information about the classes, methods, and properties available for each Firebase SDK. This is especially useful when you want to understand how to use a specific method or need details about its parameters.

The official guides and references are regularly updated with new features and best practices. The platform also offers tutorials that walk you through setting up different services, such as Authentication, Firestore, and Cloud Messaging.

Firebase YouTube Channel

The Firebase YouTube channel is another excellent resource for learning Firebase. It includes videos that explain different Firebase features, tutorials, and live coding sessions. The Firebase team frequently uploads new content to help developers stay informed about updates and learn new skills.

Key playlists to consider include:

- **Firebase Release Notes**: Regular video updates highlighting new features, changes, and improvements.
- **Firebase Tips & Tricks**: This series provides useful tips for maximizing the potential of Firebase in your projects.
- **Live Coding Sessions**: Firebase engineers and guest speakers conduct live coding sessions that showcase real-world implementations of Firebase tools.

Firebase YouTube Channel: https://www.youtube.com/firebase

Firebase Blog

The Firebase Blog is a great resource for staying up-to-date with the latest developments. The blog features announcements, success stories, feature highlights, and tutorials. It's a great way to understand how Firebase is being used in real-world projects and learn about upcoming features that could impact your application development.

The blog covers a wide range of topics, such as:

- **Feature Announcements**: New product releases, updates to Firebase services, and feature deprecations.
- **Case Studies**: Learn how developers and companies are using Firebase to solve real-world problems.
- **Best Practices**: Articles that provide insights into optimizing Firebase services for your application.

Firebase Blog: https://firebase.googleblog.com

Firebase Community and Forums

Engaging with the Firebase community can help you solve problems, discover new ways to use Firebase, and keep you motivated on your development journey. Below are some key places where Firebase developers gather to discuss issues and share knowledge:

- **Stack Overflow**: Firebase has an active presence on Stack Overflow, where developers can ask questions and receive answers from other Firebase users or even Firebase engineers. The community is quick to respond, and many common questions already have solutions available. Make sure to tag your questions with "firebase" to reach the relevant audience.
    - Firebase Stack Overflow
- **Reddit**: The Firebase subreddit is a great community space where developers share news, discuss updates, and seek help with issues. It's a useful resource for informal discussion and connecting with others who use Firebase.
    - Firebase Subreddit
- **Firebase Slack and Discord Groups**: There are also several Slack and Discord communities dedicated to Firebase. These groups often host live discussions, help sessions, and collaborative problem-solving. Search for Firebase-related channels to find groups that may interest you.

Online Learning Platforms

If you prefer structured courses, many online platforms offer Firebase-specific tutorials and courses that range from beginner to advanced levels. Here are some platforms where you can find high-quality Firebase learning material:

- **Udemy**: Udemy has a wide range of Firebase courses that cover different services, such as Authentication, Realtime Database, and Firestore. These courses are often taught by experienced developers who provide a hands-on approach to Firebase.
    - Example Course: "Firebase Firestore for Android Development" – covers the integration of Firestore with Android applications.
- **Coursera**: Firebase courses on Coursera are typically offered in collaboration with universities or leading companies. These courses provide a deep dive into the technical aspects of Firebase, as well as its practical applications in app development.
    - Example Course: "Developing Cloud Applications with Firebase" – focuses on using Firebase to build scalable cloud applications.
- **Pluralsight**: Pluralsight is an excellent resource for developers looking to enhance their Firebase skills. It offers courses tailored for different expertise levels, from beginner to advanced.
    - Example Course: "Firebase Fundamentals" – a great starting point for developers new to Firebase.

GitHub Repositories and Open Source Projects

One of the best ways to learn is by exploring open-source projects on GitHub. There are many projects that use Firebase, and studying these can help you understand how Firebase can be applied in real-world applications. Below are some useful GitHub resources:

- **Firebase GitHub Organization**: The official Firebase GitHub organization contains SDKs, sample projects, and tools for different platforms. It is a great place to explore how Firebase is implemented and see practical use cases.
    - Firebase GitHub Organization
- **Sample Projects**: The Firebase team and the community maintain a variety of sample projects that illustrate different aspects of Firebase, such as Authentication, Firestore, and Cloud Functions. Exploring these projects is a great way to see Firebase in action.
    - Firebase Samples: A repository containing quickstart samples for Firebase.
- **Open-Source Projects Using Firebase**: Searching GitHub for projects tagged with "firebase" can yield a wealth of applications using Firebase. These projects cover different platforms, such as Android, iOS, and web, and can provide inspiration for your own work.

Firebase Tools and Utilities

There are several tools and utilities that can help you work more efficiently with Firebase. Some of these tools are official, while others are developed by the community to fill specific needs:

- **Firebase CLI**: The Firebase CLI is an official command-line tool that allows you to interact with Firebase services directly from your terminal. You can use the CLI to deploy hosting, configure Cloud Functions, manage Firestore rules, and much more.

Installation Command:
sh
Copy code
```
npm install -g firebase-tools
```

  o

Common Commands:
sh
Copy code
```
firebase login          # Log in to Firebase

firebase init hosting   # Initialize Firebase Hosting

firebase deploy         # Deploy your Firebase services
```

  o
- **Firebase Emulator Suite**: This suite of tools allows you to emulate Firebase services locally, such as Firestore, Realtime Database, Authentication, and Cloud Functions. The Emulator Suite is an essential tool for testing and debugging your Firebase application before deploying it to production.
- **Firefoo**: Firefoo is a desktop application that provides a graphical user interface for interacting with Firebase services like Firestore. It allows you to easily browse, query, and edit data without needing to use the Firebase console or write custom queries.
- **Firebase Admin SDK**: The Admin SDK allows developers to interact with Firebase services from a backend environment. It's particularly useful for managing users, accessing databases securely, and integrating Firebase with other backend services.

Books and Reading Material

Books provide a deeper exploration of Firebase, including theoretical concepts, architecture, and real-world scenarios. Here are some books that you may find helpful:

- **"Firebase Essentials"** by David Martin: This book is designed for developers who are new to Firebase. It provides an overview of all the major Firebase services, including Authentication, Firestore, and Cloud Functions, along with hands-on examples and best practices.
- **"Building Mobile Apps with Firebase"** by Ethan Holmes: This book dives into how to build mobile applications using Firebase. It covers topics like Authentication, Realtime Database, Firestore, and Analytics, and includes sample projects to demonstrate these features in action.
- **"Firebase Cookbook"** by Richard Rose: This book is a collection of practical recipes for implementing Firebase in your projects. It includes solutions to common problems developers face when working with Firebase and provides guidance on topics such

as managing user authentication, implementing security rules, and using Firebase Hosting.

Firebase Meetups and Conferences

Attending Firebase meetups and conferences is a great way to learn directly from experts, network with other developers, and see how Firebase is being used across different industries. Here are some options:

- **Firebase Summit**: Firebase Summit is an annual conference organized by Google. It features talks from Firebase engineers, workshops, and hands-on labs to help you learn about new features and best practices.
- **Google I/O**: Google I/O often includes sessions dedicated to Firebase. It's a fantastic opportunity to see live demos, attend technical sessions, and meet the engineers who build Firebase.
- **Local Meetups**: Firebase meetups are held around the world and are usually organized by local developer groups. These meetups provide an opportunity to learn from other developers, discuss challenges, and share solutions.

You can find meetups through platforms like Meetup.com or by searching for Firebase-focused groups in your area. Attending these events can help you build a network of Firebase developers, which can be invaluable when facing challenges or seeking feedback on your projects.

Firebase Podcasts and Newsletters

If you prefer learning through audio content or reading curated information, Firebase podcasts and newsletters can be a great source of insights and updates:

- **Firebase Podcast**: The official Firebase Podcast features interviews with Firebase engineers and discussions about new features, use cases, and best practices. It's a great way to stay informed while commuting or exercising.
- **Google Cloud Platform Podcast**: Firebase-related topics are often covered in the Google Cloud Platform Podcast. This podcast provides insights into Google Cloud services and how Firebase integrates with them.
- **Firebase Newsletter**: The Firebase team sends out a newsletter periodically that includes information about new features, upcoming events, and notable updates. Subscribing to the newsletter ensures you won't miss any important announcements.

Firebase Newsletter Signup: https://firebase.google.com/community/newsletter

- **Weekly Firebase**: Weekly Firebase is an independent newsletter that curates articles, tutorials, and news related to Firebase. It provides a great summary of what's happening in the Firebase community, saving you time by collecting the most relevant information in one place.

Contributing to Firebase

Finally, one of the best ways to learn about Firebase is by contributing to it. Firebase is an open platform, and there are many ways you can contribute:

- **Contributing to Firebase Repositories**: The Firebase GitHub repositories are open for contributions. If you find a bug, consider submitting an issue or a pull request to help improve the SDKs.
- **Writing Articles or Tutorials**: Sharing your knowledge with others is a great way to solidify your understanding. Consider writing articles or creating tutorials on your blog, Medium, or other platforms to help other developers learn Firebase.
- **Answering Questions on Stack Overflow**: Participating in the Firebase tag on Stack Overflow helps others solve problems and can also deepen your understanding of Firebase. As you answer questions, you'll likely learn new things and encounter edge cases you hadn't previously considered.
- **Speaking at Meetups or Conferences**: If you've built something interesting with Firebase, consider sharing your experience at a local meetup or conference. This will not only help others learn from your journey but also allow you to get feedback and recognition within the developer community.

Conclusion

The journey to mastering Firebase doesn't stop at learning the basics; it requires staying updated with new features, understanding the latest best practices, and engaging with the community. By leveraging these resources—official documentation, video content, online courses, open-source projects, tools, meetups, and contributing back—you can continue to grow as a Firebase developer.

Remember, Firebase is constantly evolving, and by keeping your skills sharp, you can take full advantage of all the features that Firebase has to offer, ensuring that your applications are cutting-edge, scalable, and provide the best possible user experience.

Sample Projects and Code Snippets

Exploring sample projects and working through code snippets are essential practices for understanding how to use Firebase effectively in real-world scenarios. This section provides a collection of detailed projects and useful code snippets designed to demonstrate different aspects of Firebase, from authentication to database management, cloud functions, and beyond. Each example is presented with a clear focus on helping you understand how Firebase integrates with other technologies and can be adapted for your own projects.

Sample Project 1: Firebase Authentication and Firestore Integration

Project   **Overview**
In this sample project, we will create a simple user management system using Firebase Authentication and Firestore. Users can sign up, log in, and manage their profiles. All user information will be stored in Firestore, allowing for real-time updates and scalability.

Project Setup

- **Step 1: Set Up Firebase Project**
  Start by creating a new Firebase project through the Firebase Console. Enable **Authentication** and **Firestore Database** services.
- **Step 2: Enable Firebase Authentication**
  We will use email and password authentication for this project. In the Firebase Console, navigate to the Authentication section and enable **Email/Password** as a sign-in method.
- **Step 3: Set Up Firestore Database**
  Navigate to the Firestore Database section and create a new collection called `users` to store user information. The structure of each document will include fields like `name`, `email`, `createdAt`, and `userId`.

Code Example: User Signup and Profile Management

```
// Import Firebase libraries
import firebase from 'firebase/app';
import 'firebase/auth';
import 'firebase/firestore';


// Firebase configuration (replace with your project's config object)
const firebaseConfig = {
  apiKey: "YOUR_API_KEY",
  authDomain: "YOUR_AUTH_DOMAIN",
  projectId: "YOUR_PROJECT_ID",
  storageBucket: "YOUR_STORAGE_BUCKET",
  messagingSenderId: "YOUR_MESSAGING_SENDER_ID",
  appId: "YOUR_APP_ID"
};


// Initialize Firebase
```

```javascript
firebase.initializeApp(firebaseConfig);

const auth = firebase.auth();

const db = firebase.firestore();


// Signup function

const signUp = async (email, password, name) => {
  try {
    const userCredential = await auth.createUserWithEmailAndPassword(email, password);

    const userId = userCredential.user.uid;


    // Save user profile in Firestore
    await db.collection('users').doc(userId).set({
      name: name,
      email: email,
      createdAt: firebase.firestore.FieldValue.serverTimestamp(),
      userId: userId
    });


    console.log("User signed up and profile saved in Firestore");
  } catch (error) {
    console.error("Error signing up: ", error.message);
  }
};
```

```
// Example usage

signUp('testuser@example.com', 'password123', 'Test User');
```

Explanation
In this code snippet, we initialize Firebase using the provided configuration, and then we create a signUp function that handles user registration. The function uses **Firebase Authentication** to create a new user and **Firestore** to store the user profile information. This integration ensures that user data is well-organized and can be easily managed.

Sample Project 2: Real-Time Chat Application

Project   **Overview**
In this project, we will build a real-time chat application using **Firebase Realtime Database**. The app will allow multiple users to exchange messages in real time, and we will leverage Firebase's real-time syncing capabilities to keep all clients updated instantaneously.

Project Setup

- **Step 1: Set Up Firebase Project**
  Create a new Firebase project and enable the **Realtime Database** service.
- **Step 2: Set Up Realtime Database**
  In the Firebase Console, navigate to the Realtime Database section and create a new database. Set the database rules to allow read and write access to authenticated users:

```
{
  "rules": {
    ".read": "auth != null",
    ".write": "auth != null"
  }
}
```

- **Step 3: Implement Chat Functionality**
  Create a simple frontend where users can send and receive messages. We will use JavaScript to interact with Firebase and update the chat UI in real time.

Code Example: Sending and Receiving Messages

```javascript
// Firebase initialization (use your config)
firebase.initializeApp(firebaseConfig);
const database = firebase.database();
const messagesRef = database.ref('messages');

// Function to send a message
const sendMessage = (userId, message) => {
  messagesRef.push({
    userId: userId,
    message: message,
    timestamp: firebase.database.ServerValue.TIMESTAMP
  });
};

// Function to listen for new messages
messagesRef.on('child_added', (snapshot) => {
  const messageData = snapshot.val();
  console.log(`[${new Date(messageData.timestamp).toLocaleTimeString()}] ${messageData.userId}: ${messageData.message}`);
});

// Example usage
sendMessage('user_123', 'Hello, Firebase!');
```

Explanation

In this example, we define a sendMessage function that pushes a new message to the messages reference in the Realtime Database. We use child_added to listen for new messages, ensuring that all connected clients receive updates in real time. The **ServerValue.TIMESTAMP** is used to keep track of when each message was sent.

Sample Project 3: Firebase Storage for User-Generated Content

Project **Overview**

In this project, we will integrate **Firebase Storage** to allow users to upload images to our app. This feature is common in social media or content-sharing applications where users need to manage photos or other media.

Project Setup

- **Step 1: Set Up Firebase Project**
  Create a new Firebase project and enable **Firebase Storage**.
- **Step 2: Configure Storage Rules**
  Configure the storage rules to allow authenticated users to upload and download images. The following rules allow only authenticated users to write and read their own images:

```
service firebase.storage {
  match /b/{bucket}/o {
    match /images/{userId}/{imageId} {
      allow read, write: if request.auth != null && request.auth.uid == userId;
    }
  }
}
```

Code Example: Uploading Images to Firebase Storage

```
// Firebase initialization (use your config)
```

```javascript
firebase.initializeApp(firebaseConfig);

const storage = firebase.storage();


// Function to upload an image

const uploadImage = async (file, userId) => {

  try {

    const storageRef = storage.ref();

    const imageRef = storageRef.child(`images/${userId}/${file.name}`);

    const snapshot = await imageRef.put(file);

    const downloadURL = await snapshot.ref.getDownloadURL();


    console.log("Image uploaded successfully. Download URL: ", downloadURL);

  } catch (error) {

    console.error("Error uploading image: ", error.message);

  }
};


// Example usage (assuming file input element)

const fileInput = document.getElementById('file-input');

fileInput.addEventListener('change', (event) => {

  const file = event.target.files[0];

  uploadImage(file, 'user_123');

});
```

Explanation
In this code snippet, the `uploadImage` function allows users to upload images to Firebase Storage. The images are organized in folders by user ID, and we use `getDownloadURL` to retrieve the URL of the uploaded image. This URL can be used to display the image in the app.

Sample Project 4: Cloud Functions for Automated Tasks

Project Overview
Firebase **Cloud Functions** can be used to execute backend logic in response to events triggered by Firebase features. In this project, we will create a Cloud Function that sends a welcome email to users when they sign up.

Project Setup

- **Step 1: Set Up Firebase Project**
  Create a new Firebase project and enable **Cloud Functions**.
- **Step 2: Write the Cloud Function**
  Use the Firebase CLI to set up Cloud Functions. In your project directory, run:

```
firebase init functions
```

- **Step 3: Implement the Function**
  Edit the `index.js` file in the `functions` directory to create a function that triggers on user creation:

```
const functions = require('firebase-functions');

const admin = require('firebase-admin');

const nodemailer = require('nodemailer');


admin.initializeApp();


// Configure nodemailer for sending emails

const transporter = nodemailer.createTransport({
```

```
    service: 'gmail',
    auth: {
      user: 'your-email@gmail.com',
      pass: 'your-email-password'
    }
  });


exports.sendWelcomeEmail = functions.auth.user().onCreate((user) => {
  const email = user.email;
  const mailOptions = {
    from: 'your-email@gmail.com',
    to: email,
    subject: 'Welcome to Our App!',
    text: `Hi ${user.displayName || 'User'}, welcome to our awesome app! We're glad to have you on board.`
  };

  return transporter.sendMail(mailOptions, (error, info) => {
    if (error) {
      console.error('Error sending email: ', error);
    } else {
      console.log('Welcome email sent: ', info.response);
    }
  });
```

```
});
```

Explanation
In this example, we use **Cloud Functions** to create an automated process for sending welcome emails to new users. The function triggers when a new user signs up (functions.auth.user().onCreate) and uses **Nodemailer** to send an email to the user. This approach helps streamline user onboarding and ensures every user receives a warm welcome.

Sample Project 5: Firebase Hosting with Static Site Deployment

Project Overview
In this project, we will use **Firebase Hosting** to deploy a simple static website. Firebase Hosting provides secure, fast, and reliable hosting services, making it an excellent choice for deploying static websites or web apps.

Project Setup

- **Step 1: Set Up Firebase Project**
  Create a new Firebase project and enable **Firebase Hosting**.
- **Step 2: Initialize Firebase Hosting**
  Use the Firebase CLI to initialize hosting:

```
firebase init hosting
```

- **Step 3: Deploy the Site**
  Create an index.html file in your project directory, and then deploy it using the Firebase CLI:

```
firebase deploy
```

Example HTML Code for index.html

```
<!DOCTYPE html>

<html lang="en">
```

```html
<head>
  <meta charset="UTF-8">
  <meta name="viewport" content="width=device-width, initial-scale=1.0">
  <title>My Firebase Hosted Site</title>
</head>
<body>
  <h1>Welcome to My Firebase Hosted Website!</h1>
  <p>This site is hosted on Firebase Hosting.</p>
</body>
</html>
```

Explanation
Firebase Hosting provides a simple and efficient way to deploy static websites. By initializing Firebase Hosting and deploying an `index.html` file, you can have your website live on a secure domain in minutes. This makes Firebase Hosting ideal for quick prototyping, portfolio sites, or even full-fledged web apps.

Conclusion

These sample projects and code snippets demonstrate various use cases of Firebase, from user authentication and real-time databases to storage, cloud functions, and hosting. By working through these examples, you can gain a deeper understanding of how Firebase's services integrate to form a comprehensive development platform. Whether you're building user authentication flows, real-time features, or managing media files, Firebase provides the tools you need to develop scalable and efficient applications.

Experiment with these projects, adapt them to your needs, and continue exploring the Firebase ecosystem to unlock its full potential in your applications.

Firebase Reference Guide

Firebase is a comprehensive platform for building web and mobile applications. This reference guide is designed to help you understand the core components of Firebase and how to use them effectively. It offers an in-depth look at various Firebase features, services, and configuration options, providing practical examples and detailed explanations to guide you through the development process. This section is intended to be a valuable resource that you can refer back to as you work on your Firebase projects.

Firebase Authentication Reference

Firebase Authentication is one of the most widely used features of Firebase. It allows developers to authenticate users in various ways, including through email and password, phone numbers, and third-party identity providers like Google and Facebook. Below, we cover some of the key aspects of Firebase Authentication.

Enabling Authentication Providers

Firebase Authentication supports multiple authentication providers, such as email/password, phone, Google, Facebook, Twitter, and GitHub. To use these providers, you must enable them in the Firebase Console.

Step-by-Step Guide to Enable Authentication Providers:

1. Navigate to the **Firebase Console** and select your project.
2. Click on **Authentication** in the sidebar.
3. Under the **Sign-in method** tab, select the provider you want to enable.
4. Configure the settings for the selected provider and click **Enable**.

Implementing Email/Password Authentication

Email and password authentication is straightforward to implement and provides a secure way for users to create accounts.

Code Example: Sign Up with Email and Password

```
// Firebase initialization
import firebase from 'firebase/app';
import 'firebase/auth';


const auth = firebase.auth();


// Function to create a new user with email and password
const createUser = async (email, password) => {
  try {
```

```javascript
    const userCredential = await auth.createUserWithEmailAndPassword(email, password);

    console.log('User account created:', userCredential.user);

  } catch (error) {

    console.error('Error creating user:', error.message);

  }

};


// Example usage

createUser('newuser@example.com', 'userpassword123');
```

In the example above, `createUserWithEmailAndPassword` is used to create a new user account. The function returns a user credential object that contains information about the user.

Adding Social Authentication

Firebase makes it easy to add social authentication, such as Google sign-in, to your application. This helps improve the user experience by reducing friction during the sign-in process.

Code Example: Implementing Google Sign-In

```javascript
// Firebase initialization

import firebase from 'firebase/app';

import 'firebase/auth';


const auth = firebase.auth();

const provider = new firebase.auth.GoogleAuthProvider();
```

```javascript
// Function to handle Google Sign-In
const signInWithGoogle = async () => {
  try {
    const result = await auth.signInWithPopup(provider);
    console.log('User signed in with Google:', result.user);
  } catch (error) {
    console.error('Error signing in with Google:', error.message);
  }
};


// Example usage
signInWithGoogle();
```

In this example, we create a new instance of GoogleAuthProvider and use signInWithPopup to initiate the sign-in process. Firebase will handle the OAuth flow and return user information upon success.

Firebase Realtime Database Reference

Firebase Realtime Database is a NoSQL cloud database that allows you to store and sync data in real time. Below are some of the key operations you can perform using the Realtime Database.

Database Structure

The Firebase Realtime Database is structured as a JSON tree, where data is stored in a hierarchical format. This structure makes it suitable for storing related data, such as chat messages, user profiles, or product information.

Example Database Structure:

```
{
  "users": {
```

```
    "user1": {
      "name": "John Doe",
      "email": "john@example.com"
    },
    "user2": {
      "name": "Jane Smith",
      "email": "jane@example.com"
    }
  },
  "messages": {
    "message1": {
      "sender": "user1",
      "content": "Hello, world!",
      "timestamp": 1633036800
    },
    "message2": {
      "sender": "user2",
      "content": "Hi there!",
      "timestamp": 1633036860
    }
  }
}
```

Writing Data to Realtime Database

To write data to the Firebase Realtime Database, you can use the `set`, `update`, or `push` methods, depending on your requirements.

Code Example: Writing Data to the Database

```javascript
// Firebase initialization
import firebase from 'firebase/app';
import 'firebase/database';

const database = firebase.database();

// Function to write user data
const writeUserData = (userId, name, email) => {
  database.ref('users/' + userId).set({
    name: name,
    email: email
  }).then(() => {
    console.log('User data written successfully');
  }).catch((error) => {
    console.error('Error writing user data:', error.message);
  });
};

// Example usage
writeUserData('user1', 'John Doe', 'john@example.com');
```

In this example, we use the `set` method to write data to the specified path. If the path does not exist, it will be created.

Reading Data from Realtime Database

To read data from the Realtime Database, you can use the `once` method for a one-time read or `on` for real-time updates.

Code Example: Reading Data from the Database

```
// Function to read user data
const readUserData = (userId) => {
  database.ref('users/' + userId).once('value')
    .then((snapshot) => {
      const data = snapshot.val();
      console.log('User data:', data);
    }).catch((error) => {
      console.error('Error reading user data:', error.message);
    });
};


// Example usage
readUserData('user1');
```

In the example above, the `once` method reads the current value of the specified path. You can also use the `on` method if you need continuous updates whenever the data changes.

Firestore Reference

Firestore is Firebase's more advanced cloud database, offering better querying capabilities and scalability compared to the Realtime Database. Firestore stores data in documents and collections, which provides a more flexible structure for many use cases.

Firestore Data Model

Firestore stores data in a hierarchical format that consists of **collections** and **documents**. Collections contain documents, which in turn contain fields. Collections and documents can also contain subcollections, allowing for complex data relationships.

Example Data Model:

- **Collection**: users
    - **Document**: user123
        - **Fields**: name, email
        - **Subcollection**: orders
            - **Document**: order456
                - **Fields**: total, timestamp

Writing Data to Firestore

Firestore allows you to write data using the set, add, and update methods. The add method automatically generates a document ID, whereas set allows you to specify an ID.

Code Example: Writing Data to Firestore

```
// Firebase initialization
import firebase from 'firebase/app';
import 'firebase/firestore';

const db = firebase.firestore();

// Function to add a new user
const addUser = async (name, email) => {
  try {
    const docRef = await db.collection('users').add({
      name: name,
      email: email,
```

```
        createdAt: firebase.firestore.FieldValue.serverTimestamp()

    });

    console.log('User added with ID:', docRef.id);

  } catch (error) {

    console.error('Error adding user:', error.message);

  }

};


// Example usage

addUser('Jane Smith', 'jane@example.com');
```

In the example above, the add method is used to add a new document to the users collection. The document ID is automatically generated, and the createdAt field is set to the current server timestamp.

Querying Data in Firestore

Firestore provides powerful querying capabilities, allowing you to filter and order your data in various ways.

Code Example: Querying Firestore Data

```
// Function to get users by name

const getUsersByName = async (name) => {

  try {

    const querySnapshot = await db.collection('users').where('name', '==', name).get();

    querySnapshot.forEach((doc) => {

      console.log(doc.id, '=>', doc.data());

    });
```

```
      } catch (error) {
        console.error('Error getting users by name:', error.message);
      }
    };
```

```
// Example usage
getUsersByName('Jane Smith');
```

In this example, we use the where method to filter users by their name field. Firestore queries can be combined to create complex conditions, and the results are returned as a QuerySnapshot object.

Cloud Functions Reference

Firebase **Cloud Functions** allow you to execute backend logic in response to events from Firebase services or HTTP requests. Below, we provide examples of how to set up and use Cloud Functions.

Creating a Cloud Function

To create a Cloud Function, you first need to initialize Firebase Functions in your project. This can be done using the Firebase CLI:

```
firebase init functions
```

After initializing, you can write functions in the `functions/index.js` file.

Code Example: Basic HTTP Function

```
const functions = require('firebase-functions');
```

```
// Simple HTTP function
```

```javascript
exports.helloWorld = functions.https.onRequest((request, response) => {
  response.send('Hello from Firebase!');
});
```

In the example above, `https.onRequest` is used to create a function that responds to HTTP requests. Deploy this function using:

```
firebase deploy --only functions
```

Triggering Cloud Functions with Firestore

Cloud Functions can be triggered by events in Firestore, such as creating, updating, or deleting a document.

Code Example: Firestore Trigger

```javascript
const admin = require('firebase-admin');
admin.initializeApp();

// Function triggered when a new user document is created
exports.newUserNotification = functions.firestore
  .document('users/{userId}')
  .onCreate((snapshot, context) => {
    const newUser = snapshot.data();
    console.log('New user created:', newUser.name);
    return null;
  });
```

In this example, the function is triggered whenever a new document is added to the `users` collection. The `onCreate` method is used to specify that this function should only run when a new document is created.

Firebase Storage Reference

Firebase Storage allows you to store and serve user-generated content such as images, videos, and other files. Below are some common operations that can be performed using Firebase Storage.

Uploading Files to Firebase Storage

To upload files, you need to create a reference to the desired location in Firebase Storage and then use the `put` method.

Code Example: Uploading a File

```
// Firebase initialization
import firebase from 'firebase/app';
import 'firebase/storage';

const storage = firebase.storage();

// Function to upload a file
const uploadFile = async (file) => {
  try {
    const storageRef = storage.ref();
    const fileRef = storageRef.child('uploads/' + file.name);
    const snapshot = await fileRef.put(file);
    const downloadURL = await snapshot.ref.getDownloadURL();
    console.log('File uploaded successfully. URL:', downloadURL);
```

314 | FIREBASE FOR ABSOLUTE BEGINNERS

```
  } catch (error) {
    console.error('Error uploading file:', error.message);
  }
};


// Example usage (assuming file input element)
const fileInput = document.getElementById('file-input');
fileInput.addEventListener('change', (event) => {
  const file = event.target.files[0];
  uploadFile(file);
});
```

In this example, the file is uploaded to the uploads folder in Firebase Storage. The getDownloadURL method is used to get the URL of the uploaded file, which can be used to display the file in your application.

Downloading Files from Firebase Storage

To download files, you need to create a reference to the file and use the getDownloadURL method.

Code Example: Downloading a File

```
// Function to get the download URL of a file
const getFileURL = async (fileName) => {
  try {
    const storageRef = storage.ref();
    const fileRef = storageRef.child('uploads/' + fileName);
    const downloadURL = await fileRef.getDownloadURL();
```

```
    console.log('Download URL:', downloadURL);

  } catch (error) {

    console.error('Error getting file URL:', error.message);

  }

};


// Example usage

getFileURL('example.jpg');
```

In the example above, the getDownloadURL method is used to retrieve the download link for the specified file. This URL can be used to display the file or provide a download link to users.

Conclusion

This reference guide has covered some of the most important Firebase services, including Authentication, Realtime Database, Firestore, Cloud Functions, and Storage. Each of these services plays a crucial role in building robust, scalable, and feature-rich applications. By understanding the core features and using the provided examples, you can integrate Firebase into your projects and take full advantage of its capabilities.

Whether you're authenticating users, storing data, running backend logic, or managing user-generated content, Firebase provides all the tools you need to build powerful applications with ease. Use this guide as a reference whenever you're working with Firebase, and continue exploring the platform to unlock its full potential.

Frequently Asked Questions

Firebase, with its extensive suite of services, offers developers a comprehensive platform for building scalable and feature-rich applications. However, due to the wide range of functionalities and flexibility, developers often have questions regarding the best practices, configurations, and troubleshooting methods when working with Firebase. This section provides answers to some of the most frequently asked questions (FAQs) to help you understand Firebase better and solve common issues that you may encounter during development.

General Firebase Questions

What Is Firebase and What Are Its Primary Use Cases?

Firebase is a platform developed by Google for building mobile and web applications. It provides tools for app development, such as authentication, database management, analytics, cloud functions, and hosting, among others. Firebase is commonly used for:

1. **Real-Time Applications**: Apps that require real-time data synchronization, like chat apps or collaborative tools.
2. **Authentication**: Apps that need user identity verification, such as sign-ins using email, phone numbers, or social providers.
3. **Serverless Backend**: Cloud Functions and Firestore allow developers to implement server-side logic without managing their own servers.
4. **Analytics and Engagement**: Firebase Analytics, Cloud Messaging, and Remote Config are used for tracking user engagement and delivering personalized experiences.

Is Firebase Free to Use?

Firebase offers a **free plan** called the **Spark Plan**, which is sufficient for small projects or prototyping. The free tier includes limited usage of services like Realtime Database, Firestore, Hosting, and Cloud Functions. However, for scaling applications and enterprise-level projects, Firebase provides a **Blaze Plan**, which is a pay-as-you-go plan that offers more resources and flexibility.

Key Differences Between Plans:

- **Spark Plan**: Limited daily writes/reads to databases, restricted hosting bandwidth, and fixed number of Cloud Functions invocations.
- **Blaze Plan**: Charges based on usage, offers access to premium Google Cloud products, and removes many of the limitations of the Spark Plan.

For example, the **Realtime Database** allows 1 GB of data storage and 10 GB/month of data download for free. When scaling up beyond these limits, you will incur charges.

Can Firebase Be Used for Production Apps?

Yes, Firebase can be used for production applications. It provides the scalability, security, and reliability needed for production-level applications. Large companies like **Duolingo**, **Venmo**, and **Alibaba** have used Firebase to manage real-time data and backend services.

However, it's essential to plan your database structure carefully and implement security rules properly, especially when using Firebase in a production environment. The flexible pricing plan also means you should monitor usage closely to prevent unexpected costs.

Authentication FAQs

How Do I Set Up Social Logins in Firebase?

Firebase Authentication makes it easy to integrate social logins, such as Google, Facebook, Twitter, or GitHub. To set up a social login, follow these steps:

1. **Enable the Authentication Provider:**
   In the **Firebase Console**, go to the **Authentication** section and click on the **Sign-in method** tab. Select the desired provider (e.g., Google or Facebook) and enable it.
2. **Configure API Keys and OAuth Redirect URIs:**
   Some providers, like Facebook, require additional configuration:
   - Go to the developer portal of the social provider.
   - Add the **OAuth redirect URI** provided by Firebase to the settings.
3. **Sign in Using the SDK:**
   Here is an example for **Google Sign-In** using JavaScript:

```javascript
// Firebase initialization (assume firebase is imported)
const provider = new firebase.auth.GoogleAuthProvider();


// Function to sign in with Google
const signInWithGoogle = async () => {
  try {
    const result = await firebase.auth().signInWithPopup(provider);
    console.log('Signed in user:', result.user);
  } catch (error) {
    console.error('Error during Google Sign-In:', error.message);
  }
};
```

This code snippet handles user sign-in using Google, with Firebase taking care of the OAuth process. Similar methods can be used for other providers.

How Can I Secure Firebase Authentication Tokens?

Firebase uses **JWT (JSON Web Tokens)** for authentication, which are securely generated and include important claims such as the user's ID and expiration date. However, as a developer, there are several best practices to ensure tokens remain secure:

- **Use HTTPS**: Ensure that your app always uses HTTPS to prevent tokens from being intercepted during transmission.

- **Token Refresh**: Firebase automatically refreshes tokens before they expire. Ensure that your app can handle the refresh process without interruptions.
- **Custom Claims**: You can use **custom claims** to include additional information in your user's token, such as user roles (e.g., admin). Always validate and sanitize these claims server-side.

Firestore and Realtime Database FAQs

What Are the Differences Between Firestore and Realtime Database?

Firestore and **Realtime Database** are two NoSQL databases offered by Firebase, each with its own strengths and ideal use cases:

1. **Structure**:
   - **Firestore**: Uses a **document/collection** model, which makes data more structured and easier to query. Collections contain documents, and documents can contain subcollections.
   - **Realtime Database**: Stores data in a **JSON tree**, which can become difficult to manage as data complexity grows.
2. **Querying**:
   - **Firestore**: Supports advanced querying, including compound queries, range filtering, and indexing, making it more powerful for complex data retrieval.
   - **Realtime Database**: Provides simple filtering capabilities, but does not support complex queries as well as Firestore.
3. **Data Consistency and Offline Support**:
   - Both databases offer **offline support** for mobile and web. Firestore provides **multi-region replication** for improved data consistency and reliability.
4. **Pricing**:
   - **Realtime Database**: Charges based on the amount of data downloaded and the number of connections.
   - **Firestore**: Charges based on **number of reads, writes, and deletes**, as well as storage used.

Example Use Cases:

- Use **Firestore** for complex applications that require structured data, querying, and scalability.
- Use **Realtime Database** for simple applications that require real-time data sync and low latency.

How Can I Prevent Excessive Read Costs in Firestore?

Firestore charges based on the number of **read operations**, so optimizing reads is crucial to managing costs:

1. **Avoid Unnecessary Reads**: When you load a collection in Firestore, you incur charges for each document read. Avoid loading entire collections unless absolutely necessary. Instead, use specific **queries** to retrieve only the documents you need.

2. **Use Snapshots Carefully**: OnSnapshot listeners are used to get real-time updates, but they can generate a high number of reads if the data changes frequently. Prefer get() when real-time updates are not required.
3. **Denormalization**: Instead of querying multiple collections to assemble data, **denormalize** the data to keep everything needed for a query in one document. This can reduce the number of reads, although it comes with a storage trade-off.
4. **Cache Data Locally**: Use Firestore's **offline persistence** to cache frequently accessed data locally. This can significantly reduce read operations, especially when data changes infrequently.

Cloud Functions FAQs

What Are Firebase Cloud Functions and How Are They Used?

Firebase Cloud Functions are serverless functions that automatically run backend code in response to events. Examples of these events include:

1. **Auth Events**: Triggered when a user signs up, deletes their account, etc.
2. **Firestore Triggers**: Triggered when a document is created, updated, or deleted.
3. **HTTP Triggers**: Functions that run in response to HTTP requests, which can be used as a RESTful API.

Code Example: Firestore Trigger

```
const functions = require('firebase-functions');

const admin = require('firebase-admin');

admin.initializeApp();



// Function triggered when a document is added to 'orders'
collection

exports.newOrderNotification = functions.firestore

  .document('orders/{orderId}')

  .onCreate((snapshot, context) => {

    const orderData = snapshot.data();

    console.log('New order placed:', orderData);

    // Additional logic such as sending notifications
```

```
    return null;

});
```

In the example above, a Cloud Function is triggered whenever a new order is added to the `orders` collection. You can use this to send notifications, update analytics, or perform other backend tasks.

How Can I Debug Cloud Functions?

Debugging Cloud Functions can be challenging, but Firebase provides several tools to make it easier:

Logs: Use `console.log()` in your Cloud Function to write debug information to the **Google Cloud Console** logs. You can view logs in real time by running:

```sh
firebase functions:log
```

1.
2. **Firebase Emulator Suite**: Use the **Firebase Emulator Suite** to test Cloud Functions locally. This allows you to simulate real events, such as Firestore triggers, in a controlled environment.
3. **Error Reporting**: Google Cloud provides an **Error Reporting** tool that automatically collects and reports unhandled exceptions. You can use it to track down errors that might not be captured in standard logs.

Firebase Hosting FAQs

How Can I Set Up Custom Domains in Firebase Hosting?

Firebase Hosting makes it easy to add a custom domain to your web application. Here are the steps:

1. **Add Domain in Firebase Console**:
    - Navigate to **Firebase Console > Hosting**.
    - Click **Add Custom Domain** and enter your domain name.
2. **Verify Domain Ownership**: Firebase will provide a **TXT record** that you need to add to your domain registrar's DNS settings to verify ownership.
3. **Update DNS A Records**: Once ownership is verified, you need to add **A records** provided by Firebase to point your domain to Firebase Hosting.
4. **Wait for Propagation**: DNS changes can take time to propagate, but once they do, your custom domain will be linked to your Firebase-hosted site.

Firebase also provides **free SSL certificates**, which are automatically renewed, ensuring secure connections to your hosted site.

Can Firebase Hosting Handle Large Amounts of Traffic?

Yes, Firebase Hosting is designed to handle high traffic loads by leveraging Google's content delivery network (CDN). Key features include:

1. **Global CDN**: Firebase Hosting uses Google's CDN to distribute content across multiple data centers around the world. This ensures that users get content from the server closest to them, reducing latency and improving load times.
2. **Automatic Scaling**: Firebase Hosting automatically scales based on demand. Whether your site has a few visitors or millions, Firebase ensures that the infrastructure can handle the load without any manual intervention.
3. **Caching**: Static assets served through Firebase Hosting are cached at the CDN level, allowing for quick delivery. You can also set custom cache-control headers to manage caching behavior.

Analytics and Notifications FAQs

How Do Firebase Analytics Differ from Google Analytics?

Firebase Analytics, also known as **Google Analytics for Firebase**, is a free app measurement solution that provides insights into user behavior. Key differences from traditional **Google Analytics** include:

1. **App Focus**: Firebase Analytics is specifically designed for mobile and web apps, while Google Analytics is more general-purpose.
2. **Events-Based Model**: Firebase Analytics uses an **events-based** model, which makes it easy to track user interactions in your app, such as button clicks, screen views, and in-app purchases.
3. **Integration with Firebase Services**: Firebase Analytics integrates seamlessly with other Firebase services, such as **Remote Config** and **Cloud Messaging**, allowing for data-driven decision-making and personalized user experiences.

How Can I Send Notifications Using Firebase Cloud Messaging (FCM)?

Firebase Cloud Messaging (FCM) is a cross-platform messaging solution that lets you reliably send messages to users. You can send notifications directly from the **Firebase Console** or through code using the FCM API.

Code Example: Sending Notification Using Cloud Function

```
exports.sendPushNotification = functions.firestore
  .document('notifications/{notificationId}')
  .onCreate(async (snapshot) => {
    const notificationData = snapshot.data();
```

```
    const payload = {
      notification: {
        title: notificationData.title,
        body: notificationData.body,
      }
    };

    try {
        await    admin.messaging().sendToTopic(notificationData.topic, payload);
        console.log('Push notification sent successfully');
    } catch (error) {
        console.error('Error sending notification:', error.message);
    }
  });
```

In this example, a push notification is sent when a new document is added to the notifications collection. The **Cloud Function** uses the **Firebase Admin SDK** to send a notification to a specific topic.

Conclusion

This FAQ section has covered a range of commonly asked questions about Firebase, providing answers to help you better understand its features, best practices, and troubleshooting methods. Firebase is a versatile platform, and the more you explore and understand its components—such as Authentication, Firestore, Cloud Functions, Hosting, and Analytics—the better equipped you will be to build scalable, efficient, and engaging applications.

Whether you are troubleshooting an issue with Cloud Functions, optimizing your Firestore database for cost-efficiency, or adding a custom domain to Firebase Hosting, this guide aims to provide you with practical insights that can enhance your development experience with Firebase.

Chapter 13: Appendices

www.ingramcontent.com/pod-product-compliance
Lightning Source LLC
Chambersburg PA
CBHW071017240526
45469CB00006BD/1959